Bioethics in Africa
Theories and Praxis

Edited by

Yaw A. Frimpong-Mansoh
Northern Kentucky University, USA

Caesar A. Atuire
University of Ghana, Ghana

Series in Philosophy
VERNON PRESS

Copyright © 2019 Vernon Press, an imprint of Vernon Art and Science Inc, on behalf of the author.

All rights reserved. No part of this publication may be reproduced, stored in a retrieval system, or transmitted in any form or by any means, electronic, mechanical, photocopying, recording, or otherwise, without the prior permission of Vernon Art and Science Inc.

www.vernonpress.com

In the Americas:	In the rest of the world:
Vernon Press	Vernon Press
1000 N West Street,	C/Sancti Espiritu 17,
Suite 1200, Wilmington,	Malaga, 29006
Delaware 19801	Spain
United States	

Series in Philosophy

Library of Congress Control Number: 2018956758

ISBN: 978-1-62273-668-3

Also available:

Hardback: 978-1-62273-459-7

E-book: 978-1-62273-570-9

Product and company names mentioned in this work are the trademarks of their respective owners. While every care has been taken in preparing this work, neither the authors nor Vernon Art and Science Inc. may be held responsible for any loss or damage caused or alleged to be caused directly or indirectly by the information contained in it.

Every effort has been made to trace all copyright holders, but if any have been inadvertently overlooked the publisher will be pleased to include any necessary credits in any subsequent reprint or edition.

Cover design by Vernon Press. Cover image by Frederick Buadu, @Perfectfotosgh.

Table of Contents

List of Contributors v

Preface vii

Acknowledgements xv

Chapter 1 **A Prolegomon to Bioethics in Africa: Issues, Challenges and Commonsensical Recommendations** 1
Caesar A. Atuire
University of Ghana

Chapter 2 **Bioethics: Traditional African Perspective** 31
Yaw A. Frimpong-Mansoh
Northern Kentucky University

Chapter 3 **Ancillary Care Obligations in the Light of an African Bioethic** 57
Thaddeus Metz
University of Johannesburg

Chapter 4 **Personhood, Autonomy and Informed Consent** 77
Martin Ajei
University of Ghana

Nancy O. Myles
University of Ghana

Chapter 5 **Cultural Translation, Human Meaning, and Genes: Why Interpretation Matters in Psychiatric Genomics** 95
Camillia Kong
University of Oxford

| Chapter 6 | **The Practice of Traditional Medicine and Bioethical Challenges** | 113 |

Rose Mary Amenga-Etego
University of Ghana

| Chapter 7 | **Ethical Concerns Regarding Right of People Living with Disabilities in Ghana** | 131 |

Augustina Naami
University of Ghana

| Chapter 8 | **Bioethical Challenges in Medical Practice in Ghana: Past, Present, Future** | 145 |

Akis Afoko
*University of Development Studies;
Tamale Teaching Hospital*

| Chapter 9 | **Bioethics, Nature, the Environment and Climate Change in Africa** | 153 |

Godfrey B. Tangwa
University of Yaoundé 1

Index   161

List of Contributors

Caesar A. Atuire, Lecturer, Department of Philosophy and Classics, University of Ghana, Legon, Ghana.

Yaw A. Frimpong-Mansoh, Associate Professor, Northern Kentucky University, USA.

Thaddeus Metz, Distinguished Professor of Philosophy, Department of Philosophy, University of Johannesburg, South Africa.

Martin Ajei and Nancy Myles, Senior Lecturer and Lecturer respectively at the Department of Philosophy and Classics, University of Ghana, Legon, Ghana.

Camillia Kong, Senior Researcher, Department of Psychiatry, University of Oxford, UK.

Rose Mary Amenga-Etego, Senior Lecturer, Department for the Study of Religions, University of Ghana, Legon, Ghana.

Augustina Naami, Lecturer, Department of Social Work, University of Ghana, Legon, Ghana.

Akis Afoko, Senior Lecturer, University of Development Studies School of Medicine and Health Sciences; Consultant Urologist and Head of Urology Department, Tamale Teaching Hospital, Ghana.

Godfrey B. Tangwa, Professor and former Head of the Department of Philosophy, University of Yaoundé 1, Cameroon; retired.

Preface

This book offers a compendium of the current discourse on bioethics in Africa. The various chapters present the theoretical underpinnings, the scope, and the praxis of bioethics on the continent. The approach to bioethics envisaged by the editors of this book is a broad holistic view of the normative questions concerning human life, *bios*. As a result, the contents go beyond medical and research ethics to touch on environmental issues, economic imbalances, legal vacuums, and the philosophical foundations of ethics in Africa.

The book came out of an exciting international conference organized by the two editors on "Bioethics: African Perspectives," held at the University of Ghana in May 2017. The conference was jointly sponsored by the Department of Philosophy and Classics at the University of Ghana and Northern Kentucky University (USA). The conference drew philosophers, medical practitioners, environmentalists, social scientists and other academics and practitioners from various countries. The lively debates and discussions that followed the presentation of the papers made it evident that it was necessary to continue to research, publish and work towards a framework for bioethics in Africa that will resonate with the indigenous cultures, prevent abuses, and offer the necessary guarantees for a sustainable flourishing of life.

The main concerns that emerged from the University of Ghana conference that this book tries to address can be summed as follows: bioethics in Africa needs a framework that reflects indigenous African perspectives and values which contrasts and challenges Western ethical and normative imperialism; the scope of bioethics in Africa needs to embrace all aspects of human activities that pose a threat to health and the environment; a framework of dialogue and collaboration is needed to bridge the theoretical and practical divide between traditional medicine, spiritual healing, and Western biomedical health care; policies and enforcement are required to ensure that lives are not sacrificed due to poverty, greed and epistemological incompatibilities; traditional customs that marginalize categories of persons need to be re-visited to offer protection to all.

This book contributes African perspectives to current discussions in global bioethics. The relationship between culture and bioethics has become a central theme in recent discourse on bioethics. The discussion is raised by concerns about Western dominance and globalization of bioethics (Callahan, D., 1999). For example, it is believed that the norms of principlism (i.e. autonomy, informed consent, beneficence, nonmaleficence) with which the ethical principles of bioethics have come to be identified are informed by the dominant Western deontological and teleological ethical theories (Behrens, K. G. (2017). This raises questions about the extent to which the norms which currently define bioethical discourse and practices reflect and accommodate non-Western values, beliefs and particularities. The concern is evidenced by the recent proliferation of proposals and works on Asian and African bioethics (e.g. Ren-Zong, Q., 2004; Tangwa, G. B., 2010). These new fields of bioethics centralize domestic culture as the basis for constructing the ethical framework of bioethics. A few rich works have emerged that urge bioethics in Africa to be rooted in indigenous African values (e.g. Gbadegesin, S., 2012; Andoh, C., 2011; Tangwa, G. B., 2007; Metz, T., 2017; Behrens, K. G., 2017). However, more work still needs to be done for bioethics to be solidly grounded and adequately done in an African way. So far, existing literature on African bioethics follows the Western form of medicine to restrict discourse on bioethics to ethical issues arising from biomedical and biotechnological science. Also, the existing works tend to be centrally focused on how to ground bioethics in the foundation of African (rather than Western) moral values (e.g. Metz, T., 2010; Tangwa, G. B., 1996; Behrens, K. B., 2017; Gbadegesin, S., 1998). The attempt to ground bioethics in African indigenous values is groundbreaking but the editors of this book, *Bioethics in Africa*, believe that the theme of bioethics has to be broadened to also address non-biomedical ethical questions generated by traditional African cultural beliefs and practices toward health and health care.

We believe that restricting bioethics to ethical issues relating to biomedicine and biotechnology is problematic in the African context in at least two fundamental ways. First, it neglects the indigenous African holistic conception of health, and second, it marginalizes a crucial component of the system of health care widely consumed by Africans—i.e. African traditional system of health, broadly construed to encompass the use of plant and animal parts for the preparation of medicine as well as healing systems rooted in traditional African religious beliefs and practices. In contrast with the biomedically-based scientific health system of the Western world, non-scientific traditional medicine (popularly called "traditional medicine"—TM) is a major system of health care which is directly accessible to, and widely used by many people in African societies. It has been speculated that about more than 80% of Africans use traditional medicine (even for the treatment of HIV/AIDS) largely because of its easy access and affordability (usually freely shared) (Nyika, A., 2007). For example, it is estimated that over 70% of South Africans consult traditional healers before consulting any other type of health care professional (Bogaert, D. K. V., 2007).

Currently, a few papers are scattered in journals that debate ethical issues raised by African traditional medicine. But so far (at least as far as our research indicates) there is no single book collection that is dedicated to ethical issues raised by traditional African cultural beliefs and practices toward health and health care. Even the existing journal articles on African traditional medicine tend to concentrate on questions about its scientific status, including debates whether TM should be scientifically modernized and improved (e.g. Nyika, A., 2007; Tangwa, G. B., 2007; Bogaert, D. K. V., 2007). We think such focus defines African traditional health too narrowly. For example, it leaves out many concrete issues such as parenthood and surrogacy in traditional African traditional culture, African cultural beliefs and practices towards disability and people with disability, reproductive rights in traditional African culture, environmental health effects (on humans and animals) of traditional cultural practices. Our book seeks to fill this vacuum. It adds a new voice to calls for bioethics in Africa to be conceived and done by focusing on cultural bioethics, broadly construed to include life impacts of traditional practices such as those just mentioned above. We conceive bioethics holistically to include health issues related to all aspects of *bios*, life, including biodiversity. As Godfrey Tangwa argues in chapter 9 of this book, bioethics should be conceived as the application of ethics to all life forms, including the environment. In his observation, it was human interference in nature that originated the health and health care problems that generate ethical questions for bioethics. Our approach in this book is multidisciplinary, with chapters selected from original papers written by scholars in philosophy, social work, African studies, religious studies, psychology, medicine and health science.

Africa is experiencing a rapid socio-economic transformation. Therefore, it is becoming urgent that African countries pursue scholarly activities and establish research and study programs in bioethics in order to find appropriate solutions to the questions arising in this field. What is more, African indigenous cultures have long standing ethical standards that need to be utilized and factored into the search for solutions to African problems. Otherwise, nations run the risk of importing models that are foreign to our culture and can undermine long seated traditions and values. This book aims at contributing to such vision; it aims at encouraging and stimulating scholarly works grounded in indigenous African conception of health and moral values as a guide to inform health policy and education in African societies. The need for bioethics education and consciousness to encourage health care professionals and policy-makers to harness local materials for target health care delivery is currently of national interest among many African countries. Our focus on indigenous African systems of values and health care taps into systems that are very familiar to the people and easy to accept as an educational textbook and guidelines for public health policy.

The following is a summary of the chapters. In Chapter 1, "A Prolegomenon to Bioethics in Africa: Issues, Challenges and Commonsensical Recommendations," Caesar Atuire provides an overview of bioethical challenges facing the Sub-Saharan African region. The chapter groups these challenges under five headings: health care ethics; bioethics of communo-cultural practices; bioethics of consumerism and corruption; natural resources and environmental bioethics; bioethical neo-colonialism. Atuire outlines the peculiar African challenges in each of these areas. He concludes with a ten-point commonsensical list of recommendations for bioethics in Africa. In Chapter 2, "Bioethics: Traditional African Perspective," Yaw Frimpong-Mansoh challenges African bioethicists to expand their focus beyond ethical issues raised by biomedical and biotechnological science. The author discusses philosophical puzzles raised by the African mystical system of beliefs and practices in which African traditional medicine is fundamentally rooted. Also, the author uses a case study from traditional health care practices of the Yoruba ethnic group in Nigeria (viz. consultation of healer-diviner) to examine bioethical implications of the widespread caregiver roles that family members play in traditional African communitarian system of health care. He contends that rejection of African traditional medicine (TM) based on its grounding in African religious culture is misguided. He concludes that respect for the virtues of epistemological and value pluralism is required for a deeper understanding and open-minded appreciation of African TM, in spite of being rooted in a religious culture.

In Chapter 3, "Ancillary Care Obligations in Light of an African Bioethic: From Entrustment to Communion," Thaddeus Metz provides a new theory of ancillary care obligations, one that is grounded in ideals of communion salient in the African philosophical tradition, and that is intended to rival and surpass Richardson's model, which is a function of Western considerations of autonomy. Metz argues that the relational approach of the former has several virtues in comparison to the basic individualism of the latter. In Chapter 4, "Personhood, Autonomy, and Informed Consent," Martin Ajei and Nancy Myles examine the concept of informed consent from a Ghanaian Akan perspective. The authors examine assumptions of the notion of informed consent as a principle of bioethical practice and point to inherent inconsistencies within it. The chapter then proceeds to gesture toward the view that when examined, these assumptions indicate that the process of obtaining and validating informed consent should be contextually derived, and that theories of personhood and beliefs about the structure of existence are pivotal in the contextual knowledge that sustains these processes and validation. In Chapter 5, "Cultural Translation, Human Meaning, and Genes: Why interpretation matters in Psychiatric Genomics," Camillia Kong presents the challenges in the current globalized discourse on genomics that call for attenuated forms of translational thinking. She points out that problematic linguistic and cultural translation of concepts like genes and Western psychiatric diagnoses in the African context sheds critical light on the reductivism and decontextualisation around human behavior within the conceptual framing of psychiatric genomics, where mental disorder is treated as separable from the interpretative meanings of such behavior.

In Chapter 6, "The Practice of Traditional Medicine and Bioethical Challenges," Rose Mary Amenga-Etego, examines the life (*bio*) centeredness of traditional African belief systems and traditional medicine. She argues that African traditional medicine sees life as an interconnected chain that must not be broken (cyclical not linear that has an end-point). TM is also based on the African conception of personhood—a person is made up of many things (spirit, blood, body, etc.). In the system of African TM, saving life means more than healing; it includes rescuing, delivering, restoring and protecting (e.g. from spiritual influences against recurring sicknesses), weakening the powers of spiritual entities against causing further harms. The author concludes that the widespread belief that illnesses have both physical and spiritual causes seems to warrant a combination of Western and traditional healing processes—Western healing addressing physical problems and traditional healing addressing spiritual problems. In Chapter 7, "Ethical Concerns Regarding the Right of People Living with Disabilities in Ghana," Augustina Naami reviews studies about traditional and contemporary African beliefs and attitudes toward disability and people with disability (PWD). She focusses particularly on Ghana, and argues that Ghana is yet to align and harmonize disability laws with international laws. Because of a legislative vacuum in many areas, and lack of enforcement, PWD face a lot of challenges. For instance, in some cultures people with disabilities are stigmatized and associated with evil spiritual influences—for example, they are often stigmatized as "water babies" and bad luck. They are sometimes urged to be returned to the spiritual world; they are often killed by fetish priests (through concoctions); sometimes such rituals are carried out by family members themselves. The author concludes that aligning and harmonizing disability laws in Ghana with international laws can help minimize the dehumanizing experiences that PWD go through and secure them with good protection from abuses.

In Chapter 8, "Bioethical Challenges in Medical Practice in Ghana: Past, Present, Future," Akis Afoko discusses Western principles of bioethics and the challenges of applying them (e.g. informed consent) in the practice of medicine in the African formal and informal health care systems. He argues, for example, that because of cultural beliefs, information tends to scare patients from treatment. As a solution, the author recommends having a good surrogate to represent patients (surrogates who are not seeking their own self-interests). Also, the author strongly advocates ethics training in Africa, for example through the mass media and integration of ethics into the curriculum of the medical schools. Afoko presents the day-to-day ethical challenges that medical practitioners face in Africa: relationship with traditional medicine, herbal healers and other forms of medical care. He concludes with an overview of the future challenges of biomedical health care in Africa. In Chapter 9, "Bioethics, Nature, the Environment and Climate Change in Africa Environment (Sanitation/Nutrition/Climate Change) and Aspects of Bioethics," Godfrey Tangwa examines health implications of traditional and contemporary practices. He argues that the field of bioethics must be expanded to include environmental factors because it was human interference in nature that originated bioethics. Tangwa contends that clinging on to European models of doing things has not been helpful to African development. Global bioethics (especially Western bioethics) can be enriched by African communitarian (or Ubuntu) holistic ethics. We need Eco-bio-communitarianism: interdependent and peaceful co-existence between humans and nature.

Yaw A. Frimpong-Mansoh and Caesar A. Atuire (Editors)

References

Andoh, C., 2011, Bioethics and the challenge to its growth in Africa. *Open Journal of Philosophy,* 1 (2), 67-75.

Behrens, K. G., 2013, Towards an indigenous African bioethics. *South African Journal of Bioethics and Law,* 6 (1); 32-35.

Behrens, K. G, 2017, Hearing sub-Saharan African voices in bioethics. *Theoretical Medicine and Bioethics;* 38 (2), 95-99.

Bogaert, D. K. V, 2007, Ethical considerations in African traditional medicine: A response to Nyika. *Developing World Bioethics,* 7 (1), 35-40.

Callahan, D., 1999, Social sciences and the task of bioethics. Daedalus. *Bioethics and Beyond,* 128 (4), 275-294.

Chuwa, L. T, 2014, African Indigenous Ethics in Global Bioethics: Interpreting Ubuntu (Advancing Global Bioethics), Springer.

Gbadegesin, S., 1998, Culture and bioethics. In: Kuhse, H and Singer, P. (Eds.). *Companion to Bioethics*. Malden, MA.: Blackwell, 24-35.

Kanu, I. A., 2016, African Bioethics: An Indigenous Humanistic Perspective for Integrative Global Bioethical Discourse. LAP LAMBERT Academic Publishing.

Metz, T., 2010, African and Western moral theories in a bioethical context. *Developing World Bioethics*, 10 (1), 49-58.

Metz, T., 2017, A bioethic of communion: Beyond care and the four principles with regard to reproduction. In: M Soniewicka (ed.), *The Ethics of Reproductive Genetics*. Springer, 49-66.

Nyika, A, 2007, Ethical and regulatory issues surrounding African traditional medicine in the context of HIV/AIDS, *Developing World Bioethics*, 7 (1), 25-34.

Okpako, D., 2006, African Medicine: Tradition and beliefs. *The Pharmaceutical Journal*, 276.

Ren-Zong, Q., 2004, (Ed.), Bioethics: Asian perspectives: A quest for moral diversity, *Philosophy and Medicine*, 80.

Tangwa, G. B., 1996, Bioethics: An African perspective. *Bioethics*, 10 (3), 185-200.

Tangwa, G. B., 2004, Bioethics, biotechnology and culture: A voice from the margins. *Developing World Bioethics*, 4 (2), 125-138.

Tangwa, G. B., 2007, How not to compare Western scientific medicine with African traditional medicine. *Developing World Bioethics*, 7 (1), 41–44.

Tangwa, G. B., 2010, *Elements of African Bioethics in a Western Frame*. Mankon, Bamenda (Cameroon): Langaa Research & Publishing CIG (RPCIG).

Acknowledgements

We would like to thank the University of Northern Kentucky and the Office of Research, Innovation and Development (ORID) of the University of Ghana, Legon, whose financial contributions enabled us to organize the international conference, "Bioethics: African Perspectives," in May 2017. The faculty, staff and students of the Department of Philosophy and Classics of the University of Ghana put a generous effort into helping us to organize a successful conference. We would like to mention Nancy Myles, and in particular, Grace Addison, who also assisted in gathering the conference papers that are presented in this book. A word of thanks too to George Barimah and Robert Kenney for their contributions to the initial editorial work. As editors, we owe a good deal to our colleagues who presented interesting papers during the conference and to those who contributed to the various chapters of this book. We hope to continue to work together to create a multidisciplinary innovative platform for bioethics in the West African sub-region.

Yaw A. Frimpong-Mansoh and Caesar A. Atuire (Editors)

Chapter 1

A Prolegomon to Bioethics in Africa: Issues, Challenges and Commonsensical Recommendations

Caesar A. Atuire
University of Ghana

Abstract

An overview of bioethical challenges facing the Sub-Saharan African region. The chapter groups these challenges under five headings: health care ethics; bioethics of communo-cultural practices; bioethics of consumerism and corruption; natural resources and environmental bioethics; bioethical neo-colonialism. Atuire outlines the peculiar African challenges in each of these areas. He concludes with a ten-point commonsensical list of recommendations for bioethics in Africa.

Key Words: Sub-Sahara Africa, health care ethics, communo-cultural practices, consumerism, corruption, natural resources, environment, neo-colonialism.

1.1 Introduction

A *prima facie* impression of philosophic literature on bioethics in Africa reveals attempts to differentiate 'African bioethics' from 'Western bioethics' (Coleman 2017). African intellectuals express concern about the wholesale importation of bioethical norms from the West without sufficient input from indigenous value systems that are more consonant to Sub Saharan African (SSA) peoples. African researchers critique 'Western bioethics' in a *pars destruens* that points out the inadequacies of Western moral theories for Africa, highlighting most of all, the libertarian or individualistic bias of these theories. In the *pars construens*, they attempt to draw from some African traditions, —Yoruba, Nso, Zulu—, salient principles of a moral theory for an 'African bioethics'. There are also some African voices that propose an integrative approach which shows how

African moral theory can enrich the debate on global bioethical themes such as abortion and animal rights (Metz 2010).

My approach in this opening chapter of a volume on bioethics in Africa is different. My goal is to tease out and present the current bioethical challenges that are common and peculiar to the lives of people living in SSA. Samuel Gorovitz' definition of bioethics is particularly apt for this exercise: "the critical examination of the moral dimensions of decision-making in health-related contexts and in contexts involving the biological sciences" (Gorovitz 1977). I believe that an analysis and classification of these challenges will provide a foundation and a road map for future research and debate regarding which moral theory, or even better, theories, are most apt for addressing the bioethical questions facing SSA persons.

My underlying assumption is that ethics is an applied normative discipline; practical philosophy. At the center of ethical concerns is the rational normative reflection concerning what a good life is and how to achieve it. This means that any adequate ethical theory must be applicable to its context: it cannot be solely anachronistic or futuristic; it must be grounded in the lived conditions of those who are supposed to practice it. The same holds for bioethics as a branch of ethics. A 21st century bioethical framework for Africa can neither be ancient ethnic African bioethics nor imported Anglo-American praxis. Bioethics for Africa must respond to the lives and living ethical concerns of Africans today which are different to those of past Africans and to those of Europeans, Asians and Americans.

Bioethical challenges differ from age to age. As the capacity of humans to influence, modify and condition life continues to increase, so will the bioethical choices regarding what is good or evil, what needs to be encouraged or curbed. Bioethical questions regarding genomics and AI that were not present 50 years ago will acquire more importance during the current century. The condition of people in SSA has evolved and continues to do so. It is estimated that 56% of Africans will live in urban areas by 2050 (U. N. World Urbanization Prospects 2014). Urbanization in Africa comes along with cultural intermingling that engenders persons with multi-layered epistemic and normative frameworks. This, and the fact that most SSA populations hail from different ethnic backgrounds, calls for an amount of pluralism. Recourse to the traditions of any particular ethnic group calls for what Kwame Gyekye denominates as critical *sankofaism*.[1]

A brief look at the emergence of bioethics as a discipline in the 1960s and 1970s will buttress the point I am making. The emergence and growth of bioethics in Europe and the United States was catalyzed by three main historical factors that influenced the way the discipline was born, conditioned the themes and the nature of the ensuing debate. These catalytic conditions were (Chadwick 2017):

The rapid technological growth in the aftermath of the World War II, especially in the medical sciences where new technologies like organ transplants, kidney dialysis, contraception, among others, were leading to ethical questions concerning which lives to save and which medical choices were moral. There was also the backdrop of the abuses committed on humans through experimentation in the Nazi concentration camps.

Growth in contraceptive technologies also aided a wider separation between sex and reproduction, thereby contributing to a greater feeling of sexual freedom, whilst challenging conventional attitudes towards marriage, sexuality and reproduction.

There was a climate of greater focus on individual autonomy and civil rights which drove medical paternalism into further disrepute whilst the right of patients to be informed and to fully participate in the decisions regarding their health grew.

These factors constituted and informed a large part of the early bioethical debates in the Euro-American context: contraception; abortion; research ethics; organ transplantation and the accompanying questions about the criterion of death. The content of the debates was also influenced by the cultural climate of the late 1960s; hence it is no wonder that the first of the four principles proposed by Childress and Beauchamp was autonomy. In trying to address the challenges of the time, Western bioethicists drew from and re-interpreted the moral theories of their traditions: deontology; consequentialism; virtue ethics; religious ethics.

Mutatis mutandis, I will be looking at the bioethical issues and challenges of SSA countries. The issues are so vast and complex that I can only limit myself to introducing some of the key questions. After borrowing the Greek concept of a prolegomenon for this chapter, I imagine its contents to be a conversation from the *pronaos*. Hence, I will leave out the inner temple debates for future research. I will not try to elaborate a bioethical theory for Africa. I even hold doubts about the possibility of a single bioethical theory that can be applied across the region. It will emerge that the nature of these problems requires a multi-disciplinary and trans-cultural framework. My hope, rather, is that in highlighting the issues and challenges that are germane to an African bioethical discourse, I would have laid the grounds for dialogue within the continent and for an exchange with bioethicists from other parts of the world seeking to understand and to dialogue with the African context. At the end of the chapter, I propose 10 common-sense guidelines for bioethics in Africa.

Of course, Africa is a vast continent with countries facing different challenges. For example, the life threatening ethical questions surrounding discrimination towards albinos in parts of Tanzania are not present in Ghana, nor are the witch camps of Gambaga in Northern Ghana present in Namibia. Nevertheless, it is possible to try to identify and group the bioethical concerns of Sub Saharan African countries (SSA). Even though cultural globalization is increasingly exporting many aspects of Euro-American lifestyles, there are some bioethical issues that are hotly debated in Europe and North America, like human cloning, stem cell research, partial birth abortion, physician assisted suicide, that are less urgent in SSA.[2] Other issues that feature in SSA, such as communitarian participation in informed consent, the interdependence of the spiritual and the physical, and poverty related abuses, are less present in Europe, North America and those parts of the world generically called the West.

1.2 The Issues and Challenges

Questions of bioethical concern in SSA can be grouped under five broad themes: health care ethics; bioethics of communo-cultural practices; bioethics of consumerism and corruption; natural resources and environmental bioethics and bioethical neo-colonialism. I shall proceed to analyze why each of these areas raises bioethical concerns. In doing so, my focus will not be so much on concerns that Africa shares with other regions of the world, but to highlight the challenges that are peculiar to the SSA context.

1.2.1 Health Care Bioethics

According to the CIA factbook, 8 out of the top 20 countries with the highest death rates are in SSA.[3] All the countries where life expectancy is under 50 years are in SSA.[4] The region also ranks highest in children under-five mortality rates with a regional average of 76.5 deaths per 1000 live births as compared to the global rate of 40.8.[5] Without over estimating the capacity of bioethics to mitigate some of these problems, it is worth enquiring into ethical dimensions of these challenges. A greater attention to bioethics can improve the quality of health care and eventually reduce the morbidity and mortality rates in Africa. In many African countries, it is rare to see health practitioners being tried in law courts for bad health care delivery. Yet it would be naïve to assume that all health care practitioners in Africa are wholly virtuous.

Broadly speaking, Africans recur to three strands of health care: Western-style biomedical health care; traditional medicine; and modern religious spiritualistic healing. Each of these is an emanation of a cosmovision, an anthropology and a view of health. It would be difficult, if not unfair, to apply a single undifferentiated bioethical yardstick to all these models of health care delivery without considering the metaphysical underpinnings of their curing principles.

Western-Style Biomedical Health care. Like most parts of the world, all SSA countries have widespread state and private practitioners and centres that offer health care based on Western biomedicine. This is usually the most regulated of all health care provision systems with rules, trained personnel, professional associations, licenses, etc. Bioethical issues regarding contraception, abortion, futile therapy, organ transplant and trafficking, which are the concern of bioethicists worldwide, are present in SSA albeit with an African flavor. However, the key bioethical problem that the region faces is the lack of adequate infrastructural, material and human resources. Physicians, nurses, paramedics, and other health care practitioners in Africa are all too familiar with the burden of making life or death choices for which they often feel ethically ill-equipped.[6] Infrastructural limitations such as lack of transportation, inadequate roads, absence of ambulances, electrical power cuts and lack of adequate instrumentation can lead practitioners to assume risks and make life-changing choices for patients. Scarcity of material resources often implies choosing who to cure and who not to cure. Practitioners can find themselves with the ethical burden of deciding which life to save and which not to. An example is chronic kidney disease. In Ghana, there are 15 dialysis centres running 103 hemodialysis machines for a population of over 26 million persons. Two thirds of the hemodialysis machines are in Accra, the capital city, and its metropolitan area (Tannor, Awuku, Boima and Antwi 2018). Five of Ghana's 10 regions do not have a hemodialysis machine. The cost of dialysis at Ghana's Korle Bu Teaching Hospital is 260 cedis (about 60 US dollars) per session and it is not covered under the insurance system of the National Health Authority. A patient may require 2 to 3 sessions per week. Is it sustainable to cure a person who cannot have access to dialysis after the cure or who will not be able to afford dialysis over a prolonged period? (Shaibu 2017)

Unavailability of qualified human resources[7] often leads to work overloads that increase the possibility and frequency of errors. A 2017 study of a cross section of 145 medical practitioners in Nigeria's Abia State revealed up to 42.8% medical errors. The study revealed that: "The three most common errors committed by the participants were an error of medication prescription (95.2%), error of radio-laboratory investigation ordering (83.9%), and error of physician diagnoses (69.4%). Sixty-two (100%) of the participants who committed medical errors had a negative attitude to error disclosure to the patients and their families. Of the 62 participants who committed medical errors, 33.8% were depressed. Among those that committed medical errors, none was involved in a lawsuit for medical errors." (Iloh, Chuku, Amadi 2017)

These are bioethical issues whose solution lie not with the walls of clinics and hospitals but beyond; in the allocation of resources and in health care policy making at national levels. Yet, bioethicists are hardly ever consulted on these broader issues.

Another important bioethical question is informed consent in clinical and research ethics (Tindana, Kass, & Akweongo 2006). At the heart of the need for informed consent is the patient or research participant's right to decide whether to submit to a therapy or participate in a research project. This right to self-determination requires three elements: disclosure on the part of health care providers and researchers; capacity; and voluntariness on the part of patients and research participants to grant consent. Whereas in the Western tradition, this practice is generally accepted, with implicit assumptions that rely heavily on the person as an individual, in SSA the communitarian notion of the person calls for a careful examination of the concept of self-determination (see Ajei and Myles, chapter 4). Where the self is perceived as a communitarian being whose realization is intrinsically linked to the relational character of being-in-community, procedures for informed consent that focus on atomic individuality turn out to be inadequate. No wonder, in some cases, informed consent is reduced to patients putting a 'thumb-print' on a form without fully understanding what they are consenting to (see Afoko, chapter 8).

Moreover, the underlying assumption that both patient and therapist subscribe to a similar epistemological framework is not always the case in the African context. In rural communities, where medical practitioners sometimes work through translators, it is often difficult to obtain enough information from a patient to make a correct diagnosis. Persons who are uninformed of the various anatomic components of the human body find it difficult to describe the symptoms of their ailment. And even when the physicians eventually arrive at the physiological causes, the patients, holding on to a different causal framework, may believe that the physical ailment can ultimately be attributed to a non-physical cause (Gyekye 1995). This leads to a different evaluation of the information offered by the practitioner that can vitiate the consent granted by the patient. There are cases where patients with clearly diagnosed physiological conditions have been known to request to be released from hospitals, or have simply abandoned hospitals, in order to visit spiritual healers who, they believe can attend to the root cause of their ailments.[8, 9] Such behavior, which has been known to lead to tragic consequences, presents ethical dilemmas for biomedical health care providers.

An important driving factor for informed consent in the Western context is the fight against paternalism in health care. In most traditional African contexts, the role of the 'medicine-man'[10] is that of a person who holds esoteric knowledge and exercises a sacred ministry to the community using herbal and spiritual powers. The 'medicine-man' is perceived as a 'sacred minister', not a salaried professional who owes allegiance to an institution or a business practitioner who makes commercial gain from the exercise of his profession. The items required for the cures—foodstuffs, poultry or livestock—are not conceived as a payment for the services but as elements necessary to placate, ingratiate and obtain healing from the divinities. Personal gifts to the 'medicine-man' are a sign of gratitude usually given after the patient has regained health. 'Medicine-men' carry out their practice in a way that will be described as paternalistic within the context of Western health care. They decide what is wrong with the patient without necessarily divulging how they arrived at the diagnosis and they prescribe therapies without detailed explanations of each element of the treatment. The underlying bond between patient and healer is trust. The patient knows and trusts that the healer is neither an employee of a corporate body nor a private business person for whom there could be a potential conflict of interest between the patient's health and corporate or personal gain. Hence, there is trust-based paternalism, which does not have a negative connotation so long as the 'paternal' figure is acting as a true and genuine *pater*, a father.

Western biomedical practice, for historical motives linked to abuse and manipulation, has turned paternalism into a negative value. This is justifiable where trust in the *pater's* good and unbiased judgement is broken and when the *filius*, son, is grown enough to decide for himself. The solution that is often chosen, that is, greater autonomy of the patient, relies more on the second part of the statement, that is the capacity of the *filius* and less on the first part, that is repairing the broken trust in the *pater*. A possible solution could be to work on both aspects of the problem. In fact, the choice of placing greater emphasis on patient autonomy can and does, in the long run, fuel further lack of trust in medical practitioners and can also lead to a certain amount of professional disengagement on the part of practitioners who, for fear of legal retorsion, off-load the burden of ethical decisions to patients –or caregivers— who are hardly qualified to take those decisions.

It is true, as seen illustrated above, that there is bad medical practice in Africa. It is also true that informed consent as is generally perceived in the West is not the answer. A more adequate solution might require critically incorporating the value of trust into the exercise of the medical profession, as was the case with traditional medicine. But restoring trust, as has been pointed out by Onora O'Neill (O'Neill 2002), cannot be achieved in the abstract. It necessarily requires the fostering of trustworthy persons. In this light the necessity of adequate bioethics in the training programs of medical personnel becomes vital. This is currently not the case. In many SSA countries, bioethical training programs are yet to be incorporated nationwide in the curricula for training medical personnel.

Traditional medicine. The WHO defines traditional medicine as 'diverse health practices, approaches, knowledge and beliefs incorporating plant, animal, and/or mineral based medicine, spiritual therapies, manual techniques and exercises applied singularly or in combination to maintain well-being, as well as to treat, diagnose or prevent illness.' (WHO Traditional Medicine Strategy 2002–2005: 7) The same document estimates that traditional medicine is used by 80% of Africans sometimes in conjunction with other forms of medicine. The expression Traditional and Alternative Medicine (TAM) is also often used to refer to the group of medical practices that do not fit into the Western biomedical model. This expression is unhappy because the addition of the word 'alternative' carries connotations of estrangement.

I prefer to distinguish between traditional medicine and modern religious spiritual healing. Traditional medicine, as the name suggests, is linked to ethnic customs and belief systems that are indigenous to African peoples. Traditional medicine has a holistic view of the human person that does not allow for a net distinction between the spiritual and the physical or the natural and the supernatural (Wiredu 2003). The various branches of traditional medicine rely on plants and herbs as well as spiritual forces to cure the sick. In traditional medicine, the diagnosis usually entails establishing both physiological and non-physical causes. The latter can be done through spiritual divination by consulting the gods to establish the reason behind the present ailment and to establish the best line of cure (see Rose Mary Amenga-Etego, hapter 6). It is important to underline that in most SSA contexts, the cosmological framework presupposes a constant interaction and causality between the physical and non-physical worlds, the visible and invisible (Gyekye 1995).

Modern spiritual healing, on the other hand, is practiced mainly by Christian Charismatic Spiritualists and some Muslim healers. This form of health care is not traditional to Africa; it is a recent development of Christianity that draws from some charismatic interpretations of Scripture and ethnic beliefs. Mallams who claim to be able to draw mystical powers from the Quran practice the Muslim equivalent. These religious spiritual healers generally embrace the separation between the spiritual and the physical, a position as we have said earlier that is not innate to many African cultures. Religious spiritual healers generally believe that the root cause of many ailments is spiritual and that until the spiritual problems are settled no definitive cure can be given to physical ailments. Their emphasis is on curing the spirit of the person. Theirs is a position of 'doctors' of the spirit; in fact, some would like to be given the same recognition as biomedical physicians.

Even though there is an increasing drive to incorporate traditional medicine into the health care systems of SSA countries (Cfr. Kofi-Tsepo 2004), there are underlying bioethical issues that need to be addressed as this process develops. Academics and researchers often try to study the active ingredients of the herbal mixtures used by traditional healers. The goal of this exercise is to identify and extract the active ingredients and where possible, produce them on a purer, larger and, quite often commercial scale. Two ethical questions arise from this practice. The first is the question of intellectual property. Traditional unwritten formulae are not usually protected by patents. Researchers and scientists who are capable of decoding and formalizing these formulae can be hailed for discovery and awarded rights and benefits which in reality belong to others. Secondly, some attempts at integrating traditional medicine to mainstream health care are in reality forms of Westernization of traditional medicine. This process can be useful in providing knowledge about the curative powers of natural herbs and elements hitherto unknown. It also raises standards of hygiene of these products and mitigates undesired side effects. Nevertheless, the ethical question remains as to whether this is a form of emptying the holistic metaphysics of traditional medicine. A visit to a traditional healer is an experiential encounter, usually carved into a ritual of greetings, prayers, incantations, sacrifices, among others. The herbs and their active ingredients are important elements that contribute to the treatment, but they are not necessarily the essential element of the experience. An important part of the healing aspect of traditional medicine, the psychological, emotional, and faith experiences—is eliminated when traditional medicines are packaged and distributed like other pharmaceutical products.

Disclosure is one of the three conditions of informed consent. The power of the traditional healer lies in holding secret powers and knowledge that ordinary persons do not possess. What level of disclosure can be requested from a traditional healer for informed consent to be valid? A traditional healer can inform a patient about the anticipated effects/symptoms that will occur after undergoing a certain therapy. Disclosing the secrets of the art may be a form of demystification. Traditional healers are genuinely concerned about the what may happen to age-old guarded secret formula and knowledge were this to be rendered public. For example, 'bone-setters' in the Bulsa tradition of Northern Ghana who cure fractures usually break a stick, give it a ritual burial and then unearth it after a number of days. They then 'read' the behavior of the stick that has been buried before determining if and how to cure the fractured bone of the person. Even though one might and can search for 'scientific' explanations of this 'reading', it would be difficult to expect the 'bone-setter' to reveal the secret of his art.[11] It might even be the case that there are no rational categories that can offer an exhaustive explanation.

As said earlier, traditional medicine relies a good deal on trust. The patient believes and trusts that the healer is in possession of gifts and powers that are at the service of the community and the gods. Persons who recur to traditional medicine in some way are manifesting trust in this belief system. There is implicitly a form of consent here (Van Bogaert 2007). And if patients are to be protected from abuse, the rules must be elaborated from within that belief system to ensure that the persons to whom trust is attributed are indeed *trustworthy*.

Lastly, it must be said that in contemporary SSA traditional medicine is also succumbing to the drive for economic gain. As a result, there are cases of persons who under the guise of traditional medicine harm patients.[12] In some countries like Ghana, Western-based biomedical practitioners cannot advertise themselves whereas traditional healers can (see Afoko, chapter 8). Some studies claim that up to 70% of healers in rural Africa are charlatans who manipulate and cheat patients (Serbulea, in Van Bogaert 2007). What is more, it is relatively easy for some traditional and spiritual healers to abscond from taking responsibility for their errors and failures by attributing failure to non-measurable and uncontestable factors such as the other intervening spirits or failure on the part of the patient to fully adhere in mind and body to the prescribed therapy or simple lack of 'faith' on the part of the patient. South Africa in 2017 has tried to establish a legislative framework for licensing traditional healers. However, there is still debate on the adequacy and efficiency of the adopted criteria (Van Bogaert 2007). Many other SSA countries are yet to begin this process.

Modern Religious Spiritualistic Healing. A relatively recent strand of medicine that is found practically in all SSA countries is the art of healing through prayers, fasting, chanting and invocations practiced mainly by Christian Charismatic communities and in some Muslim communities. Renowned pastors or prophets offer medical consultations, often at a fee, to help patients diagnose the spiritual causes of their ailment. The ensuing therapy usually includes prayers by the pastor over the patient; prayers by the patient at established times and places; fasting; anointment with spiritual oils; sprinkling or drinking of holy water; wearing specially blessed objects or artefacts to spurn malignant spirits; bathing in the ocean; vigils; reading specific sacred passages; among other things.

This form of therapy is not restricted to health in the strict sense. Believers recur to pastors/prophets/mallams and other 'women and men of God' to find solutions to all types of life problems: finding a spouse; keeping the spouse; succeeding in business or at school; travelling blessings; obtaining a visa to the USA or Europe; sexual dysfunction; sterility and barrenness; safe childbirth; and, in general, happiness and well-being. Predominant among areas covered by religious spiritual health care practitioners is mental health. The treatment gap for mental disorder is many SSA countries is over 90%. Ghana, for example, has a treatment gap of 98%.[13] It is estimated that 96% of Ghanaians are religious believers. Christians constitute over 70% of the population whilst Muslims account for about 18%. There are officially only three psychiatric hospitals in the country situated around the capital, Accra, with 1332 beds.[14] A large part of mental health care in Ghana is provided by Christian spiritual prayer camps. The exact number of these is unknown. Conservative estimates from 2014 claim there are hundreds (Edwards 2014), but the current number could well be over a thousand. "Camps are commonly thought to vary in size, from small shack-like structures to entire village-communities with large church halls, facilities, and commerce. Most prayer camps are under-resourced, lacking adequate shelters, bedding, mosquito nets, cleaning supplies, and improved sanitation facilities. Prayer camps are often staffed by caretakers, pastors, and church elders, and may be led by a prophet or prophetess, who acts as the chief healer, spiritual leader, and administrator of the camp" (Arias, et al. 2016). The living conditions and therapeutic methods employed in these camps have been the object of concern. There have been cases of abuse including corporal punishment and chaining of mental health patients.[15]

Even though there have been attempts to integrate the activities of prayer camps into the main government recognized health care system, so far little has been achieved. The theoretical frameworks are still too wide apart as can be seen from the following declarations by persons working in prayer camps regarding the causes of mental disorder (Arias, et al. 2016):

1. *Some causes are physical. Substance abuse, like cannabis, cocaine, alcohol...It is the spirit that asks them to do it. You tell the spirit to stop, that you will not do this again, but you can't. Unless you add prayer, you don't have the strength to overcome the thing.* —Pastor
2. *There are a lot of causes. Some [patients] are cursed...in the blood...before you trace [the mental illness], you can see that you find it in the family [of the patient]...when you trace it back, you see that maybe that person who had it [earlier in the family history] was cursed.* —Senior prayer camp pastor
3. *In mental illness, 98% of the time it is spiritual. There is a verse from the Bible, Ephesians 6:12. 'For we wrestle not against flesh and blood, but against principalities, against powers, against the rulers of the darkness of this world, against spiritual wickedness in high places.' That is our philosophy [about] mental illness.* — Prayer camp prophetess

For most persons operating within prayer camps, the key to curing mental disorder lies in the spiritual realm. Even though they recognize the efficacy of biomedical therapy, most believe that ultimate cure must come from the spiritual:

When you go to the hospital, and they say you are okay, that means every month, or every three weeks or so, you have to go for medicine. Without the medicine for two weeks, you will fall back into your sickness... That is why you are being controlled. It is the medicine which is controlling you. Here, there is no medicine, just spiritual healing. If you are healed, you are healed forever" (Church elder).

Some prayer camp healers believe that collaboration ought to be established with biomedical health care providers. However, they also insist that spiritual health care be recognized and given a status equivalent to biomedical health care:

We should work together, thus using the hospital and the prayer camps, because God created himself in many ways. He's the creator of the universe. There is [a] physical side to everything, and there is [a] spiritual side. Let those in the prayer camp handle the spiritual aspect, [and let] the physicians handle the physical aspect" (Prophetess).

From a bioethical view, there are at least three areas of concern that need to be addressed. First is the question of physical abuse of patients: unhealthy living conditions; fasting by persons who are physically unfit; chaining and corporal punishment. This challenge which is often denounced by human rights activists is perhaps the least difficult to address. It can be overcome by creating and enforcing a normative framework of standards to be observed in prayer camps. More challenging is the possibility of moral and psychological abuse through manipulation. When patients are led to believe that the cause of their condition is due to hereditary factors or the presence of malignant spirits whose existence cannot be empirically verified, room is created for dishonest practitioners to manipulate patients and their families. In the process of diagnosis at spiritual camps, patients are often led to believe that there is some human agency that is partly or efficiently responsible for their conditions. For example, a patient suffering from schizophrenia might be told that the reason for her present condition is that a colleague at her place of work is using spiritual powers to impede her from succeeding in her career. Even though the pastor/prophet may not give a specific name, the patient will try to pin a name to the suggestion. In such a case, another person, a colleague, might find herself suspected or even victimized without understanding why. There are many cases of families that have been torn apart because of this form of diagnosis. Yet, there is no legal framework to protect persons from being accused unjustly under these circumstances.

The process of establishing a normative framework for the practice of religious spiritual health care remains unexplored. Criteria for discerning the authenticity of practitioners in this field will have to be established in collaboration with faith-based organizations. Practical randomized trials of collaboration have not yet yielded enough results to constitute a working model (Ofori-Atta, et al. 2018). The epistemic challenge of finding or elaborating a framework that embraces both the spiritual and biomedical sectors especially in the area of mental health care remains.

1.2.2 Bioethics of communo-cultural practices

Traditions, cultural practices and norms are part of the fabric of every society. These, even when they arise from pragmatic needs, eventually end up being woven into the belief systems that form part of the metaphysical framework of the society. For example, during the period of the transatlantic slave trade, the Bulsa people of Northern Ghana, who descend from the Mamprusi, used tribal scars on the faces of children as a distinguishing mark. In this way, Bulsa people who were captured into slavery could recognize each other in any part of the world. Later, the marks evolved into having other functions such as the power to protect children from evil spirits that caused infant mortality, among others. Among the various ethnic groups of SSA, there are communo-cultural practices that foster a healthy sense of identity, encourage sharing, and protect the environment. An example is the ban on going out to sea to fish on specific days (usually Tuesday) and seasons (around August) practiced by various fishing communities along the Gulf of Guinea. The taboos around these bans claim that the recreational activity of the sea gods is not to be disturbed by fishing activities at those particular times. The norm however also has many benefits such as promoting sustainability of fishing by allowing time for marine species to regenerate and offering a mandatory period of rest for fisher folk as well as introducing the performance of rituals that help to unite communities and enhance a sense of identity.

Nevertheless, some communo-cultural practices raise bioethical concerns. For example, despite official governmental prohibitions, female genital mutilation is still highest in SSA,[16] persecution of persons with albinism is still prevalent in some parts of East Africa,[17] *trokosi* or ritual servitude is still practiced in some parts of Ghana, Togo and Benin.[18] Communo-cultural practices that require giving a ritual burial to dead contributed to the spreading of Ebola during the 2014 outbreak in Guinea, Liberia and Sierra Leone (Frimpong-Mansoh, chapter 2). The *dipo* puberty rites among the Krobo in Ghana, where young girls have to undergo a test of virginity, raise questions regarding a woman's right to the privacy of her body.[19] In January 2018, the river Ofin gods of the Upper Denkyira East district of Ghana issued, through their priest mediators, a ban on girls crossing the river during menstruation. The girls who need to cross the river to get to school daily saw their access to education curbed by this taboo.[20]

Communo-cultural practices that lead to discrimination against some members of society based on sex, sexual orientation, genetic abnormalities, tribal origin, psychiatric and physiological conditions, call for ethical examination. The most common approach to eliminating or curbing these practices of discrimination has so far been through legislation and punishment. Yet some practices continue even when they are officially illegal. At least twenty-nine countries in Africa do not recognize polygamous marriages. However, in many of these countries, polygamy is *de jure* illegal but practiced and decriminalized *de facto*.[21] Without getting into the debate concerning the immorality of polygamy, I would like to point out that that the inefficiency of programs dedicated to eliminating certain traditional practices can be attributed to cultural impositions stemming from metaphysical and anthropological presuppositions that are foreign to African peoples. Usually, the motivations, theoretical and historical, that might have led to these practices are not carefully examined. It is all too easy to classify these practices with derogatory terms like 'primitive' or 'backward'. Even when NGOs carry out 'educational' programs to reduce or curb these practices, there is often little effort put into integrating the new models into the existing value system and offering holistic solutions.

Coming back to the example of polygamy, in some communities, marriage is a protection for women against social vulnerability. Where polygamy is rendered illegal and no framework has been put into place to guarantee the rights of women against this vulnerability, a new series of problems are generated. For example, women who conceive with a married man, may find themselves and their children in a more precarious situation because they are not only derided by society and their own families for having children out of wedlock,[22] but they may also be exposed to grave economic and social hardship since there are no efficient systems to ensure that both mother and child receive enough social and economic protection. Of course, the solution is not polygamy. But the point is that an understanding of the cultural institution of marriage and the organization of children and mother's rights needs to be factored into a normative framework for the abolition of polygamy.

In sum, bioethics in SSA faces the challenge not only of trying to ensure standards, praxis and norms that protect persons and communities, but to do so efficiently, there is the need to engage in the difficult task of cultural anthropology and to find new paradigms and terms of reference for a normative discourse.

1.2.3 Bioethics of consumerism and Corruption

A new visitor to the major cities of most SSA countries is surprised by the pervasive presence of billboards advertising all kinds of products and services. The advertisements range from larger-than-life photographs of pastors offering miracles to pharmaceutical companies promoting contraceptives and day-after pills; from companies offering funeral insurance policies to politicians promising a brighter future to citizens in exchange for votes. Recent economic growth and globalization has turned SSA into a fertile market. Unfortunately, some of the products on sale in the African markets are either fake or sub-standard and harmful to health. Companies that would not sell the same merchandise in their countries of origin sometimes sell these products in Africa. A 2016 BBC report named five Swiss companies that are linked with exporting diesel containing high levels of toxins that would not be acceptable in Switzerland.[23] Other studies have revealed that in Ghana and seven other African countries, the sulfur content of imported diesel products is 150 to 1000 times higher than current European limits.[24] In the pharmaceutical field, large quantities of substandard and falsified products are currently being sold in SSA. In a region where malaria is a widespread threat, it is worrying that: "Since 2013, WHO has received 1500 reports of cases of substandard or falsified products. ... Of these, substandard antimalarial drugs and antibiotics are the most commonly reported. Most of the reports (42%) come from Sub-Saharan Africa, 21% from the Americas and 21% from the European region."[25]

Apart from the question of false and sub-standard products, there is also the use of products, especially in the cosmetic sector, that are harmful to health. Driven by overt and subliminal advertising, some Africans recur to beauty products such as skin bleaching creams and pills that are known to have adverse effects on health (de Souza 2008). Even though there is enough medical evidence to show the dangers of this practice and several attempts are being made to dissuade the practice, several skin-bleaching products are sold freely without prescription across the region. What is more, advertisers and entertainers on the continent continue to privilege fair-skinned models over darker ones thereby reinforcing the beauty myth associated with fairer skinned people.

Since the ethical practices of pharmaceutical companies regarding access to retroviral drugs for the cure of HIV in Africa has been widely discussed, I will not dwell on that topic (Ahn, et al., 2003) (ibid.). The underlying ethical question is behavior that would seem to attach less value to the lives of Africans by both foreign and local companies. It would seem that profit making is a much stronger value than concern for the well-being of communities and persons. The current debate going on in many SSA countries regarding the use of GMOs as a solution to the need to increase local agricultural food yields and to reduce dependence on imported food items,[26] is also a new frontier where economic concerns are playing an important role in the debate (Komparic 2015).

One might ask whether there are regulatory bodies in SSA countries. The answer is both yes and no. In many cases the bodies and the regulatory framework exist, however, enforcement is a challenge due to lack of resources and corruption.[27] In others, the existing rules are inadequate, and there is inertia in changing and updating because some persons do derive benefits and advantages from the normative gaps. In the case of the diesel products, the Swiss companies mentioned in the BBC report defended their actions by pointing to the fact that the high level of toxins contained in the diesel products sold to African countries were legal and within the limits set by the SSA countries. The local regulatory counterparts echoed by saying that if Ghanaians wanted better fuel, they should prepare themselves to pay higher for fuel.

The bioethics of consumerism and corruption in SSA ultimately brings to the fore the imbalance of economic power of SSA countries with regards to other parts of the world. There is a question of justice when sub-standard products are intentionally produced and dumped on a region. The challenge is also internal to SSA countries where the colonized appropriate and imitate the culture of the colonizer to overcome a feeling of inadequacy and fit into the standards of the latter. This, in turn, fuels the market for sub-standard products that are unhealthy but within the purchasing power of citizens of low-income countries.[28]

1.2.4 Natural Resources and Environmental Bioethics

According to the World Bank listing of 2017, only five African countries belong to the Upper category of Upper Middle-Income Economies.[29] The rest are either Lower or Lower Middle-Income Economies with a per capita of less than 4,035 dollars per annum. Africa also has the highest population growth rate of 2.55 percent per annum; above twice the world average.[30] The continent holds a large percent of the world's natural resources.[31] It not surprising that the budgets of many SSA are sustained by natural resources. Apart from the endemic problems of corruption and mismanagement that hamper a fair distribution of the gains from these resources, there are also questions of degradation of the environment, pollution, child labor and poor working conditions for laborers.

Added to this is the fact that rapid urbanization, population growth and inadequate waste management are causing health hazards for people living in cities in SSA. Air pollution is high[32] and the ocean in some parts has become a rubbish dump, particularly with plastic waste. This creates health risks especially for populations whose main source of nutrition and income is fishing.

From an ethical viewpoint, the first most general question is: given that most natural resources are irreplaceable, what does the current generation owe to future ones, if it consumes all the available resources? Then there are the more particular bioethical concerns regarding the environment, health and sustainability. Of particular bioethical concern also are the working conditions of persons along the production line of the exploitation of Africa's natural resources. A good example is the spread of HIV/AIDS among workers in the mining sector in South Africa (Campbell and Williams 1999), where mining towns are populated with youthful male migrant workers from rural communities. The gender imbalance of these towns contributes to a higher incidence of promiscuity, mainly through prostitution. Infected miners, in turn, spread the disease upon return to their original communities. Mining companies have launched initiatives to reduce the spread of the virus through awareness, testing and screening programs.[33] The question, however, remains concerning the justice of fostering the growth of these towns where young males, driven by poverty, migrate to, to earn a living but cannot afford to take their families along with them. Other examples are the exploitation of child labor and the pollution of water bodies in DRC along the cobalt supply chain.[34] Similar examples are found in the informal gold mining sector in Ghana, popularly known as *galamsey*.[35] The persons who work in these sectors are constantly exposed to health risks, disabling accidents are common and longevity is heavily compromised.[36] Also of concern is damage to the environment, including the water bodies which are the source of livelihood for humans and animals in many communities that are not even directly involved in the mining activities.

The exploitation of natural resources for human use has been present in Africa for millennia. Nevertheless, the current situation of population growth and mass commercialization of these resources calls for a pondered balance between immediate and the longer-term health benefits of peoples.

1.2.5 Bioethical neocolonialism

Among the five areas of bioethical concern in Africa, the question of neo-colonialism is perhaps the one most written about in scholarly literature. It also the most difficult to conceptually delineate. Almost all major African bioethicists have expressed concern about the imposition of Western models of bioethics on Africans: Andoh; Murove; Gbadegesin; Metz; Tangwa; Fayemi; Widdows; and Behrens; to mention a few. Neo-colonialism as a form of control or pressure exercised by wealthier economic powers on developing countries, especially former colonies can be economic, political and cultural. Bioethics is not the only realm in which Africans experience neo-colonialism. Indeed, it is hard to prove that bioethics has an explicit neo-colonial agenda. However, as Widdows (Widdows 2007) and Bamford (Bamford 2016) have both pointed out, the historical origins and the practical implementation of bioethics reveal that there is a real risk of cultural neo-colonialism, fueled by economic and political forces. This happens when so-called global models and criteria are imposed with a superiority complex on parts of the world without regard to indigenous values systems. The imposition need not be explicit, but it can be implicit, as Camillia Kong points out when she challenges the reductivist and de-contextualized enframing of psychiatric genomics (see Camilla Kong, chapter 5).

Pinning down the exact *modus operandi* of bioethical neo-colonialism in Africa is elusive. The discourse is often tinged with ideology, prejudice and emotions arising from the historical imbalance of power in the relationship between Africa and the West. Nevertheless, on the theoretical and practical levels respectively, three challenges that can be enucleated.

On the theoretical level, the first challenge can be traced back to the individual versus community debate that has been at the heart of African philosophy. As pointed out at the beginning of this chapter, the question of individual autonomy was a key element in the emergence and development of bioethics in the West. In the 1970's debate surrounding abortion in Italy, the pro-abortion slogan among Italian women was '*l'utero è mio e lo gestisco io!*" (the uterus is mine and I gestate/manage it). An African response might have been "*l'utero è tuo, e la gestisci per tutti noi*" (the uterus is yours and you gestate/manage it for all of us). The 1973 United States Supreme Court ruling on Roe v. Wade regarding the constitutionality of laws prohibiting or restricting abortion was based on the 14th Amendment, Due Process Clause, that the right to privacy could extend to a woman's decision to have an abortion. Even though the ruling made room for state intervention to protect health and life, the overriding factor that made abortion legal was the woman's right to decide with regards to her body. No wonder pro-abortion movement in the United States is called pro-choice. There is no doubt that the underlying arguments used to legalize abortion under these circumstances were tinged with libertarianism.

The question of neo-colonialism arises when the results of these debates are exported and imposed on African societies through political, cultural and economic pressure without making room for any discussion on their theoretical underpinnings. Regarding abortion, in particular, Metz has demonstrated how abortion could be upheld, with some restrictions, arguing from an African philosophy of *Ubuntu*. Some human rights activists and donor agencies have been known to chastise and to hold African governments for ransom for not replicating normative standards that have been set based on assumptions and arguments that most Africans do not share. For example, in the current debate surrounding the laws against homosexuality that exist in many SSA countries, arguments based on the right to express one's sexuality so long as it does not violate other persons' rights to do same, have so far proven to have little resonance among most Africans. Neither is economic blackmail of African governments[37] nor 'naming and shaming' of African leaders a thoroughly ethical solution. African scholars, for example Dr Martin Ajei,[38] have shown, arguing from various African traditions, that homosexuality can be upheld or at least not persecuted. Another example is how Gbadegesin tries to uphold euthanasia arguing from the communitarian Yoruba value of *Ikuyajesin* instead of the more frequent individualistic 'right to die' discourse that is frequent in Western theorizations (Gbadegesin 1993).[39] All the above-mentioned African authors, Metz, Ajei and Gbadegesin have come under criticism from fellow African scholars (e.g. Fayemi & Akintunde 2012). Notwithstanding the differences, it is these internal debates that can generate a normative framework whose theoretical underpinnings, being African, can resonate more with the peoples of SSA. The differences of interpretation even of same ethnic traditions, as in the case of Gbadegesin and Fayemi, can only go a long way to enrich the African bioethical deliberations.

The second theoretical challenge with neo-colonialism is the positivistic assumption that underlies many Western theories in the biomedical sciences. Compte's claim "that each of our leading conceptions – each branch of our knowledge – pass successively through three different theoretical conditions: the Theological, or fictitious; the Metaphysical, or abstract; and the Scientific, or positive,"[40] thereby making supernatural and metaphysical explanations obsolete, is all too present in the life sciences. African cosmology is deeply spiritual (Gyekye 1995). Neo-colonialism creates models that deride attempts to explain events and ailments by appealing to supernatural or theological forces. The neo-colonial approach does not only exclude these elements, but it also proposes to hound them out by degrading them to the level of myths and tales of no scientific value. And when there is something good that can be obtained from these non-positivistic frameworks as is the case of traditional herbal medicine, the neo-colonial approach is to 'positivize' it by emptying it of all supernatural content. This form of positivism is a cultural imposition that is at odds with the beliefs of many African peoples.

The third and final theoretical aspect of neo-colonialism in the field of bioethics is Western dogmatism. It is ironic that societies founded on libertarian principles can be so dogmatic especially in relation to persons who are not members of the same societies. The dogmatic version of Western biomedical sciences refuses to consider any plausible causes of illness of disorder that cannot be attributed to biochemical or genetic causes.

The theoretical manifestations of neo-colonialism in bioethics and other similar fields are all based on the assumption of intellectual supremacy that Western civilization has arrogated to itself. Granted that the scientific and technological achievements of the West are unparalleled, it does not necessarily derive that there could be nothing the West could learn from other traditions.

The theoretical assumptions of neo-colonialism have practical consequences in the lives of SSA citizens. First among these is normative misalignment which in turn generates dysfunctionality and encourages corruption. The current legal systems of many SSA countries is a continuation of laws put into place by colonial rulers. For example, Ghanaian law still considers attempted suicide a punishable act of misdemeanor (Criminal Code, 1960; 29.57.2). A recent study of nine African countries, mostly former British colonies, shows how laws prescribing the prosecution of suicide survivors are framed in almost identical language (Adinkrah 2016), pointing to their colonial origin. Ironically, in 1961 the United Kingdom repealed her laws regarding the prosecution of suicide survivors, but many former colonies are still holding on to the colonial heritage. No wonder, the result is a good deal of underreporting of suicides attempts by both family members and health care practitioners in some African countries.

Bioethical neo-colonialism does not only affect laws passed during the colonial era. In recent times, as new ethical challenges emerge, legislators often adopt and enact *ad litteram* laws that were created in other jurisdictions, mainly in the West. For example, laws regarding biosafety in Kenya can be traced back to the Cartagena Protocol whose premises are based on principlism (Fayemi and Macaulay-Adeyelure 2016:5).

The second practical issue regarding the bioethical neo-colonialism is found especially around research. A good part of research carried out in SSA countries is funded by organizations outside the region. The amount of funding available locally for research is extremely limited. For this reason, researchers in the region have to align their themes and methods to the demands of funders even where the criteria do not completely address local exigencies (e.g. Ssali, et al 2016). Bioethical concerns have also been raised about the activities of researchers from foreign countries who carry out research on human subjects in Africa. These concerns and others led to the publication in 2014 of the volume on *Research Ethics in Africa: a Resource for Research Ethics Committees.*[41] The work in this volume is yet to be adopted by many centres across the continent.

Another form of bioethical neo-colonialism on the practical level, closely linked to dogmatism on the theoretical, level is what Tangwa denounces when he says: "Western civilization and culture has a big mouth and loud voice which it knows how to use very well and small ears which are scarcely ever used" (Tangwa 2010: 153). He continues: "The main underlying problem with the Western background and outlook is its epistemological over-confidence, bordering on arrogance and often resulting in recklessness. The constant perennial overturning and correction of past 'knowledge' by new 'knowledge' has not necessarily led to tentativeness by Western scientists and technologists in their claims or to more circumspection and caution in their interventions in nature. On the other hand, and by contrast, the main underlying value of the African world-view and outlook is its epistemological humility and respectful caution, as befits fallible beings, even if it also has the strong tendency toward conservatism and lack of progress" (Ibid. 161)

African bioethicists have tried to respond to some of these neo-colonial challenges by proposing solutions that vary from resistance to Western bioethics (Onouha 2007), to rewriting the bioethics principles of Beauchamp and Childress (Behrens 2013) and to adopting what is often called 'African bioethics'. This latter question of African bioethics has become a debate issue that re-echoes some of the questions of the 20th century debate surrounding the existence and nature of African philosophy.

Whilst Tangwa, Behrens, Murove and Andoh would see African bioethics rooted in African values and traditions as a route to decolonizing bioethics, others such as Coleman express "doubts as to an established body of knowledge that can be referred to as 'African bioethics'. Coleman, referring to the proponents of African bioethics says that: "There is clearly an attempt by these SSA authors to project a traditional African anthropological and philosophical contribution, towards presenting an African worldview of current hot issues in contemporary bioethics (issues as euthanasia, abortion). This is a more hermeneutic exercise, which sometimes is complicated by the very different interpretative views of different African authors" (Coleman 2017: 44). Fayemi and Macaulay-Adeyelure also note that "the attempt to decolonize bioethics in Africa by opting for Africanizing bioethics exclusively in Africa has the danger of 'dichotomizing different cultures as 'radical others' on one another, promoting the tyranny of existing cultural practices, and obscuring the real issues at stake. Values that are advocated in bioethics such as respect for human dignity, human freedom and care are not only universal in scope; they are also eternal values. Thus, cultural differences can be seriously misconceived and misused in ways that some moral judgments and practical matters become easily entangled. The appeal to cultural differences as 'colonial distance' and serving as an ethical justification for rejecting those norms perceived as originating in the West and strongly advocated there is logically unsound" (Fayemi and Macaulay-Adeyelure 2016:8). They advocate, in my opinion, rightly, for a greater focus on the bioethical problems of Africans today and to critically examine both traditional and imported models to see how to contribute to improving the lives of peoples. This he calls bioethics in Africa, in contrast with African bioethics. This is what we have tried to explore in this chapter. And I would add further that it is carrying out this exercise that a school or way of doing bioethics in Africa can emerge that may eventually become 'African bioethics'.

1.3 Conclusions and recommendations

In the light of the foregoing challenges, it is evident that the field of bioethics in SSA is vast and requires urgent attention. It is also clear that a multi-disciplinary approach is required. This multi-disciplinarity, due to the ethnic, cultural, religious and philosophical pluralism that is reality in Africa, will need to be more embracing and perhaps less dogmatic than some approaches to bioethics in other parts of the world. Bioethicists from different disciplines will have to elaborate a common grammar that will favor fruitful dialogue between traditions and worldviews that seem miles apart. In this way, bioethics in Africa will not only serve the African peoples better but could also be a model for other parts of the world where bioethical schools tend to follow parallel discourses.

1.3.1 Ten Common-sense recommendations

In this vein, I would like to end this prolegomenon proposing 10 common sense guidelines to doing bioethics in Africa.

1. Health is both an individual and communitarian good. The WHO definition of health as a state of complete physical, mental and social well-being and not merely the absence of disease or infirmity, ought to be taken fully especially in the aspect of social well-being. Hence, the ethical decisions regarding the health of a person cannot be divorced from communitarian considerations.
2. The healing experience is greater than the biomedical or the genomic. An understanding of the treatment of disease and disorder that is limited only to comprehending the biomedical or genomic is partial. For most African traditions, visiting a health care practitioner to seek a cure is much more that seeking biochemical solutions to a bodily dysfunction or mental disorder. The art of healing is an experience that aims at re-establishing a harmony which includes all aspects of the person.

3. *Corpore sano in mens sana.* As Kwame Gyekye points out referring to Akan ontology (Gyekye 1995), a good number of African traditional worldviews are spiritual. Hence, an unhealthy body is unlikely to be found in an unhealthy *mens* (spirit). So, unlike the common Latin view expressed as *mens sana in corpore sano*, it is sometimes more appropriate to look at health from the angle of a sound spirit in a healthy body.
4. Bioethics is about prevention. The history of bioethics in the Western world has mostly been reactionary: responding to ethical challenges of new technologies in biomedicine. SSA countries are in the process of rapid cultural, social and technological evolution that requires new policies. Bioethicists in Africa will do well to anticipate and participate in bringing the discipline into policy-making forums rather than react after poor or inadequate choices have been made.
5. Critical Sankofaism. It is very well to appeal to ethnic traditions and values when making bioethical choices. However, traditions and cultural norms must also be subjected to critical analysis and where necessary updated to contemporary contexts. Old solutions to new problems are not always the best.
6. Inclusion. The search for solutions to bioethical problems in Africa as mentioned above needs to have a more communitarian dimension. There is a difference between communitarianism and tribalism which advocates community within the tribe and margination outside the tribe. An authentically communitarian bioethics combats the margination of categories of persons for social, health, sexual, racial, ethnic, and cultural reasons. Given that Africa today is part of the 'global community', the communitarian spirit needs to be ecumenical towards Western culture, despite any resistance from persons who might be described as 'individualists' or 'recalcitrant communitarians'.
7. Courage in the face of economic tyranny. The economic poverty that bedevils most SSA countries can often lead to choices that privilege immediate financial and economic gain over long-term sustainability. This is particularly relevant for those bioethical choices that have to do with protecting the physical and immaterial environment. Courage is required to avoid this pitfall.
8. Emergency cannot be a permanent state. It is commonplace to appeal to situations of emergency –acute lack of resources, epidemics, natural disasters—to justify omitting recourse to proper bioethical considerations in making choices. However, choices must be made to ensure that states of emergency do not

become permanent, the norm, or an excuse for overlooking bioethical considerations.
9. Ethics is not mathematics. Aristotle in the *Nichomachean Ethics* reminds us that if ethics is about the good of humans, the nature of that good cannot be determined with the exactitude of a mathematical problem, because the subject matter, human actions in themselves, leave room for uncertainty (Aristotle 1094, b 11-27). African scholars have criticized Western bioethics as being over-certain and even arrogant. The same danger applies to African bioethics within the region. SSA is made up of many peoples from different ethnic backgrounds and cultures with different religious traditions. Bioethicists within the continent need to ensure that the traditions of one ethnic tradition, albeit a majority, are not imposed on minority traditions. Bioethics is Africa should appeal to the plurality of traditions as a source of ethical reflection. The truth, as Hans Urs Von Balthasaar proposes, is symphonic.
10. *Salus populi suprema lex esto* (Cicero *De Leggibus*, III, III, VIII). Cicero's maxim, "The health (welfare, good, salvation, felicity) of the people should be the supreme law." Even though there can be differing views about the content of *salus populi*, this generic recommendation, when adopted as an underlying motivation, makes room for healthy and constructive dialogue.

1.4 Notes

[1] *Sankofa* in the Twi language of Ghana means "Go back and get it", it refers to the Asante Adinkra symbol represented by a bird with its head turned backwards while its feet face forward carrying a precious egg in its mouth. *Sankofaism* is the appeal to ethnic traditions and values when making decisions in the present and for the future. However, traditions and cultural norms must also be subjected to critical analysis and where necessary updated to contemporary contexts, hence the term 'critical sankofaism'.

[2] This has led some such as Fayemi and Macaulay-Adeyelure, (2016) to question whether there are even bioethics in Africa.

[3] Viewed 04 June 2018, from https://www.indexmundi.com/g/r.aspx?v=26&t=20

[4] Viewed 04 June 2018, from https://en.wikipedia.org/wiki/List_of_countries_by_life_expectancy

[5] Viewed 04 June 2018, from http://apps.who.int/gho/data/node.sdg.3-2-viz?lang=en

[6] Discussions with participants at bioethics conference held at the University of Ghana. May 2017.

[7] Doctor to Patient ratios range from as low as 3 (Niger) to 77 (South Africa) per 100,000 people. In the UK the figure is 271 doctors per 100,000 people.

[8] Viewed 04 June 2018, from https://www.reuters.com/article/us-health-ebola-congo/ebola-patients-slip-out-of-congo-hospital-as-medics-try-to-curb-outbreak-idUSKCN1IO1AW

[9] Discussion during bioethics conference 2017 held at the University of Ghana

[10] **Medicine man**, also called **medicine person** or **healer**, member of an indigenous society who is knowledgeable about the magical and chemical potencies of various substances (medicines) and skilled in the rituals through which they are administered (viewed 04 June 2018, from https://www.britannica.com/topic/medicine-man)

[11] Recourse to '*mysteria*' is a part of almost all religious traditions.

[12] Guinea healer held over faking hundreds of pregnancies, viewed 04 June 2018, from http://www.bbc.com/news/world-africa-42718604

[13] World Health Organization (WHO). Mental health situational analysis in Ghana, viewed 04 June 2018, from http://www.who.int/mental_health/policy/country/ghana/en/

[14] World Health Organization (WHO). WHO-AIMS Report on Mental Health System in Ghana [Internet]. 2011. Viewed 04 June 2018, from http://www.who.int/mental_health/who_aims_country_reports/ghana_who_aims_report.pdf.

[15] Human Rights Watch. Like a Death Sentence: Abuses against Persons with Mental Disabilities in Ghana, 2012, viewed 04 June 2018 from https://www.hrw.org/report/2012/10/02/death-sentence/abuses-against-persons-mental-disabilities-ghana.

[16] Viewed 04 June 2018 from, https://www.unicef.org/wcaro/overview_4571.html

[17] Viewed 04 June 2018 from, http://www.latimes.com/world/africa/la-fg-malawi-albinos-hunted-2017-story.html

[18] Viewed 04 June 2018 from, https://www.ghanaweb.com/GhanaHomePage/NewsArchive/Trokosi-practice-still-popular-in-Ghana-Research-146003

[19] Dipo is celebrated in the month of April every year. The festival is used to usher girls who are virgins into being of age to be married. Girls to go through rituals and tests to prove their chastity before they qualify to partake in the festival. They are the cladded with cloth to just their knee level and paraded before the entire community as the initiates (dipo-yi).

[20] Menstruating girls banned from crossing Ghana river. Viewed 04 June 2018, from http://www.bbc.com/news/world-africa-42652314

[21] Viewed 04 June 2018, from https://en.wikipedia.org/wiki/Legality_of_polygamy#cite_note-genderindex.org-81

[22] Born ones, they are called in Ghana

[23] Fuel 'too dirty' for Europe sold to Africa. Viewed 04 June 2018, from

http://www.bbc.com/news/world-africa-37373414

[24] Viewed 04 June 2018, from https://www.graphic.com.gh/news/general-news/ghana-imports-substandard-diesel-fuel.html

[25] WHO news release, 2017, 1 in 10 medical products in developing countries is substandard or falsified, viewed 04 June 2018, from http://www.who.int/news-room/detail/28-11-2017-1-in-10-medical-products-in-developing-countries-is-substandard-or-falsified

[26] Ghana imported some 689,000 metric tonnes of rice in 2016. Viewed 04 June 2018 from https://www.ghanabusinessnews.com/2017/05/11/ghana-imports-300m-worth-of-rice-in-2016/

[27] Corruption In Food and Drugs Authority (FDA) in Ghana and Nigeria.

[28] Viewed 04 June 2018, from https://philarchive.org/archive/MILGBA-2v1

[29] Viewed 04 June 2018, from http://www.iscb2017.info/uploadedFiles/ISCB2017.y23bw/fileManager/CFDC%20World%20Bank%20List.pdf

[30] Viewed 04 June 2018, from UN http://www.un.org/en/sections/issues-depth/population/

[31] 99 percent of the world's chrome resources, 85 percent of its platinum, 70 percent of its tantalite, 68 percent of its cobalt, and 54 percent of its gold, among others. Viewed 04 June 2018 from, https://www.google.com.gh/search?q=percentage+of+natural+resources+in+africa&oq=percentage+of+natural+resources+in+africa&aqs=chrome..69i57j0.33734j0j4&sourceid=chrome&ie=UTF-8

[32] Review of Urban Air Quality in Sub-Saharan Africa Region: Air Quality Profile of SSA Countries. Viewed 04 June 2018 from, https://doi.org/10.1596/26864

[33] Viewed 04 June 2018, from https://www.miningglobal.com/operations/hivaids-mining-industry-what-are-we-doing-about-it

[34] Viewed 04 June 2018, from https://www.cbsnews.com/news/cobalt-children-mining-democratic-republic-congo-cbs-news-investigation/

[35] Galamsey or artisanal mining involves rudimentary techniques of mineral extraction, highly manual processes, hazardous working conditions and low levels of environmental and health awareness.

[36] Viewed 04 June 2018, from https://www.ghanaweb.com/GhanaHomePage/NewsArchive/Galamsey-In-Ghana-And-Its-Health-Implications-375099

[37] In 2011 during a Commonwealth meeting, the Prime Minister of UK David Cameron threatened to cut aid to commonwealth African nations that did not grant gay rights. This position was viewed by most Africans as a form of neo-colonialism.

[38] Martin Ajei is a senior lecturer in the Department of Philosophy and Classics in the University of Ghana. He has presented at various seminars papers on the tenability of homosexuality within an African context.

[39] Gbadegesin (1993), "Bioethics and culture: an African perspective."

[40] From *The Positive Philosophy of Auguste Comte* (trans. Harriet Martineau; London, 1853), Vol. I, p. 1.

[41] Viewed 04 June 2018, from https://www.sun.ac.za/english/faculty/healthsciences/paediatrics-and-child-health/Documents/9781920689315%20Research%20Ethics.pdf

1.5 References

Adinkrah, M., 2016, 'Anti-suicide laws in nine African countries: Criminalization, prosecution and penalization', *African Journal of Criminology and Justice Studies, AJCJS*, 9(1), 279.

Arias, D., Taylor, L., Ofori-Atta, A., & Bradley, E. H., 2016, 'Prayer camps and biomedical care in Ghana: Is collaboration in mental health care possible?' *PLoS ONE, 11*(9), e0162305. http://doi.org/10.1371/journal.pone.0162305

Aristotle, 1925, *The Nichomachean Ethics*, transl. W.D., Ross, Oxford, Vol.IX.

Andoh, C. T., 2011, Bioethics the challenge to its growth in Africa, *Open Journal of Philosophy*, 1, 67-75, viewed 04 June, from https://doi.org/10.4236/ojpp.2011.12012

Ahn, M.J., Grimwood, A., Schwarzwald, H. and Herman, A., 2003, 'Ethics and the AIDS pandemic in the developing world', *Journal of the International Association of Physicians in AIDS Care*, 2(2), 81-87.

Behrens, K.G., 2013, 'Towards an indigenous African bioethics', *South African Journal of Bioethics and Law*, 6(1), 32-35.

Campbell, C. and Williams, B., 1999, 'Beyond the biomedical and behavioral: Towards an integrated approach to HIV prevention in the Southern African mining industry', *Social Science & Medicine*, 48(11), 1625-1639.

Coleman, A.M.E., 2017, 'What is "African Bioethics" as used by Sub-Saharan African authors: An argumentative literature review of articles on African bioethics', *Open Journal of Philosophy*, 7(01), 33.

Comte, A., 1853. *The Positive Philosophy of Auguste Comte*, Transl. H. Martineau, London, Vol. I, p. 1.

de Souza, M.M., 2008, 'The concept of skin bleaching in Africa and its devastating health implications', *Clinics in Dermatology*, 26(1), 27-29.

Fayemi, A.K. and Macaulay-Adeyelure, O.C., 2016, 'Decolonizing bioethics in Africa, *BEOnline: Journal of the West African Bioethics Training Program*', 3(4), 68.

Gbadegesin, S., 1993, 'Bioethics and culture: An African perspective', *Bioethics*, 7(2-3), 257-262.

Gorovitz, S., 1977, 'Bioethics and social responsibility', *The Monist*, 60(1), 3-15.

Gyekye, K., 1995, '*An essay on African philosophical thought: The Akan conceptual scheme*', Temple University Press, Philadelphia.

Iloh, G.U., Chuku, A., Amadi, A.N., 2017, 'Medical errors in Nigeria: A cross-sectional study of medical practitioners in Abia State', *Arch Med*

Health Sci, viewed 04 June 2018, from http://www.amhsjournal.org/text.asp?2017/5/1/44/208180

Komparic, A., 2015, 'The ethics of introducing GMOs into Sub-Saharan Africa: Considerations from the Sub-Saharan African theory of Ubuntu', *Bioethics*, *29*(9), 604-612.

Metz, T., 2010, 'African and Western moral theories in a bioethical context', *Developing World Bioethics*, *10*(1), 49-58.

Ofori-Atta, A., Attafuah, J., Jack, H., Baning, F., Rosenheck, R. and Joining Forces Research Consortium, 2018, 'Joining psychiatric care and faith healing in a prayer camp in Ghana: Randomised trial', *The British Journal of Psychiatry*, *212*(1), 34-41.

O'neill, O., 2002, *Autonomy and trust in bioethics*, Cambridge University Press.

Onouha, C., 2007, 'Bioethics across borders: An African perspective', *Studies in Social Science*, Upssala.

Pine, B.J., Pine, J. and Gilmore, J.H., 1999, *The experience economy: Work is theatre & every business a stage*, Harvard Business Press.

Tangwa, G.B., 2016, 'Ebola Vaccine Trial', in D. Schroeder, J. Cook Lucas, S. Fenet, F. Hirsch, (eds), *"Ethics Dumping" – Paradigmatic case studies'*, *a report for TRUST*, viewed 04 June 2018, from http://trust-project.eu/deliverables-and-tools/.

Tangwa, G.B., 2010, *Elements of African bioethics in a Western frame*. African books collective.

Tannor, E.K., Awuku, Y.A., Boima, V. and Antwi, S., 2018, 'The geographical distribution of dialysis services in Ghana, *Renal Replacement Therapy*, *4*(1), 3.

Tindana, P. O., Kass, N., & Akweongo, P., 2006, 'The informed consent process in a rural African setting: A case study of the Kassena-Nankana district of northern Ghana', *IRB*, *28*(3), 1–6.

Van Bogaert, D.K., 2007, 'Ethical considerations in African traditional medicine: A response to Nyika, *Developing world bioethics*, *7*(1), 35-40.

Widdows, H., 2007, 'Is global ethics moral neo-colonialism? An investigation of the issue in the context of bioethics'. *Bioethics*, *21*(6), 305-315.

Wiredu, K., 2003, 'On decolonizing African religions', in P. H. Coetzee & A. P. J. Roux (eds.), *The African philosophy reader*, p. 21, Routledge, London.

Chapter 2

Bioethics:
Traditional African Perspective

Yaw A. Frimpong-Mansoh
Northern Kentucky University

Abstract

Challenges African bioethicists to expand their focus beyond ethical issues raised by biomedical and biotechnological science. The author discusses philosophical puzzles raised by the African mystical system of beliefs and practices in which African traditional medicine is fundamentally rooted. Also, the author uses a case study from traditional healthcare practices of the Yoruba ethnic group in Nigeria (viz. consultation of healer-diviner) to examine bioethical implications of the widespread caregiver roles that family members play in traditional African communitarian system of healthcare. He contends that rejection of African traditional medicine (TM) based on its grounding in African religious culture is misguided. He concludes that respect for the virtues of epistemological and value pluralism is required for a deeper understanding and open-minded appreciation of African TM, in spite being rooted in a religious culture.

Key Words: African bioethics, culture, traditional medicine, communitarian, supernatural, family, personhood, autonomy, informed consent.

2.1 Introduction

A central theme in recent discourse on bioethics involves a discussion of the relationship between culture and bioethics. The discussion is raised by concerns about the globalization of Western bioethics (Callahan 1999:284). It is believed that bioethics, in its orthodox form, is dominated by and globalizes Western ethical principles, norms, and issues. For example, it is believed that Beauchamp and Childress' groundbreaking norms of principlism (i.e. autonomy, informed consent, beneficence, non-maleficence) with which the ethical principles of bioethics have come to be defined are informed by the dominant Western deontological and teleological ethical theories (Behrens 2017:96). The norms adopted from the theories are assumed as universally valid and binding. This raises questions about the extent to which the norms which currently define bioethical discourse and practices reflect and accommodate non-Western values, beliefs and particularities. The concern is evidenced by the recent proliferation of proposals and works on Asian and African bioethics. These new fields of bioethics centralize domestic culture as the basis for constructing the ethical framework of bioethics. In African bioethics, in particular, many rich works have emerged that urge bioethics in Africa to be rooted in indigenous African values (e.g. Andoh 2011; Behrens 2017; Gbadegesin 2012; Metz 2017; Tangwa 2007). However, more work still needs to be done for bioethics to be solidly grounded and adequately done in an African way. So far, much of the literature on African bioethics follows the Western form of medicine to focus on discourse on bioethics on ethical issues arising from biomedical science.

The themes of African bioethics have to be broadened also to address non-biomedical ethical questions generated by African traditional health practices. The restrictive focus on biomedically-related bioethics is problematic in the African context in at least two fundamental ways. First, it neglects indigenous African holistic conception of health and health care, and second, it marginalizes a crucial aspect of bioethical issues distinctive and dominant in African cultures: bioethical issues raised by African traditional system of health and health care, broadly construed. African traditional medicine (TM) has been widely discussed in the emerging field of African bioethics, but the discussions tend to concentrate on questions about its scientific status, including debates whether TM should be scientifically modernized and improved (e.g. Bogaert 2007; Nyika 2007; Tangwa 2007). This paper adds a new voice to calls for bioethics in Africa to be conceived and done in African ways by focusing on cultural bioethics, distinguished from the mainstream biomedically-centered bioethics. I argue that African bioethics must be distinctively African in at least two fundamental ways: a) African bioethics must be distinctively African in terms of indigenous African conception of health and health care; b) for it to be genuinely African, the ethical norms and values of African bioethics must come from the indigenous African moral system. Regarding the first, I discuss philosophical puzzles raised by the African mystical system of beliefs and practices in which African traditional medicine is fundamentally rooted. About the second, I use a case study from traditional health care practices of the Yoruba ethnic group in Nigeria (viz. consultation of healer-diviner) to examine bioethical implications of the widespread caregiver roles that family members play in the traditional African communitarian system of health care. I begin the discussion with an examination of the importance of grounding bioethics in a cultural context.

2.2 African and Western Bioethics

Critical responses to attempts to develop bioethics from African perspectives are usually generated by questions whether morality in itself is not a system of objective norms or principles universally applicable and binding independent of contingent particular contexts—cultural, gender, race, etc. For example, in a forum organized by *Developing World Bioethics* (2010) on "Bioethics and Culture," Thaddeus Metz contributed a discussion on "An African Theory of Bioethics." Defending a moral theory grounded in indigenous African values salient in the Sub-Saharan region, he articulated a communitarian African moral theory which defines the moral rightness of an action in terms of actions that "express respect for communal or, equivalently, friendly or (broadly) loving relationships, ones in which people both identify with each other (share a way of life) and exhibit solidarity with each other (care for others' quality of life)" (Metz 2010:158). In response, Macpherson and Macklin (2007) questioned "why something counts as 'African'," and "whether an individual right to informed consent is consistent with Sub-Saharan values." About Metz's argument that African moral theory entails a right to informed consent comparable to utilitarianism and Kantianism, Macpherson and Macklin asked: "[I]f the African and two Western moral principles all point to the same outcome of an ethical issue, what does it matter (except to philosophers) if the underlying justifications differ" (quoted by Metz 2010:158-159). Macpherson and Macklin's concern is rooted in their belief that an attempt to develop an African moral theory is "an ambiguous task given the complexity and size of the population and geography of African cultures and nations" (Metz 2010:159).

Three salient themes in Macpherson and Macklin's objections to attempts to develop a system of bioethics rooted in African moral theory are particularly noteworthy: why something counting as African matters to the theoretical foundation of bioethics; why does it matter if diverse perspectives lead to the same ethical conclusion; and that the idea of "African morality" (and also the idea of "African bioethics") misleadingly reduces the wide divergent African societies into one culture. Essentially, the arguments have a common theme: they all express a concern whether culture actually matters to doing ethics and bioethics. The concern is consistent with general criticisms that are often raised about attempts to develop a system of philosophy contextually in cultural terms. It is not only non-African outsiders who share such sentiments; it is also a central issue in African philosophical thought debated by African writers. For example, Kwame Anthony Appiah criticizes the very idea of African philosophy based on his belief that it falsely entails "cultural unanimism." By this, he means that the idea of African philosophy falsely suggests that African societies are culturally homogenous- "the belief that there is some central body of folk philosophy that is shared by black Africans quite generally" (Appiah 1992:24). In the emerging field of African bioethics, Segun Gbadegesin (2012) is among the prominent pioneers of African bioethics, but he is also ambiguous and skeptical about the philosophical soundness of grounding ethics in a cultural foundation.

Macpherson and Macklin's concern about the potential reduction of all African societies into one homogenous culture is a legitimate issue. It is certainly true that, for a continent as diverse as about fifty-four different countries (with each made up of multiple ethnic and tribal groups), Africa is rich with cultural diversity. African societies are among the most complex pluralist communities in the world, constituted mostly by "a diversity of tribal, ethnic, cultural and religious groups, different traditions, and people divided along urban and rural lines" (Adelman 1998:73). But what Macpherson and Macklin fail to recognize is that cultural diversity does not necessarily imply cultural isolationism. Sub-Saharan African countries tend to share various cultural beliefs, values and practices that unite them as Africans. One particular shared culture salient in all African societies is the communitarian system of thought and life, which is sometimes called the philosophy of Ubuntu.

Culture matters to bioethics, particularly in terms of the moral framework by which bioethical norms and values are constructed, including how the notion of health and the medical system that sustains it are conceptualized. This observation is supported by the fact that culture (as an institution) is a resource from which members of a community cash out ideas regarding what constitutes a meaningful and fulfilled life (including healthy life). As Coetzee (2002:274) puts it, "Culture is an open-ended resource of social meanings on which members of a community draw to mediate the contingencies of their everyday lives". By definition, "A culture denotes the resources of a community's material and moral worlds. It is through these resources that a certain group of people delimit themselves as a cultural group" (Coetzee 2002:274). In the same vein, Oruka (2002:58) treats culture as a material capital for members of a community: "Culture often is a property, a way of life of a society as a whole.... Culture is man's contribution to the nature of environment. It is a general way of life of a people which, among other things, demonstrates their celebrated achievements in thought, morals, and material production". He elaborates: "These three summarize the content of culture which in totality is a people's body of knowledge, beliefs and values, behavior, goals, social institutions plus tools, techniques, and material constructions".

The conception of culture as a material resource that defines and determines "a way of life of a society as a whole" is very true, for example in the area of health and health care. For example, the cultural systems of the Western and African worlds uniquely determine their system of health care and the bioethical issues that confront them. Undeniably, the health care system in all cultures of the world (but especially in non-Western cultures) is largely constituted by a mixture of biomedically-based scientific and tradition-based non-scientific medical practices. But in the Western world, the health care system is dominantly driven by biomedical science (compared with non-scientific traditional healing practices), and medical consumption is predominantly in the area of biomedical clinical science.

The dominant theme of bioethics in any culture reflects or aligns with the ethical dilemmas raised by the system of health care and health care practices dominant in the culture. So, bioethical issues in the Western world are dominated and driven by advancements in biomedical and biotechnological science. The historical development of Western bioethics is actually closely linked with revolutionary developments in biomedical and biotechnological science. As Kuhse and Singer (2012:3) describe it, "Since the 1960s ethical problems in health care and the biomedical sciences have gripped the public consciousness in unprecedented ways. In part, this is the result of new and sometimes revolutionary developments in the biomedical sciences and in clinical medicine."

In contrast with the biomedically-based scientific health system of the Western world, non-scientific traditional medicine (popularly called "traditional medicine"—TM) is the major system of health care which is directly accessible to, and widely used by, many people in African societies. It has been speculated that about more than 80% of Africans use traditional medicine (even for the treatment of HIV/AIDS) largely because of its easy access and affordability (usually freely shared) (Nyika 2007; Tangwa 2007). For example, it is estimated that over 70% of South Africans consult traditional healers before consulting any other type of health care professional (Van Bogaert 2007). Although rural and traditional communities are the biggest consumers of traditional medicine (TM), the rate and number of people using these methods are also relatively high in urban cities as well.

Now, since the dominant theme of bioethics (in any culture) is dictated and driven predominantly by ethical dilemmas relating to the system of health care and health care practices dominant in the culture, the salient bioethical themes in African bioethics should include bioethical problems or issues that are distinctively and predominantly African (widespread in Africa but least confronted elsewhere). The issues that are and should be at the center stage (or deserve a serious attention) in African bioethics are substantively different and need not be construed as the same as those that are at the center of Western bioethics (or predominantly discussed in Western bioethics). For example, the various kinds of bioethical issues (especially in reproductive medicine such as genetic testing) in America have their foundational root in the ideological debate about abortion. However, in the African context, issues related to reproduction (or reproductive technology) tend to be of a lesser concern. As Andoh points out,

> many in Africa consider the field of bioethics a Western discipline or field of study that deals with issues on High-Tech and addresses directly issues arising from or related to the use of High-Tech, health related issues and practice in the West and modern medicine which does not affect African countries (Andoh 2011: 68).

For example, currently there is not much debate in Africa (unlike in the West) on bioethical dilemmas arising from the biotechnology involving dialysis machines, artificial ventilators, organ transplants (biomedical breakthroughs that enable patients who would otherwise be dead to be potentially kept alive), as well as bioethical debates on *in vitro* fertilization and reproduction techniques. Certainly, people in Africa may face similar issues as advances in biomedicine and biotechnology penetrates deeply into the African culture and system of health. But currently, the potential reality of that forecast is in the remote future.

The search for African bioethics is justified by a need to neutralize the globalization of Western bioethics and bioethical principles. Daniel Callahan, one of the founding fathers of American bioethics, in reference to what he calls "the culture of bioethics," describes the Western dominance of bioethics this way:

> The more interesting story perhaps concerns the culture of bioethics itself. It is a discipline with some discernible biases, some unmistakable signs of heavily American origins, and some long-standing internal struggles.... It has been accepted in great part because it is so compatible with American culture, at least that well-rooted liberal part of the culture.... Bioethics is often too American, too culture-confronting, too prone to float along with the tide (1999: 284).

Another prominent American bioethicist, Edmund Pellegrino, also points out at least three distinctive areas of Western values that dominantly define the themes of bioethics: the values of empirical science, principle-based ethics and the liberal democratic political philosophy. And he identifies these values as often alien and antipathetic to non-Western worldviews (Andoh 2011:68).

The demand for bioethics in Africa to be conceived and done in an African way is also supported by the emerging openness to and widespread respect for cultural diversity and moral pluralism in the contemporary liberal world. Such trends challenge convictions about global bioethics—a system of bioethics founded upon universalistic assumptions about objective moral facts derived from shared or common human nature. The demand for African bioethics was born out of a discontent with Western dominance and universalization of bioethics. The effort is not just to avoid another form of intellectual imperialism but to also reaffirm Africa's rich and distinctive values and identities. Such reaffirmation also helps to counter and correct the negative effects and legacies of colonialism. This nationalistic philosophy is a renewal of a classic theme in post-colonial African thought which calls for modern African societies to be reconstructed on the foundation of indigenous African cultural values and institutions. Since regaining their independence, post-colonial Africans have pursued efforts to recover, revive, and preserve their African dignity, values, and identity. For example, the desire for the revival and preservation of authentic indigenous African values and identity was an underlying ideology of the negritude movement, a movement of black intellectuals (e.g. Aimé Césaire and Léopold Sédar Senghor) which started in France in the 1930s and 1940s to advocate and assert their black cultural identity. Early post-colonial African leaders, such as Nkrumah, Senghor, Nyerere, in various ways, embraced and supported the philosophy of black nationalism. They considered African distinctive identity, defined by cultural values which truly reflect and represent authentic African beliefs, as the normative guiding framework by which post-colonial African social reforms and policies ought to be formulated and pursued. It is a similar sentiment that underlies recent calls by African intellectuals for bioethics in Africa to be conceived and done in African way (or consistent with African indigenous values). As Andoh emphatically puts it,

> In order that African traditional ethical values are not seen as irrelevant for contemporary society and researchers, there is a serious need for bioethics in Africa to reclaim and return to the roots of African thinking so as to reconsolidate a true African

authenticity. For bioethics to be authentically African, Africans must endeavor to root it, ground and fashion it according to their cultural norms as well as practical realities.... There is a need ... for Africans to reclaim their worldview if they want to maintain their identity in the face of change. The attempt to define and do bioethics in Africa in an African way contributes to the post-colonial efforts to reaffirm, protect and preserve African values and identities (Andoh 2011:74).

2.3 Traditional African Health Care

African bioethics must be distinctively African in terms of indigenous Africans' conception of health and health care. Traditional African medicine is one such system. This section examines ethical and epistemological puzzles about TM. I approach the discussion from the context of traditional African culture. Particularly, I discuss philosophical puzzles raised by the African mystical system of beliefs and practices in which African traditional medicine is fundamentally rooted. I argue that African TM (in all its forms) is fundamentally rooted in the supernatural beliefs that characterize African traditional culture. I conclude that respect for epistemological and value pluralism is required for a deeper understanding and open-minded appreciation of African TM, in spite of it being rooted in a religious culture.

African traditional medicine is among the major traditional healing systems (e.g. the traditional Indian system—*Ayurvadeda* and *Unani*, and the traditional Chinese medicine) that have survived the influence of modern biomedicine and biotechnology (Okpako 2006:26). The "traditional" nature of African traditional medicine is defined by the fact that the beliefs and rituals that characteristically embody the system evolved indigenously from traditional African beliefs and practices and orally (but also literally in a minimal sense in recent years) transmitted from generation to generation. By definition, the World Health Organization's (WHO) General Guidelines for Methodologies on Research and Evaluation of Traditional Medicine (2000:1) describes TM as "the sum total of the knowledge, skills, and practices based on the theories, beliefs, and experiences indigenous to different cultures, whether explicable or not, used in the maintenance of health as well as in the prevention, diagnosis, improvement or treatment of physical and mental illness". Generally, TM covers a broad set of medical knowledge and health care practices that formally fall outside of the mainstream health care system of a country. In the African context, the South African Traditional Health Practitioners Act (2007) describes TM broadly to encompass traditional health practices relating to "the performance of a function, activity, process, or service based on a traditional philosophy that uses indigenous African techniques and principles." As captured by the South African Traditional Health Practitioners Act, examples of traditional medical practices include "the physical or mental preparation of an individual for puberty, adulthood, pregnancy, childbirth, and death" (*ibid.*). Particularly, people who can legitimately register and be recognized as traditional medical "professionals" under the South African Traditional Health Practitioners Act1, include "herbalists (*izinyanga* or *amaxhwele*), diviners (*izangoma* or *amagqirha*), traditional surgeons (*iingcibi*) who mainly do circumcisions, and traditional birth attendants (*ababelethisi* or *abazalisi*)" (*ibid.*). The definition and the sample list of the areas of health and people that legitimately qualify for the designation of traditional medicine and medical practitioners are consistently held across African cultures.

Although TM is practiced in various ways in different African societies, generally African traditional healing practices share at least the following four distinctive features: a) belief that serious illnesses are caused by a supernatural agency, b) widespread use of plant and animal parts for the preparation of medicine, c) divination (i.e. diagnosis through consultation of an oracle, usually ancestral spirits), d) incantation (i.e. rituals, in the form of medical poetry—a collection of carefully chosen words that accompany the diagnosis, preparation, and administration of traditional medicine) (Okpako 2006:26). These distinctive features suggest that the most dominant form of African traditional medicine can be divided into two broad categories: 1) natural substances (viz. plant, animal parts, etc.), and 2) mystical or supernatural beliefs and practices. Let us examine deeply the relationship between the natural and supernatural aspects of TM.

The supernatural aspect of TM is one for the basis of skepticisms toward the therapeutic credibility of TM. African traditional religious beliefs and practices are often stereotyped as superstitious, and are generally branded and smeared negatively as acts of witchcraft. For example, describing the supernatural aspect in a distorted language, Nyika (2007) criticizes the practices of TM as involving 'necromancy', 'superstition', 'witchcraft', 'magical', 'bogus', 'crude mixtures', 'paternalistic', 'trial and error', 'poorly designed experimentation' (Tangwa 2007:42). As Keith Thomas notes in his marvelous work, *Religion and the Decline of Magic*, mixed feelings about supernaturalism has, in recent years, led a host of religious intellectuals to develop a habit of explaining away supernatural claims by urging religious concepts not to be interpreted literally but rather construe them as a metaphorical or symbolic figure of speech for explaining mysterious events (Appiah 1992:114). Similarly, some intellectuals who strongly support TM often make strenuous efforts to disentangle and disassociate TM from supernaturalism. Godfrey Tangwa is a good example. Tangwa is one of the vocal voices among distinguished African intellectuals who strongly advocate respect for the value of African TM and its integration into the mainstream health care systems. But in his insightful criticism of Nyika's misleading analysis of TM from the perspective of Western medical science, Tangwa minimizes the degree of supernaturalism in African TM. Tangwa (2007:43) argues that Nyika's description of traditional medicine, especially in the sections which Nyika entitles "Supernatural TM" and "Herbalism," is "simplistic and lacking in inside experience or sympathetic outside observation". For example, he argues that Nyika exaggerates the degree of supernaturalism in African traditional medical practices. In his observation, "only a relatively small part of African TM involves the need to look beyond the purely physical causes or treatment of ailments" (Tangwa 2007:43). He concludes that "[m]ainstream African TM uses herbs and other natural substances in treating diseases, and few indeed are the patients who need divination and other spiritual procedures with the art of healing" (Tangwa 2007:43).

It is true that the widespread use of traditional herbal healing in ordinary (or common) life does not overtly involve spiritual practices. Therefore, it may seem misleading to draw a close relation between the two. It is also true that herbal and other natural substances (minus spiritual consultation) constitute the largest part of the traditional medical system which is widely used by many people in African societies. So, Tangwa is right that, in contemporary African societies, only a few people directly seek traditional healing through consultation with traditional priests and shrines. Consultation of shrines and other occult worships constitutes only a very tiny part of African TM, especially for non-critical and non-serious (non-extraordinary) illnesses. But this does not necessarily imply a rejection of the supernatural aspect of traditional medicine. It is difficult to draw an incommensurable separation between supernatural medicine and natural medicine.

Typically, the cause of serious medical problems (such as blindness, crippling disabilities, etc.) are often attributed to spiritual agents, and spiritual help is often sought. Also, even with herbal and natural medicines in the context of ordinary health care, people often interpret their medical effects as having spiritual meaning and implications (especially in terms of ancestor spirits). Generally, medical knowledge and the healing power of traditional medical substances (including herbs) are believed to have a spiritual origin. For example, there is a widespread belief among indigenous Africans that knowledge of the therapeutic power of herbal and other natural substances is a special gift (e.g. from ancestors) revealed to particular favored individuals (e.g. distinguished family elders, people believed to have been reincarnated, etc.). Also, traditional medicine (especially the herbal type) in Africa is, in its genuinely traditional sense, distributed and shared non-commercially. A token fee may be collected, but this is usually not seen as a payment for treatment but it is rather regarded symbolically as part of the required ritual healing process. This shared culture has led traditional healing (especially herbs) to become a common knowledge in the routine lives and health practices in many African family homes and communities. This has further led a knowledge of herbal healing (i.e. knowing what particular herb is suitable for a particular ailment) to become naturalized in the people's sub-consciousness. The naturalization of the common knowledge and use of medicinal herbs and other natural treatments largely accounts for why many people do not consciously and directly relate to and perceive herbal medicine in a spiritual sense. Their supernatural beliefs about natural medicine are implicitly embedded in their sub-consciousness.

I think a successful argument for the credibility of TM does not need an effort to demystify it from supernaturalism. For, it is difficult to disentangle TM from supernatural beliefs, especially given the religious foundation of African traditional culture. In other words, attempts to demystify the supernatural aspect of African TM is a very difficult task, given that the African traditional culture in which TM is rooted is in itself a religious culture. In African cosmological worldview, the world which human beings occupy is a complex community constituted of an interconnected and interdependent set of natural and supernatural entities and relations (Okolo 2002:213). As Mbiti describes it:

> Religion is a difficult word to define, and it becomes even more difficult in the context of African traditional life.... [F]or Africans it is an ontological phenomenon; it pertains to the question of existence or being. [W]ithin traditional life, the individual is immersed in a religious participation which starts before birth and continues after his death. For him, therefore, and for the larger community of which he is a part, to live is to be caught up in a religious drama. This is fundamental, for it means that man lives in a religious universe. Both that world and practically all his activities in it, are seen and experienced through a religious understanding and meaning (Mbiti 1996:67).

Kwame Gyekye echoes a similar description:

> It would be correct to say that religion enters all aspects of African life so fully—determining practically every aspect of life, including moral behavior—that it can hardly be isolated. African heritage is intensely religious. The African lives in a religious universe: all actions and thoughts have a religious meaning and are inspired or influenced by a religious point of view. The African world into which European Christian missionaries entered in the late seventeenth century was a religious world... (Gyekye 1996:3)

As Appiah (1992:108) also observes, "the marks of traditional life is the extent to which beliefs, activities, habits of mind, and behavior in general are shot through with what Europeans and Americans would call 'religion'". For example, ancestral veneration is a common practice in many traditional societies. The Urhobo tribe in southern Nigeria is a good illustration. The Urhobo tribe (as is typical in many other tribal communities in Africa) believes that one can experience a serious misfortune such as serious illness if a family member fails to honor his or her duties toward his or her ancestors (Okpako 2006:240). Given that the lives and thoughts of the people in African traditional cultures are saturated with religious beliefs and practices, it would be misleading to isolate and separate their beliefs and attitudes toward the herbal part of traditional medicine from their religious beliefs and practices.

The traditional African naturalistic and supernaturalistic approach to health care is consistent with traditional Africans' holistic conception of health and personhood. The notions of illness, medicine and healing, in the African traditional worldview, are not restricted to the physical condition of the patient; they have a spiritual meaning as well. Regarding the African holistic view of health and health care, Sogolo (2002:192) writes, "in every culture, what counts as an acceptable explanation of illness is tied to the people's general conception of health and disease. It largely depends on their overall world-view. The firm assumption has always been that African cultures hold a *holistic* conception of diseases and illness" (italics in the original). To the traditional African, health refers to any condition related to a person's ability to function and execute his or her regular activities. In Sogolo's words, in reference to the African holistic view of health, "people are considered ill if they display a state of unusual feeling, suffering pain or incapacitation, or being in danger of death or mutilation. Once day-to-day life activities (e.g. the ability to work or to perform other social duties) are affected by this general feeling, such a person is said to be ill, whether or not the causes are traceable to specific structural changes in the cells of the body" (Sogolo 2002:195-196). For example, in the Yoruba community of Nigeria, the word health (*Alafia*) "embraces the totality of an individual's physical, social, psychological and spiritual well-being in his total environmental setting" (Ademuwagun 1978:89). The African holistic view of health supports the belief that health care is more than a technical concern about the biomedical condition of the patient. Health is not exclusively a bio-scientific concept; health has supernatural meanings and implications as well.

Now, skepticisms about the veracity of supernatural claims relating to TM (such as the belief that serious illnesses can be inflicted by an anger from an ancestor spirit) are sometimes based on questions about the possibility of proving them by empirically-based objective evidence. For example, are there spirits? Can the prayers invoked in libation pouring really influence (or entice) spirits to come and inhabit the shrines? Can the spirits really answer (or explain) questions such as "What made this person ill?" Such questions may be raised based on an interpretation of religious claims as lacking an empirical content. For example, a reference to a god or an ancestor spirit may be understood as a reference to mysterious entities whose claim of existence transcends the spatial-temporal empirical world. I think such an interpretation of religious claims may be true in the Western Christian world but not so in the African traditional world. Although traditional African belief systems (including beliefs about health) are religious, it must be noted that religion in African traditional culture is human-centered. The reality of anything that exists (e.g. spirits, trees, stones) is conceived or interpreted in terms of its meaning, impact or relation to humanity (or human existence). As Mbiti (1996:68) put it, "Africans have their own ontology, but it is a religious ontology, and to understand their religions we must penetrate that ontology.... [I]t is an extremely anthropocentric ontology in the sense that everything is seen in terms of its relation to man." So, references to spirits in African traditional healing practices are not claims about transcendental entities or forces that exist beyond the natural world.

In African cosmological thought, mystical terms like gods, spirits, ancestors, divinities, describe mystical entities or forces which are all part of and play an active role in the spatial-temporal empirical world. In fact, it has even been observed that, in the African traditional worldview, *supernaturalism* and *naturalism* are intertwined—it does not distinguish between the natural and the supernatural, or natural entities and spiritual entities. For example, Wiredu argues:

> The word 'nature' is, perhaps, misleading in this context, in so far as it may suggest the complementary contrast of supernature. Here, we come, in fact, face to face with an important aspect of the cosmology of the Akans [in Ghana]. God is the creator of the world, but he is not apart from the universe: He together with the world constitutes the spatial-temporal totality of existence. In the deepest sense, therefore, the ontological chasm indicated by the natural/supernatural distinction does not exist within Akan cosmology (Wiredu 2003:21).

Spirits are real invisible forces and entities that together with natural or physical forces and entities constitute the totality of reality (the concrete empirical world). The real existence of spirits may take the form of existence in attachment to human beings and natural objects. In other words, human beings, as well as some natural objects and forces, can have both physical and spiritual aspects (in quality and power).

Since the natural and supernatural are intertwined, mystical accounts (or explanations) and naturalistic accounts or explanations in African epistemological thought are not distinguishable; it is difficult to separate them. So, the laws of nature (natural laws) and spiritual laws are two ways of conceptualizing the forces that control and regulate the order of the universe, including human health. Since the existence of spiritual entities and forces depend on their relationship with, or embodiment in, human and natural entities, a confirmation of their empirical reality is not, from the perspective of an impartial observer who is experientially-acquainted with African traditional culture, difficult to obtain. For example, an impartial observer can test their empirical reality by observing the manifestations of spirits in people (e.g. patients, priests) or animals and objects. Also, as Horton (1995) is famously known in African philosophy of science for arguing, references to spiritual forces in traditional cultures are comparable to references to theoretical entities in scientific explanations. The spiritual beings and forces of African belief systems (e.g. ancestors, gods) are theoretical entities analogous to the elementary particles and fields (gravitational, electromagnetic—atoms, molecules, waves, germs, etc.) of modern scientific belief systems. For Horton, the ancestors, gods, and other spiritual entities of African traditional thought function to connect concrete events into intelligible patterns much in the same way that modern science appeals to elementary particles and fields/forces to connect concrete into intelligible patterns to explain natural occurrences. In his view, spirits, in African traditional thought, are forces (i.e. theoretical entities) that operate 'behind' or beneath common-sense (observable) events or phenomena. Sogolo (2002) agrees that Western science and

African mystical thoughts are complementary: both seek to explain and predict causes by an appeal to different kinds of theoretical entities.

Doubts about the empirical content of mystical claims are intertwined with questions about the rationality of mystical beliefs. Can traditional beliefs be rationally justified, especially when rooted in mysticism? Kwasi Wiredu raises similar questions about the rationality of traditional African supernatural epistemological system of thought. Referring to what he calls "the backward aspects of our culture," Wiredu writes:

> the analytical dimension seems to be lacking in their enthusiasm. So we have, among other distressing things, the frequent spectacle of otherwise enlightened Africans assiduously participating in the pouring of libation to the spirits of our ancestors on ceremonial occasions …under the impression that in so doing they are demonstrating their faith in African culture (Wiredu 2003:194).

Wiredu's point of contention is that mystical beliefs are held uncritically. Unlike the habit of arguing for the ontology of abstract entities before believing or rejecting them, African traditionalists blindly and unscrupulously entertain their spiritistic beliefs in ancestors without a critical analysis or argumentation. As he illustrates it, "That our departed ancestors continue to hover around in some rarefied form ready now and then to take a sip of the ceremonial schnapps is a proposition that I have never known to be rationally defended" (Wiredu 2003:162).

The notion of rationality does not have only one agreeable criterion, but generally philosophical questions about rationality entail issues about factual truth. So, the question about the rationality of supernatural explanations invariably involves puzzles about the truthfulness of claims about medical diagnosis and treatment rooted in beliefs in spiritual forces and entities. Is the truth (or truthfulness) of such claims factually or evidentially or objectively verifiable? Do the claims track any facts in reality? In response, it seems fair to also ask: Why have people believed in such mystic rituals and have been asking the spirits to perform such tasks for at least several hundreds of years? Shouldn't they know by now, if they are rational enough, that the rituals don't work, and that the beliefs (behind the rituals) are false? Certainly, false (or untrue) beliefs cannot endure for far too long as supernatural medical beliefs have existed and thrived in human history (in all cultures of the world, including the West). In other words, the supernatural medical beliefs could not survive over time, if the beliefs were false (in the sense of not having a reliable factual evidential support). Logically and pragmatically, it must be that the healings work. Empirically, the issue may be settled teleologically by pointing to testimonies about the healing efficacy of supernatural practices. For example, consider Appiah's (1992:118) testimony, based on his experience of growing up in the traditional Asante royal kingdom in Kumasi, Ghana:

> The evidence that spirits exist is obvious: the priest goes into a trance, people get better after the application of spiritual remedies, people die regularly from the action of inimical spirits. The reinterpretation of this evidence, in terms of medical-scientific theories or in terms of psychology, requires that there be such alternative theories and that people have some reason to believe in them; but again and again, and especially in the area of mental and social life, the traditional view is likely to be confirmed (Appiah 1992:118).

Now, the Africans' belief in the healing power of spiritual forces must not be misconstrued to imply a distrust and rejection of bio-scientific medicine. They depend on both. As we saw from their holistic conception of health and personhood, traditional Africans see bio-scientific explanations relating to illnesses as necessary but not sufficient in accounting for all the complexities and mysteries surrounding health and illness. Causal explanations of events for them are not just a psychological attitude (as David Hume conjectured), and neither do they believe that natural-scientific explanations of efficient cause (as Aristotle postulated) fully exhaust all there is to know and account for natural occurrences, such as bodily and psychological ailments. As people whose cosmological worldview is deeply rooted in religion, for them, naturalistic explanations at best account for efficient causes but they do not go far enough to account for the first cause (i.e. the ultimate origin) of the problem. Misfortunes like serious illnesses are accountable in terms of both efficient and first causes. For example, a psychological illness may be explained naturalistically by alluding to certain neurochemical imbalances in the brain. Perhaps this can be traced back to a genetic problem in the patient's family history. But the explanation, in the traditional African view, cannot end here. The traditional African would further probe into how the family came to inherit the genetic problem, and she may regard this as a mystery that transcends the limits of naturalistic scientific account. Consultations beyond a biomedical scientist, such as consultation of an ancestor spirit through a traditional priest or a family elder, for help may be considered.

People who do not believe in religion and other people raised and/or trained to cultivate a natural-scientific mindset or system of belief may hardly be convinced of the soundness and credibility of supernaturalistic explanations of the sort inherent in a traditional system of medicine. However, the persuasiveness and credibility of supernaturalistic worldview is a fundamental *epistemological dilemma* in the history of philosophy. It all comes down to a question about the acceptability of epistemological pluralism: can knowledge and values (including medical knowledge) be constructed and validated from multiple perspectives or worldviews? The logic of intellectual humility requires a respect for epistemological pluralism that acknowledges that our epistemic interpretations and value judgments at best are theory underdetermined by experiential observation, and that, inversely, observation is theory-laden, as the French philosopher-physicist Pierre Duhem noted in the early part of the twentieth-century (Appiah 1992:119). What this means is that "the application of a whole set of other beliefs relies on a whole host of other beliefs, not all of which can be checked at once" (ibid.). Relatedly, the theory is value-laden in the sense that "our theories both contribute to forming our experience and give meaning to the language we use for reporting it" (ibid.).

The summary is that our experiential backgrounds, including our cultural contexts and inherited beliefs, inform our worldviews, hence, we need to respect epistemological and value pluralism. Equally, scientific and traditional medicine (along with its supernatural rootedness) have an explanatory system of beliefs that share the problem of underdetermination. Hence, one system cannot be reasonably judged as epistemologically superior to, and better than, the other. This does not mean that the African traditional system of medicine is a perfect system which does not need further work for improvement. As is the case with scientific medicine (in Western as well as non-Western worlds), the practice of traditional medicine is filled with a whole host of financially greedy charlatans, quacks, and conmen. The remedy and improvement, however, need not come from Western bioethics and advancements in scientific medicine (for reasons such as the danger of the scientific system swallowing up and annihilating TM eventually). This challenge needs to be an integral part of the core theme of African bioethics—i.e. calls for experts of TM and other stakeholders (e.g. governmental agencies) to do more indigenously to help to rigorously advance and improve the quality of traditional medicine, its safety, and protection of patients from medical malpractices.

It must be clarified that, by defending traditional African medicine against objections to its rootedness in African religious culture, I do not imply that African traditional religious beliefs and practices are without ethical problems. There are many questionable traditional religious beliefs and practices that are dehumanizing and pose serious threats to human health and life. Consider for example the practice of ritual servitude in some places in West Africa. This dehumanizing cultural ritual is typically practiced in West Africa, especially in Ghana, Togo, and Benin. Among the Ewes who practice the ritual in Ghana, variations of the practice are also called *trokosi, fiashidi,* and *woryokwe,* with "trokosi" being the most common of those terms. In Togo and Benin it is called *voodoosi* or *vudusi.* In this practice, traditional religious shrines (popularly called fetish shrines in Ghana) take human beings, usually young virgin girls, in payment for services or in religious atonement for alleged misdeeds of a family member. (We see here one of the abuses of the African communitarian ethics.) These shrine slaves serve the priests, elders and owners of a traditional religious shrine without remuneration and without their consent, although the consent of the family or clan may be involved. Those who practice ritual servitude usually feel that the girl is serving the god or gods of the shrine and is married to the gods of the shrine. If a girl runs away or dies, she must be replaced by another girl from the family. Some girls in ritual servitude are the third or fourth girl in their family suffering for the same crime, sometimes for something as minor as the loss of trivial property. Currently, ritual servitude is still practiced in the Volta Region of Ghana, in spite of it being outlawed in 1998, and despite carrying a minimum three-year prison sentence for conviction. How does the practice of ritual servitude square with African egalitarian ethics of care in the African communitarian cultural system? This is also a subject that deserves the attention of African bioethicists.

2.4 African Bio-Communitarian Ethics

In addition to grounding African bioethics in African indigenous conception of health, and for it to be genuinely African, the ethical norms and values of African bioethics must come from indigenous African moral systems. In this section, I use a case study from traditional health care practices of the Yoruba ethnic group in Nigeria (viz. consultation of healer-diviner) to examine bioethical implications of the widespread caregiver roles that family members play in traditional African communitarian system of health care.

In recent decades, lessons from events in the history of powerful Western countries (e.g. the Nazi medical experimentation on Jews in the early to the middle of the 1940s in Germany and the Tuskegee syphilis experimentation on African Americans between 1932 and 1972 in the United States) have led ethics to evolve to become a prominent institution in the practice of medicine in the Western world. To protect medical patients from potential abuses, ethical codes, principles, and committees have been formed to serve as formidable watchdogs to provide oversight over medical decisions and practices (Frimpong-Mansoh, 2006). This transformation has revolutionized medical practice in the Western world by shifting away from the traditional authoritarian paternalistic form of physician-patient relationship that assumed that "doctors know best" to a heightened moral recognition and respect for patients' rights of self-determination and autonomy in health care. Obtaining the voluntary informed consent of competent individual patients (or their designated representatives) is now in principle a fundamental ethical expectation in medical practice in the Western world. Africans need to go through a similar transformation to adopt ethical consciousness in their medical practices. But the dilemma is that globalization of Western biomedical and bioethical norms, principles and methodologies is a genuine threat to African indigenous thoughts, norms and practices. Bioethics in Africa have to be done in an African way. African bioethical principles and norms have to be consistent with indigenous African moral thoughts and institutions. Such African bioethical norms and principles may or may not share similarities with Western bioethical norms and principles, but they cannot just be copied from the West and implanted in the African system of health care. Prominent pioneers of African bioethics, such as Godfrey Tangwa, Cletus Andoh, Thaddeus Metz, and Kevin Behrens, have initiated concerted efforts to develop African bioethics grounded in African indigenous moral worldviews. I add to their efforts by examining ethical questions relating to traditional African communitarian health practices in which family and community members tend to serve as health caregivers and participate in patients' care, usually even without the expressed consent of the patient.

African bioethics is rooted in indigenous African communitarian system of ethics which is defined by the values of solidarity, harmony and communal (family-centered) living. Traditional African societies are community-centered, and the cultural systems foster egalitarian virtues of collective responsibility, community participation and engagement. (For a sample of classical literature that describes African social identity as communitarian, see Gyekye 1997; Nkrumah 1967; Nyerere 1967, 1968; Wiredu 2008.) African communitarian culture is egalitarian in the sense that the social groups are regarded as a community of equals in which people see their well-being in the welfare of the group (Nkrumah 1967). This cultural system is clearly illustrated by the role of family and family members in patients' care. In traditional communities, families and family members play an active role in patient care. Family members often serve as surrogate caregivers or home "nurses" and they usually participate in family members' health care, usually without the request and authorization of the patient. The family caregiving roles and responsibilities often occur unanticipated, and assumed voluntarily, when a close relative or community member suddenly falls sick. The roles and responsibilities are often voluntarily and automatically assumed willingly just by virtue of being a family or community member. For example, studies show that many of the people who were infected in the Ebola Virus Disease (EVD) outbreak in West Africa in 2014 were family member caregivers (For example, see a study by Nielsen, Kidd, Sillah, Davis, Mermin & Kilmarx 2015). The caregiving role of the family members extends to include burial preparations and services.

As a virtue of Africanness, the African sentiment (or expression) of care has a normative content: an expected fulfillment of one's share of the burden (obligation) of collective responsibility—the actualization of *ubuntu* (or communitarian character) in ensuring mutual flourishing or collective wellbeing. For example, consider the activity of *enoboa* (i.e. mutual helping-hand in farming activities) practiced by traditional farmers in the Akan tribe in Ghana. When I was growing up (in the 1970s and 1980s), I vividly remember the practice whereby my father and a group of farmers would seasonally team up to help each other by taking turns in weeding their farms and harvesting their crops. This was motivated by the wisdom they saw in the power inherent in communal or group tasks and efforts. The joint venture also facilitated a faster harvest and minimized the risks of wastage and spoilage. Such communal venture was mutually beneficial. It is a similar communitarian sentiment towards a sense of mutual fulfillment which underlies the familial expressions of health care towards family members.

The health caregiving role of family members in traditional African cultures is not necessarily something necessitated or compelled by poverty and limited health care resources (e.g. professional health care workers such as professional nurses). Certainly, African societies are poor, and they face a tremendous problem of limited health care professionals. But the caregiver role of African families is a responsibility motivated by a culturally and ethically ingrained communitarian sentiment of care. As Wiredu writes about the kinship lineage and clan institutions that define the structural character of traditional African communitarian cultures:

> In terms of feeling and sentiment, people are brought up to develop a sense of bonding with large groups of relatives at home and outside it from very early childhood. This evolving sense of bonding is a learning process in which the individual comes more and more to see herself as the center of obligations and rights. At the level of the lineage, one is already affiliated with quite a substantial population (Wiredu 2008:333).

The caregiving role of the family usually occurs even in the mainstream professional health care system (along with the traditional counterpart). For example, family and extended family members accompany patients to the hospital, and they are usually present and actively involved in the consultation room. Also, the communal sentiment of care is not restricted only to health care practices. Communitarian expression of care is an expression or a mark (and a test) of African character. In a sense, it is un-African, that is, out of African character, to be uncaring or un-communitarian.

Now, what bioethical lessons can be drawn from the traditional African communitarian system of health care in which family members typically serve as caregivers and participate in patients' health care without an explicitly expressed consent from the patents? A story narrated by Gbadegesin about a traditional health care practice of the Yoruba ethnic group in Nigeria illustrates widespread caregiver roles that family members play in African traditional health care. Gbadegesin writes:

> Let us start with a picture of a traditional approach to health care in Yorubaland. Consider the following case that I have referred to as Mother as Daughter's Surrogate. An adult daughter, Laide, is seriously ill. Her Mother, Sade, goes to consult Healer-Diviner on behalf of Laide, the daughter. By the time that Mother gets to the diviner, other clients are waiting to see him. Mother takes her place on the queue. When it is her turn, she presents her problem to the healer by whispering to the divination chain. Healer takes the chain and consults with the oracle, chants some verses of the corpus until he strikes at Mother's problem: illness in the family. Healer tells Mother what to do—offer sacrifice to the gods and give some herbal medicine, which he supplied, to Daughter. Later Healer visits Daughter in Mother's presence, listens to her complaints and gives her more herbal remedies…. First, it is clear that this is a typical occurrence in Yoruba traditional health care systems (Gbadegesin 2013:7).

The traditional Yoruba health care system offers a further illustration of the traditional African communitarian health care system in which family members play active roles in patient care. Certainly, the traditional Yoruba communitarian health care system is, as Gbadegesin puts it, "is a different world entirely" from the Western medical system (2013:7). It seems to be a world that does not take the standard bioethical principle of respect for patient autonomy, privacy, confidentiality, and informed consent seriously. The traditional Yoruba communitarian health care system reflects actual health practices common across traditional societies in Africa. So, it seems to suggest that typical bioethical norms in standard (Western) bioethics, especially the principle of informed consent, are irrelevant and even impossible to obtain in the traditional African communitarian system of health care. For the rest of the discussion, I focus mainly on the values of autonomy and informed consent.

The answer to the question whether the traditional African communitarian system of health care accommodates and recognizes standard bioethical norms, typically autonomy and informed consent, depends on how those norms and the notion of personhood are conceived. The notion of informed consent would be problematic for the African communitarian ethical system if the concept is analyzed from the perspective of Western individualistic conception of personhood. But as we saw earlier, in the African communitarian cultural system, the idea of personhood is holistic. We learn from the Yoruba traditional health care system a comprehensive, communal conception of humanity, particularly self-identity and autonomy. As Gbadegesin points out, "there is an expansive notion of self in Yoruba worldview which makes the patient see her *Mother* as part of her extended identity.... [T]here is an enlarged notion of patient autonomy, which includes Daughter and Mother as one entity. It is a notion that Daughter, like Mother, internalizes and accepts" (Gbadegesin 2013:8).

The case study and the analysis give us a glimpse of one way in which the Western-oriented orthodox bioethics is not entirely consistent with traditional African communitarian health care system, especially given the large role that family members play in the system. Westernized bioethics is built on ethical principles geared toward atomistic individuals and their autonomous rights. Alternatively, given the communalistic nature of African cultural and ethical frameworks, bioethics and bioethical principles in the African system of health care are consistently communalistic. Contrary to the atomistic framework of Western bioethics, the Africans take a holistic or communalistic approach to health care. Self-identity in African worldview is not constituted of an egoistic atomic subjectivity. Rather, self-identity, in the authentic African sense, is social in nature. African communitarian ethics sees a person as a holistic being; a person is not just an isolated solitary atomic individual. As Xhosa's (a culture in South Africa) Ubuntu philosophy maintains, '*Umntu ungumntu ngabantu,*' which means that "a person is a complete person only through humane dealing with other people" (Nama & Swartz 2002: 294). This is what is captured in African Ubuntu metaphysics: *I am because we are, and since we are, I am.*" Or as it is now often simply phrased in Sub-Saharan

African discourse, "A person is a person through other persons." John Mbiti (1969: 108-109), a prominent cultural anthropologist, interprets the African social identity this way: in the African culture, "only in terms of other people does the individual become conscious of his own being, his own duties, his privileges and responsibilities towards himself and towards other people." African communal self, rooted in the communal maxim of "I am because we are," is a direct contrast to the Western individualistic culture in which self-identity is defined in terms of the Cartesian maxim, "I think, therefore, I am".

2.5 Conclusion

The arguments defended in this paper call for bioethics to be conceived more broadly than the way it is currently restricted to ethical issues relating to biomedical and biotechnological science. Particularly, in the less advanced worlds, such as Africa, traditional medicine is an important component of the health care systems, and traditional beliefs and practices toward health and health care equally raise fundamental ethical dilemmas that cannot be simply ignored. In this paper, I have defended a model of traditional African communitarian bioethics rooted in indigenous African communitarian practices. I have argued that rejections of TM on the basis of its rootedness in African religious culture are inspired by a lack of epistemic empathy and humility toward epistemological and value pluralism. But it must be clarified that the arguments defended in this paper are not intended to argue for cultural relativism, especially of the form of cultural isolationism. Rather, my defense of African bioethics on the basis of epistemological and value pluralism situates African bioethics in inter-culturalism. Convergence of epistemological and moral worldviews, contingently, is possible. For example, Africans may share with the Western world the importance of autonomy and informed consent in health care, but their particular cultural conceptions of health and personhood may lead them to construe and apply such bioethical concepts differently. For example, as we have seen in this paper, the individualistic cultural ontology of the Western world leads them to construe the notions of autonomy and informed consent purely from the perspectives and interests of atomistic individual patients. On the contrary, as we have seen, the African communitarian cultural ontology leads them to hold a holistic conception of health and personhood, and this further leads them to construe the notions of autonomy and informed consent communally. On these holistic and communalistic beliefs and attitudes toward health and personhood, family members are seen as an extension of oneself, and therefore a family member's unauthorized participation in one's health care is not necessarily seen as a violation of personal autonomy. These differences in worldviews toward health and personhood justify the need to be pluralistic in bioethics by acknowledging and respecting non-Western perspectives of bioethics such as bioethics from an African perspective.

2.6 References

Ademuwagun, Z. A., 1978, '"Alafia"--the Yoruba concept of health: implications for health education', *International Journal of Health Education*, 21(2), 89-97.

Andoh, C.T., 2011, 'Bioethics and the challenges to its growth in Africa', *Open Journal of Philosophy*, 1(2), 67-75.

Appiah, K.A., 1992, *In my father's house: Africa in the philosophy of culture*, Oxford University Press, New York.

Behrens, K.G., 2013, 'Towards an indigenous African bioethics', *South African Journal of Bioethics and Law*, 6(1), 32-35.

Behrens, K.G., 2017, 'Hearing sub-Saharan African voices in bioethics', *Theoretical Medicine and Bioethics*, 38(2), 95-99.

Van Bogaert, D.K., 2007, 'Ethical considerations in African traditional medicine: A response to Nyika'. *Developing World Bioethics*, 7(1), 35-40.

Burger, A.P., 1996, *Ubuntu: Cradles of peace and development*, Kagiso Publishers, Johannesburg.

Callahan, D., 1999, 'The social sciences and the task of bioethics', *Daedalus*, 128(4), 275-294.

Chuwa, L.T., 2014, African indigenous ethics in global bioethics: Interpreting Ubuntu (1), Springer.

Frimpong-Mansoh, A., 2008, 'Culture and Voluntary Informed Consent in African Health Care Systems. *Developing World Bioethics*, 8(2), 104-14.

Gbadegesin, S., 1998, 'Culture and bioethics', in H. Kuhse, & P. Singer, (eds.), *Companion to bioethics*, pp. 24-35, Blackwell, Malden, MA.

Gbadegesin, S., 2013, 'Bioethics and an African value system', Keynote address: *Teaching Skills in International Research Ethics*, Indiana University Center for Bioethics, TaSkR V Workshop, from [https://scholarworks.iupui.edu/bitstream/handle/1805/4422/Gbadegesin-Keynote_Bioethics_and_an_African_Value_System.pdf?sequence=1&isAllowed=y].

Gyekye, K., 1996, *African cultural values: An introduction*, Sankofa Publishing Company.

Gyekye, K., 1997, Tradition and modernity: Philosophical reflections on the African experience, Oxford University Press

Kanu, I. A., 2016, African bioethics: An indigenous humanistic perspective for integrative global bioethical discourse, LAP LAMBERT Academic Publishing.

Kuhse, H. & Singer, P., (eds.), 2013, *A companion to bioethics*, 2nd ed., Wiley-Blackwell, Malden, MA.

Mbiti, J., 1996, 'African religions and philosophy', in E. Parker, & K. Kibujjo, (eds.), *African philosophy: A critical approach*, Prentice Hall.

Metz, T., 2010, 'African and Western moral theories in a bioethical context', *Developing World Bioethics*, 10(1), 49-58.

Metz, T., 2017, 'A bioethic of communion: Beyond care and the four principles with regard to reproduction', in M. Soniewicka, (ed.), *The ethics of reproductive genetics*, 49-66, Springer.

Nama, N. & Swartz, L., 2002, 'Ethical and social dilemmas in community-based controlled trials in situations of poverty: A view from a South African project'. *Journal of Community & Applied Social Psychology*, 12(4), 286-297.

Nielsen, C.F., Kidd, S., Sillah, A.R., Davis, E., Mermin, J. & Kilmarx, P.H., 2015, 'Improving burial practices and cemetery management during an Ebola virus disease epidemic-Sierra Leone 2014', *MMWR, Morbidity and Mortality Weekly Report*, 64(1), 20-27.

Nkrumah, K., 1967, 'African socialism revisited', *Africa: National and Social revolution*, p.88.

Nyerere, J.K. & Tanzanie, President, 1977, *The Arusha Declaration ten years after* (No. 9). Government printer, Dar es Salaam.

Nyerere, J.K., 1968, Freedom and socialism: Uhuru na ujamaa; a selection from writings and speeches, 1965-1967, Oxford University Press.

Nyika, A., 2007, 'Ethical and regulatory issues surrounding African traditional medicine in the context of HIV/AIDS'. *Developing World Bioethics*, 7(1), 25-34.

Okolo, C. B., 2002, 'Self as a problem in African philosophy', in P. H. Coetzee & A. P. J. Roux (eds.), *The African philosophy reader: A text with readings*, p. 213, Routledge/Taylor & Francis Group, New York, NY.

Okpako, D., 2006, 'African medicine: Tradition and beliefs', *The Pharmaceutical Journal*, 276, 239-240.

Sogolo, G., 2002, 'The concept of cause in African thought', in P. H. Coetzee & A. P. J. Roux (eds.), *The African philosophy reader: A text with readings*, pp. 192-199, Routledge/Taylor & Francis Group, New York, NY.

South African Traditional Health Practitioners Act 2007, *Government gazette*, viewed 30 June 2008, from http://uscdn.creamermedia.co.za/assets/articles/attachments/11034_tradhealpraca22.pdf.

Tangwa, G.B., 1996, 'Bioethics: An African perspective', *Bioethics*, 10(3), 183-200.

Tangwa, G.B., 2004, 'Bioethics, biotechnology and culture: a voice from the margins', *Developing World Bioethics*, 4(2), 125-138.

Tangwa, G.B., 2007, 'How not to compare Western scientific medicine with African traditional medicine', *Developing World Bioethics*, 7(1), 41-44.

Tangwa, G. B., 2010, *Elements of African bioethics in a Western frame*, Langaa Research & Publishing CIG (RPCIG), Mankon, Bamenda, Cameroon.

'Transforming a barren ethics landscape in Nigeria', 2011, in *Global Health Matters*, Fogarty International Center, National Institutes of Health, Department of Health and Human Service, p. 10.

Van Bogaert, D.K., 2007, 'Ethical considerations in African traditional medicine: A response to Nyika, *Developing World Bioethics*, 7(1), 35-40.

Wiredu, K., 2003, 'On decolonizing African religions', in P. H. Coetzee & A. P. J. Roux (eds.), *The African philosophy reader*, p. 21, Routledge.

World Health Organization, General Guidelines for Methodologies on Research and Evaluation of Traditional Medicine (WHO/EDM/TRM/2000.1), viewed on 3 August 2016 from http://www.who.int/medicines/areas/traditional/definitions/en/

Chapter 3

Ancillary Care Obligations in the Light of an African Bioethic

Thaddeus Metz
University of Johannesburg

Abstract

Not long ago Henry Richardson published the first book ever devoted to ancillary care obligations, which roughly concern what medical researchers are morally required to provide to participants beyond what safety requires. In it, Richardson notes that he is presenting the "only fully elaborated view out there" on this topic, which he calls the "partial-entrustment model." In this chapter, I provide a new theory of ancillary care obligations, one that is grounded in the ideals of communion salient in the African philosophical tradition, and that is intended to rival and surpass Richardson's model, which is a function of Western considerations of autonomy. I argue that the relational approach of the former has several virtues in comparison to the basic individualism of the latter.

Key Words: African bioethic, ancillary care, autonomy, clinical trials, communion, partial-entrustment model, relationality, research ethics.

3.1 The Underexplored Controversy about Ancillary Care Obligations

What does a medical researcher (or, more carefully, her team, which includes sponsors and fieldworkers) morally owe participants in her study when it comes to resources and not just matters such as informed consent and privacy? Virtually no one doubts that the researcher owes participants information and materials that would prevent them from being harmed by the study, at least if the cost of providing them would be reasonable and the avoidance of harm would be consistent with obtaining the information sought. In addition, there is no debate that if the study does end up harming the participants, the researcher normally must compensate them for it. That applies not merely to the time taken and inconvenience caused, but also for any unforeseen physical or psychological injury produced by the study.

Now, is there any additional respect in which a medical researcher has a moral obligation to provide resources to participants in her study? The debate about how to answer this question is underdeveloped. There is a lack of consensus in the field, intuitions pull in opposite directions, and little theory has been applied to the matter. The debate concerns what is sometimes called "ancillary care obligations" or "ancillary standards of care," with the "ancillary" indicating what beyond harm caused by the study might warrant the provision of aid to participants.

In this chapter, I do not really try to argue for the existence of ancillary care obligations, but, instead, mainly seek out a theory that would make the best sense of them, supposing they exist. If the theory is independently attractive, then there would in effect be an argument for their existence. However, my main aim is not to establish that they exist, but rather to identify which moral principle would entail and best explain their existence.

As Henry Richardson pointed out not long ago in the first and only book-length discussion of ancillary care obligations, his is the "only fully elaborated view out there" on this topic (2012: xi). Richardson calls his theory the "partial-entrustment model." Ultimately grounded on the value of autonomy, it is roughly the view that, upon waiving privacy rights and providing information to the researcher, the latter becomes obligated to support participants' health in light of the information acquired from them, even if their need for medical assistance has not been caused by the study.

I argue here that the partial-entrustment model is vulnerable to criticism, and that a new theory is attractive for being able to avoid and to explain the objections facing the former. This novel approach is grounded on some ideas salient in the African philosophical tradition, which are fundamentally relational and, more specifically, communal. Very roughly, it is a community, construed as an end in itself, that explains ancillary care obligations better than autonomy.

I start by clarifying what the debate is about, providing a more thorough account of what ancillary care obligations are, or, more carefully, would be if they existed. Then, I expound an African bioethic, a principle grounded on a characteristically Sub-Saharan value of communion (initially advanced in Metz 2010a, 2010b), and show how it does a prima facie strong job of entailing and explaining ancillary care obligations. I next briefly expound Richardson's partial-entrustment model, note some of its weaknesses, which are largely a function of its individualism, and contend that the African relational approach is much less vulnerable to these weaknesses. Finally, I respond to some criticisms of the communal approach to ancillary care obligations, which Richardson himself has raised, and close by noting some issues that need to be addressed elsewhere to continue the debate between us.

3.2 Ancillary Care Obligations: What the Debate Is about

Ancillary care obligations, supposing they are real, are moral duties binding on a medical researcher (and her team) to provide information, treatment, funds, or other resources to study participants for reasons other than scientific soundness, participant safety, or compensation for study-caused harm. More roughly, they are responsibilities of those conducting medical research to aid study participants for diseases or injuries that were not caused by the study.

There are two familiar illustrations of ancillary standards of care (found in Slack et al. 2005; Stobie and Slack 2010; Richardson 2012). First, someone conducting research on malaria might encounter evidence of long-standing schistosomiasis in a given participant. Must the researcher disclose to a participant that he has this disease and even provide treatment, supposing she could do so at little cost to herself?

Second, consider a scholar researching an HIV vaccine who finds out that some study participants have acquired HIV during the course of the study. Suppose, though, that she did everything she could have in order to help them avoid becoming HIV+, providing information about how to avoid it, offering free condoms, and the like. Even though her study did not cause the harm of acquired HIV, should the researcher provide ARVs or other relevant treatments, again, if she could do so at little cost to herself?

Although some answer "no" to both questions, friends of ancillary care obligations answer "yes." Most of the latter believe that there are often obligations between a researcher and her participants that are *positive* rather than negative (i.e., are not merely to avoid doing harm or interfering), *special* rather than general (i.e., are owed to particular individuals[1]), and *unassumed* rather than intentionally acquired (say, by having made a promise either explicitly or implicitly[2]). Even if not all ancillary care obligations take this form, for most in the debate these days, they do on many occasions.

This kind of obligation would be unusual, given a background of characteristically Western moral categories. Quite often, positive obligations to particular others are assumed, e.g., by having made a promise, and unassumed positive duties are general, e.g., one can have a duty of beneficence to help anyone facing an emergency or who is amongst the worst off. Can one really have an obligation to provide aid to a specific person that one did not elect to take on?

Remember that I do not seek to answer this question definitively in this essay. Instead, I aim to explore two theoretical explanations of how one might plausibly make sense of such ancillary care obligations and to argue that a new one, grounded in African mores, is particularly promising.

3.3 An African Bioethic

Elsewhere, I have advanced an approach to medical ethics that is relational, somewhat like the ethic of care, but that is theoretical, in the manner of the Four Principles, Kantianism, and utilitarianism. In contrast to all these Western approaches, my approach is grounded on a characteristically African value of communing, which is not reducible to caring, promoting well-being, and so on.

As one is obliged to point out when discussing Sub-Saharan Africa, it does not manifest a uniform culture, with more than 50 countries, thousands of different ethnic and linguistic groups, and cultural influences from Euro-America, the Middle East, and the Indian subcontinent. Even so, most anthropologists and historians note *salient* (present neither everywhere in Africa, nor only there) patterns amongst indigenous ways of life below the Sahara, that is, norms that are not a function of what has come to it from other regions. In particular, most readers beyond Africa will likely have heard that its moral belief systems are characteristically communitarian, focused on relational values such as harmony or cohesion. In the following, I expound a moral theory that specifies the nature of this relationship and that roughly takes it to be something that merits pursuit for its own sake.[3]

For some rough expressions of this perspective, consider the claim by Peter Kasenene, a Ugandan-based scholar of Sub-Saharan religious and moral thought: "in African societies, immorality is the word or deed which undermines fellowship" (1998: 21). Consider also the remarks about indigenous Africans made by Desmond Tutu, "Social harmony is for us the *summum bonum*—the greatest good. Anything that subverts or undermines this sought-after good is to be avoided like the plague" (1999: 35).

With these terse statements, which I unpack below, Kasenene and Tutu are seeking to provide an accurate description of African beliefs about ethics, whereas I draw on one major Sub-Saharan approach to morality in order to advance a normative theory, one that is particularly revealing with respect to bioethics. According to this prescriptive ethic, *an act is right insofar as it honors (people's natural capacity for) communal relationships, ones of identity and solidarity.*

To begin to spell out what I mean by "communal" relationships, or ones of "fellowship" or "harmony" as per the quotations above, consider some representative comments about it from Sub-Saharan African intellectuals. According to the Ghanaian Kwame Gyekye, the most influential African political philosopher of the past 20 years, "The fundamental meaning of community is the sharing of an overall way of life, inspired by the notion of the common good" (2004: 16). Pantaleon Iroegbu, a Nigerian theologian, maintains that "the purpose of our life is community-service and community-belongingness" (2005: 442). Former South African Constitutional Court Justice Yvonne Mokgoro remarks, "Harmony is achieved through close and sympathetic social relations within the group" (1998: 17). Finally, the Kenyan historian of African philosophy Dismas Masolo highlights what he calls the "communitarian values" of "living a life of mutual concern for the welfare of others, such as in a cooperative creation and distribution of wealth ... (of) feeling integrated with as well as willing to integrate others into a web of relations free of friction and conflict" (2010: 240).

The above characterizations of communion suggest two distinguishable properties (first reconstructed in Metz 2007). On the one hand, there is what I call "identity," a matter of sharing a way of life, belonging, being close, and feeling integrated. On the other hand, one finds reference to promoting the common good, engaging in service, being sympathetic, and living a life of mutual concern for others' welfare, which I call "solidarity."

More carefully, it is revealing to understand identifying with another (or being close, belonging, etc.) to be the combination of exhibiting certain psychological attitudes of "we-ness" and cooperative behavior. The attitudes include a tendency to think of oneself as a member of a group with the other and to refer to oneself as a "we" (and not merely as an "I"), a disposition to feel pride or shame in what another member does, and, at a higher level of intensity, an emotional appreciation of the other's nature and value. The cooperative behaviors include being transparent about the terms of interaction, allowing others to make voluntary choices, acting on the basis of trust, adopting common goals, and, at the extreme end, choosing for the reason that "this is who we are."

Exhibiting solidarity with another (or acting for others' good, exhibiting concern for their welfare, etc.) is also usefully construed as the combination of exhibiting certain psychological attitudes and engaging in helpful behavior. Here, the attitudes are ones positively oriented towards the other's well-being and include a belief that the other merits aid for her own sake, an empathetic awareness of the other's condition, and a sympathetic emotional reaction to the empathy. And the actions are not merely those likely to be beneficial, that is, to improve the other's state, but also, in the ideal case, are ones done for that reason and for the sake of making the other a better person or for the sake of communal relationship itself.

Figure 3.1: Schematic Representation of Communion[4]

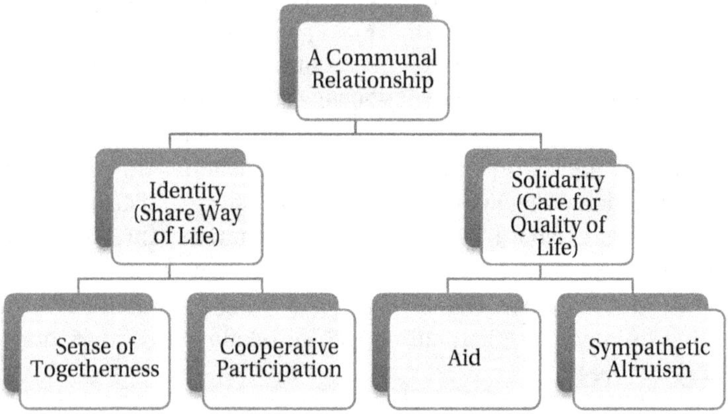

```
                    A Communal
                    Relationship
                   /            \
          Identity               Solidarity
          (Share Way             (Care for
          of Life)               Quality of
                                 Life)
          /        \              /         \
    Sense of    Cooperative    Aid      Sympathetic
    Togetherness Participation           Altruism
```

These specifications of what it is to commune with others, schematically presented in Figure 3.1, ground a fairly rich and promising normative ethic with a Sub-Saharan pedigree. A prescription to honor communion (or, more carefully, people in virtue of their ability to commune) means, in part, respecting actual relationships of identity and solidarity. To honor a relationship means producing, sustaining, and enriching it, but not in whatever way one can, as consequentialism would prescribe. For example, honoring the value of communion would normally mean not seeking to advance it by means of discord, the opposite of communion comprised of division ("me versus you" and subordination) and ill will (harmful behavior consequent to indifference or cruelty), at least when it comes to those who have not been discordant.

To begin to appreciate the explanatory power of this moral principle, consider its implications for the nature of wrongdoing. The relationship of identifying with other people in combination with that of exhibiting solidarity with them is basically what English-speakers mean by "friendliness," or even a broad sense of "love." Hence, this African moral theory implies that wrong actions are, very roughly, those that are not friendly. What makes acts such as killing, coercing, deceiving, exploiting, cheating, breaking promises, and the like typically impermissible is that they are (extremely) unfriendly, indeed, ways of prizing division and ill will (discordance).

It is not merely that these actions are uncaring but also that they typically involve subordination done out of a divisive attitude. This Afro-communal ethic includes everything that care ethicists prize, as it prescribes acting to improve others' quality of life consequent to certain attitudes of sympathy and altruism. However, it also includes a certain kind of relationship that care ethicists typically do not prize, or at least not in the way they normally expound their view. African moralists tend to value both caring for others' quality of life and sharing a way of life with others, where the latter is more or less the combination of enjoying a sense of togetherness and participating in cooperative projects. Elsewhere, I have argued that this latter condition must be brought into a relational morality in order to avoid concerns about paternalism, exploitation, and similar objections that plague the ethic of care because of its exclusive focus on welfare (Metz 2013). For example, considerations of informed consent are plausibly captured by the idea that conducting research on or treating someone without his consent would essentially be to degrade his capacity to genuinely *share* a way of life, and not so much a failure to care for him.

Note that the present normative interpretation of African morality is not vulnerable to one of the most frequent criticisms of Sub-Saharan ethics, namely, a demand for uniformity or an inability to account for the value of the liberty to be different from others. For one way to see that it avoids this problem, recall what I have said about the meaning of the phrase "identify with others" or "share a way of life," namely, that it by definition includes coordinating behavior, such that honoring this value prima facie means not subordinating others. Forcing others to be like oneself or a group is not to *share* a way of life, which in this context implies voluntariness, at least on the part of adults. For another, consider what it means to prize friendliness, which I suggested above is a rough equivalent of my Afro-communalism. To be friendly with someone hardly means pressuring him to become like someone else. Instead, part of the value of friendship (an intense form of friendliness) is that two adults have elected to come together, and to stay together, of their own accord. Another part of its value is that friends help one another to "do their own thing," not to become the same. What goes for the good of friendship goes for a normative ethic of friendliness.

Lastly, I point out that as a relational approach (and like the ethic of care), there is a clearly partial dimension to African ethical thought.

Traditionally speaking, in Sub-Saharan societies, blood ties were deemed grounds for having a greater claim to aid than those lacking such relationship (Appiah 1998). However, a more attractive reconstruction would imply that those who are already in a communal relationship with one have a somewhat greater claim to one's aid than others who are not in such a relationship with one. Such a principle plausibly explains why a patient already being treated by a medical professional is entitled to continued attention, relative to someone not yet in treatment, even in the absence of a promise to provide it. It also explains why a medical professional can be obligated to cover for a colleague with whom he works, but not for one at another hospital whom he does not know, again, even without any explicit agreement.

I lack the space to spell out and defend this principle any more, or to bring out its African pedigree. Although the quotations above indicate that this ethic is founded largely on ideas from the Sub-Saharan region, it is not meant to be only for people with such a cultural background. Although friendliness has not served as a salient principled ground of moral thought in the West (or in the East), I presume readers from a variety of traditions can appreciate its prima facie appeal. If one were sympathetic to the idea that there are ancillary care obligations of the form adumbrated above, and if the Afro-communal principle did turn out to account for them well, then that would serve as some additional evidence in its favor.

3.4 Ancillary Care Obligations as Ways of Honoring Communion

In this section, I apply the Afro-communal ethic to ancillary care obligations, indicating that it entails and plausibly explains them. It is only in the following section that I argue that it does a better job than the partial-entrustment model at doing so.

Here is the basic rationale for thinking that a medical researcher can have obligations to aid her patients beyond what safety or a promise requires.[5] Upon sharing a way of life with participants, a researcher has established part of a morally significant relationship that demands respect and hence full-blown realization in the form of caring for their quality of life as well. Once a researcher and a participant have begun to think of themselves as a "we" engaged in the joint project of a study, they have formed a tie that imposes special obligations to care for one another's quality of life that can go beyond those listed in a participant agreement form (with the one in a greater position to aid naturally having more of a duty to do so). Just as extant patients are normally entitled to treatment from a given medical professional and with some priority relative to strangers, extant participants have a claim to receive aid from a medical researcher, such that it would be pro tanto wrong for her to allocate it to strangers with whom she has not related communally.

In addition to providing an explanation for who it is that a medical researcher must aid, an appeal to communion can account for how to aid. Basically, the form that caring should take is determined by considerations of the way of life that has been shared.[6] That is, the proper way for one person to seek to benefit another is in large part a function of the nature of the relationship of which they have both been a part. Since a medical researcher and participants have been involved in a joint project of discovering information about health, health-related care is the appropriate sort.[7] When a medical professional owes a colleague aid, it is for help with such matters as taking over her shift when she has family obligations, and not, say, assistance with cleaning her garage. By analogy, if indeed a medical researcher owes participants aid, it is a matter of informing them about unknown diseases and treating them.

Finally, consider the question of how much a medical researcher is required to aid participants. Researchers are already often concerned about the costs of their studies, and they might reasonably be worried about being deemed to have obligations to aid participants beyond what research ethics committees currently tend to expect. There are two respects in which researcher obligations would be limited by the present bioethic.

For one, the Afro-communal ethic plausibly entails that researchers are more obligated, the more they can help others without imposing great costs on themselves. Honoring communion does not mean maximally promoting it; it is not utilitarian, demanding that a moral agent sacrifice up to the point that he would be as badly off as the worst off he is seeking to help (as per Peter Singer's 1972 view). Instead, honoring the capacity to commune means giving all of one's extant relationships their due, which, for a medical researcher, include ties to his employer and the scientific community. It also means protecting one's own *capacity* to commune, which has value, a dignity, apart from the way it has been actualized. Given, then, that one is not to treat oneself merely as a means to the ends solely of one's participants, or indeed to those of anyone with whom one is communing, there are limits to what can be expected of a researcher and her team.

Of course, speaking of "no great cost" or of "little cost" is vague. To say a bit more, the thought is that a given agent has trivial, moderate, and urgent interests, and that she can be required to sacrifice at least her trivial interests when the urgent ones of others are at stake. What counts as a trivial interest will depend on the agent. Spending a million dollars would not be trivial for most human beings, but it could well be trivial for a pharmaceutical company with profits in the billions.[8]

A second principle that follows from the basic one advanced here is this: the closer the relationship between two parties, the greater the obligation to aid. The moral reason why one is required to give one's family the lion's share of one's resources is plausibly that one is closest to them, not that one has promised or that one could do the best by helping them rather than others. Even if one had not promised to do so, and even if one would not maximize good outcomes by doing so, one would still have some weighty duty to help one's family before non-family. And an appeal to communion makes good sense of that.

By extension, the closer a researcher becomes to participants, e.g., by virtue of having engaged in a longitudinal study with the latter, the more that is owed to them in comparison to, say, those subjected to a once-off drawing of blood. Of course, often, it is not literally the researcher who develops ties with participants, but rather those acting under her direction, such as fieldworkers and nurses. However, insofar as the latter's agency is a function of those who have conceived and funded the study, the ties they form with participants are also plausibly considered to be those of the principal investigator and her sponsors.

In sum, the appeal to communion provides powerful explanations of an array of positive, special, and unassumed obligations in a medical context, not merely those between a researcher and participants. It explains why a researcher can be obligated to aid participants apart from any agreement to do so, but not, say, those who work at a shop till. It accounts for the intuition that a researcher can be obligated to aid participants with regard to their health, but not for everything they might need in life. And it also makes good sense of how much a researcher owes different participants. It, therefore, merits being paired up against the dominant theory of ancillary care obligations.

3.5 Communion versus Entrustment

Here, I briefly expound the partial-entrustment account of standards of ancillary care, most often associated with Richardson's (2012) book, but also advanced by others (Richardson and Belsky 2004; Stobie and Slack 2010: 155–157), and I provide some reasons to favor communion as their ground. I maintain that Richardson's individualist foundation, viz., his appeal to autonomy, is not as powerful as a relational dimension of communion at accounting for the intuitive contours of ancillary care obligations. I also respond to objections to my approach, some of which have recently come from Richardson himself (2015).

According to Richardson, ancillary care obligations arise when patients' autonomy is reduced or threatened by virtue of disclosing intimate information about themselves with a researcher. "The central claim of the partial-entrustment model is that, simply by providing researchers with these special permissions (to conduct research on them), participants effectively entrust the researchers with special responsibilities to look after needs they discover by acting on those permissions" (Richardson 2012: 35). The entrustment is only partial, as participants naturally retain significant responsibility for looking after their own needs. However, upon receiving private information from participants, which places them in a vulnerable position, according to Richardson, the researcher becomes obligated to help participants, even if their need for help was not caused by the study.

Self-governance is the value at the bottom of Richardson's explanation of ancillary care obligations. Roughly, since the researcher has compromised the participants' autonomy, she has a duty to protect them in other ways. As Richardson says, "The basis of the special ancillary-care obligation, then, lies in the special responsibility for protecting participants' autonomy that falls to researchers when they accept the participants' waivers of their privacy rights" (2012: 96). Upon giving informed consent to participate in a study, participants waive their right to retain certain kinds of information about themselves (e.g., about their body and intimate behaviors as they pertain to the object of study) and thereby put themselves in a compromised position, which, for Richardson, means that the researcher incurs an obligation to protect them from harm discovered by means of that information. The obligation would be all the weightier if the researcher (or her team) asked participants to become a part of the study.

Rather than point out the advantages of this model, which Richardson (2012) has done quite ably, I focus on what I think are new and important weaknesses,[9] so as to show the superiority of the communal alternative. One of these problems is that there are places in Richardson's complete theoretical account where autonomy does not do the sole—or even the main—justificatory work, as it is supposed to do according to the official line of argument adumbrated above; autonomy is supplemented by an *ad hoc* appeal to an altogether different, relational value.

For one, according to Richardson, a researcher has a duty to offer treatment or funds to participants only after, and because, she has warned them of harm that she discovered in the course of the study about them. Once she notifies them of a sensitive matter, *the relationship becomes more intimate*, which is what obligates the researcher to offer aid as well.

As the point is important, I quote several passages from Richardson to this effect:

> The warning or, more generally, the broaching of the sensitive issue deepens the relationship between these two parties.... Insofar as the demandingness of beneficence obligations varies directly with the depth of relationships, this deepening of the relationship is itself a basis for firmer obligations of beneficence (than merely warning) (2012: 92).

> (T)he morally required warning ... has transformed this situation from one in which the best and most apt way of promoting these autonomy concerns would likely have been to back off and keep one's distance into one in which one is instead called upon to be supportive.... While we would typically prefer that such support comes from our close intimates, broaching the issue *makes* the accepter an intimate (2012: 93–94).

> Once one has warned the other about a new problem that one discovers on the basis of private information ... the morally best way to address these underlying concerns becomes not to duck out, but rather to help.... (T)he duty to warn (or its cognates) further deepens the incipient relationship begun by the initial intimacy, providing a clear locus for a special obligation of beneficence. The upshot is a special ancillary-care obligation (2012: 95–96).

My point is this: it is *not* so much the fact of reduced privacy or compromised autonomy that, by Richardson's full account, generates the duty to aid beyond providing a warning of a discovered illness, but rather, the intensity of the relationship between the parties. Richardson's appeal to the intensity of relationship in order to ground obligation fits naturally in a communal ethic, but not in an autonomy-based one that makes no essential reference to other persons.

Continuing the dialectical move against Richardson, notice that he also appeals to the depth or intensity of the relationship, e.g., how close the parties are and how long the relationship has lasted, in order to determine how much a researcher is obligated to aid participants (while also including a "little cost" rider) (2012: 42, 48–49, 188). However, this factor again has nothing inherently to do with the participant's autonomy, and rather fits best within a fundamentally relational ethical framework.

In reply, Richardson could seek to give up the appeal to intimacy as a factor determining the ground and content of obligations. He might instead maintain that it is indeed a reduction of autonomy, or threat of such, that creates the obligation for a researcher to aid a participant. Sometimes, for example, Richardson contends that when a researcher warns a participant of a disease revealed in the course of the study, "the gaze of another threatens to inhibit how one deals with particularly sensitive matters" (2012: 93), or that the participant "will likely feel temporarily at a loss when suddenly confronted with the issue" (2012: 94). Imposing these autonomy-related risks on participants, the researcher incurs a duty to make up for them, by offering treatment for the disease.

This approach would be more coherent for Richardson, but, I maintain, less plausible. The obligation to offer treatment to participants, it seems to me, existed *before* such threats to autonomy obtained. My intuition is that if the researcher has a duty to warn participants of a disease they are revealed to have in the course of the study, then she also has a duty to offer more than that *at the same time, prior to having actually warned them* and thereby having negatively affected their autonomy. And if the duty to offer treatment existed prior to the participants being warned, then it, of course, was not the warning that created the duty. It must have been something else that created it, plausibly the fact that the researcher and the participant shared a way of life or came to identify with one another with respect to medicine.

Finally, I suggest that autonomy is a prima facie poor explanation of a special, positive, and unassumed obligation. If a person makes a fully free and informed choice to give something to a party, then, *in the light of autonomy*, he is responsible for any foreseeable vulnerability that doing so may entail, and the one who now has the information is not liable to aid *on that basis*. Consider that when I provide money to a seller on the internet, I freely reduce my autonomy to some degree, as I no longer have the money and hence cannot make a wide array of other purchases. My range of choice is now limited merely to using that purchased object; I am unable now to acquire any number of other objects to use. Yet, the seller normally incurs *no* liability as a result, with respect to any autonomy-related issues.

Similar remarks seem to apply to someone who makes a free and informed choice to give information to a researcher. So long as the participant was not exploited, i.e., had little or no choice but to become a participant, and so long as the participant was neither deceived nor otherwise ignorant of key facts, autonomy-based factors mean that it is his responsibility to bear the cost of having disclosed the information about himself. When thinking from the perspective of autonomy, there is no difference between deciding to put personal information about oneself on the internet and giving the same information to a researcher. In both cases, others do not become obligated to help one because one's autonomy has been compromised. If a researcher has some liability towards participants, it is probably not because their autonomy has been reduced in the course of making a free and informed decision, but rather, more promisingly, the fact of having related in a certain way.

I agree that contractual exchanges can sometimes give rise to supra-contractual obligations, as Alan Wertheimer has argued (2010: 255–320). My claim is that *autonomy* provides a poor account of when and why such exchanges do so, and that, on the face of it, relational considerations do a better job of explaining them. For example, communion is a plausible reason why an internet seller incurs no liability to provide aid to a purchaser who loses some autonomy in making a purchase, and why one might plausibly owe the kid who mows one's lawn over time more than one could get away with by paying him (cf. Wertheimer 2010: 256).

To sum up this section so far, I have more or less argued that where the partial-entrustment model appears strong in accounting for ancillary care obligations, it is so by illegitimately invoking relational values that are distinct from autonomy, and that where it is weak, it is so because of its appeal to autonomy as the ground of ancillary care obligations. Before closing, I address three important objections that prima facie apply to my appeal to communion as a way to account for ancillary care obligations. The first two have been suggested by Richardson himself (2015).

Richardson's two worries concern who, precisely, is owed aid from a researcher and under what conditions. One of the criticisms is that my appeal to a relational value is too narrow, unable to account for cases in which there is interaction, but not a relationship, between a researcher and participants. For example, imagine a case in which researchers have merely asked some demographic questions of a person and then taken a cheek swab to collect a DNA sample. Suppose that analysis of the sample has revealed a fatal condition and that the researcher has a duty to warn the patient of that. Partial-entrustment appears to make good sense of this duty, since the disease was revealed in the course of the researcher having obtained health-related information from the patient, whereas an appeal to communion has more difficulty, on the face of it, since there is no real relationship yet between the parties.

In reply, the first thing to note is that, even if there is a duty to warn the participant, there is probably no duty to treat her, at least if there is some real cost to doing so. The brevity of the length, and the weakness of the intensity, of the relationship (if there is one at all, of course), plausibly explain why. But partial-entrustment cannot appeal to these relational factors, at least if seeking to ground considerations on the individualist value of autonomy. Indeed, considerations of autonomy (at least as Richardson is inclined to understand them) are likely counterintuitively to entail a duty to provide treatment, supposing that revelation of a fatal illness was foreseeable to the researcher, and especially if conveyed to the participant prior to taking the swab.

Secondly, note that, strictly speaking, the appeal to communion does not require a full-blown relationship in order to ground a duty to aid. It is one thing to relate in a certain way, and another to be party to a certain kind of relationship. To be sure, the African ethic instructs moral agents to form communal relationships (amongst other things), but that does not mean that relationships alone obligate within a relational ethical framework (*contra* the view advanced in Olson 2016); weaker ways of relating can also obligate.

Suppose, for example, that the crossing-guard at my son's school cannot afford the fees to send his own son there. I see the guard most days, obeying his instructions and exchanging a nod and a smile, but not much beyond that. Despite our lack of relationship, we enjoy a sense of togetherness and we cooperate in the shared aim of protecting school-bound pedestrians. That, I submit, is enough to obligate me to help if he were to ask parents at the school to each contribute a small amount to enable his son to attend, at least more than if he were a stranger. This obligation is one that partial-entrustment cannot capture, given the lack of intimate information disclosed. And the case is similar to the putative counterexample of the cheek swab participant with whom there is a lack of relationship but with whom there is a sense of togetherness and coordination in pursuit of shared ends.[10]

The second criticism of the communal theory of ancillary care obligations is the converse of the first one, namely, the approach is too broad, such that it cannot avoid entailing that a medical researcher has duties towards her local bartender, with whom she might well have a relationship. Even if a full-blown relationship is not necessary to have a special duty to care for another, by the African ethic, it is surely sufficient. So, it appears that a researcher could be obligated to aid her local bartender just as much as, if not more than, a participant in her study, which is counterintuitive.

Or is it? Recall my proposal that the nature of caring is properly determined by the nature of the sharing, i.e., that the ends sought out by the parties are what largely fix the content of the kind of aid that they must provide each other, such that a medical colleague can be obligated to cover another's shift, but not to clean his garage. It follows that if the researcher did have an obligation to help her bartender, it would not be to provide him with health care. Instead, at most, it would be to assist in tending the bar. Is that such an odd idea? Suppose the researcher has indeed formed a trusting, somewhat intimate relationship with the bartender, sharing stories about their lives over some years. Then, if the bartender needs to take an urgent call, and the researcher can help to keep things running for 20 minutes, I find it plausible to think that she would be wrong to refuse to do so (even if not the sort of wrong that would call for the use of force or punishment).

A third objection to the communal account of ancillary care obligations is that its rationale is too weak to ground an actual obligation on the part of a researcher. Aid to participants is never to be too costly, and it is only in the case of having intense ties with them that providing aid would really "pinch" a researcher and her team. Perhaps, then, providing ancillary care is not really a duty, but something beyond the call of duty.

I make two replies, here. First, one should distinguish between what duty calls an agent to do and how strong the duty is. A duty might be strong in the sense of not being easily overridden by other moral considerations, but not in the sense of requiring all that great a sacrifice. The objection presumes that if one need not provide much aid, then one lacks a duty (or a strong duty) to provide it, but that either conflates two issues or supposes a closer tie between them than intuitively obtains. After all, I might well have an actual (strong) duty merely to return a book that I borrowed from you.

Second, my aim in this chapter is to weigh Richardson's partial-entrustment model of ancillary care obligations against a new, Afro-communal alternative. Insofar as both of these theories include similar accounts of how much aid is required, the present objection cannot provide grounds for choosing between them.

3.6 Conclusion: Further Topics to Be Addressed

In this chapter, I have sought to mine the African philosophical tradition for ideas that can make sense of ancillary care obligations, giving the dominant view of them a run for its money. Relational values are known for their salience in Sub-Saharan philosophy, and I have argued that they account well for the existence of special, positive, and unassumed duties that a researcher has with respect to participants in her study. Specifically, I have articulated an ethic according to which a moral agent must honor communion (or, more carefully, treat people as special in virtue of their capacity to relate communally), which means identifying with others and exhibiting solidarity towards them. I have also provided reasons to think that the ethic not only provides a plausible ground for ancillary care obligations, but also is in several ways more promising than Richardson's influential partial-entrustment model, which is grounded on the value of autonomy.

I close by pointing out some ways in which the debate between communion and entrustment can be furthered, supposing that the former is indeed promising. One way would be to consider which approach best handles additional cases in which there are intuitively positive, special, and unassumed obligations. In this essay, I have mentioned some, for instance, the duty to aid a medical colleague, a crossing-guard, and a bartender. Are there indeed duties to aid particular individuals that are not a function of promise-keeping in these and a variety of other cases? If so, which theory does better at capturing them? On the face of it, the appeal to communion is going to have a much broader reach than entrustment, for which the duty to aid is triggered by the disclosure of intimate information.

Another issue worth discussing, and which I did not address here, is who, precisely, can be the proper object of aid in a medical research context. For example, suppose a woman brings her sick child to a study. Can a researcher be obligated to treat the child? If so, why? Is it because the researcher has threatened the autonomy of the mother or the child? Or is it because the researcher has related communally with her or the child?

Finally, there needs to be more analysis of the limits to aid. I briefly addressed them, suggesting that respect for oneself as a being capable of communing can ground a distinction between what is dutiful, which can require sacrificing trivial interests, and what is beyond the call of duty, which would involve giving up urgent ones. However, I accept that the analysis merits further consideration, particularly in relation to the idea that it might be, in fact, the researcher's autonomy that deserves self-respect.

3.7 Acknowledgements

This essay was first published as 'Ancillary Care Obligations in Light of an African Bioethic: From Entrustment to Communion' *Theoretical Medicine and Bioethics* 38 (2017): 111-126 and has been reprinted with permission of Springer.

For oral comments on a talk based on this research, I thank participants at the Conference on Giving a Voice to African Thought in Medical Research Ethics hosted by the University of the Witwatersrand, Steve Biko Centre for Bioethics, in 2015. For written comments on a previous draft, I am grateful to Kevin Behrens, Henry Richardson, and an anonymous referee for *Theoretical Medicine and Bioethics*. Research for this essay has been supported financially by the South African National Research Foundation (NRF), and any opinion, findings, conclusions, or recommendations expressed in it are those of the author, with the NRF not accepting any liability in regard thereto.

3.8 Notes

[1] Hence, this account of the nature of ancillary care obligations assumes from the start, with Richardson, that they are not merely obligations of general beneficence, the approach that had been deemed most promising by some in early discussions more than ten years ago (Slack et al. 2005)

[2] Hence, this account of the nature of ancillary care obligations assumes from the start, with Richardson, that they do not merely "arise from implicit and explicit commitments, such as promises and roles" that have been taken on with the expectation of providing aid, as per some others in the recent debate (Stobie and Slack 2010: 153).

[3] Some other African philosophers consider communion merely to be a means towards the realization of other values such as well-being (Gyekye 2010) or vitality (Bujo 1997), particularly that in one's society.

[4] Slightly modified and reprinted with permission from Metz (2016: 178).

[5] I first briefly suggested this reasoning in Metz (2010a: 55–57), but do much more to spell it out and defend it here. It would be interesting to compare my approach with another relational account that Nate Olson (2016) has recently advanced, according to which the concept of respect for meaning in people's lives as it inheres in their relationships is key.

[6] It need not take the form of a *role*, the strategy largely employed in Stobie and Slack (2010: 153); and Olson (2016).

[7] I first advanced this rationale in Metz (2010a), and it has recently been echoed in (Olson 2016: 323–324).

[8] A fuller account would require a theory of what is good for a human being, which I lack the space to provide here. However, I note that in the African tradition, the human good is usually conceived objectively, i.e., in terms of needs and not so much pleasant experiences or satisfied desires (see, e.g., Gyekye 2004). A need-based theory of the human good would provide the ultimate basis for evaluating an agent's claim that a certain degree of sacrifice is too great.

[9] A weaker objection is that Richardson overemphasizes the role of free and informed consent to conduct the study. Suppose researchers did not seek out such consent, or suppose they sought it out but actually failed to obtain it (unbeknownst to them). Even so, ancillary care obligations would still obtain. This is not a deep problem for Richardson, I believe, since he could say that the violation of autonomy imposes all the more responsibility on the researcher to make up for it. What really does the work in Richardson's theory is not the *giving* of informed consent or a

waiver of privacy, *contra* his phrasing (2012: 34–37, 65), but the *taking* of private information, whether consensually or not.

A stronger objection, but one already made in the literature, is that the partial-entrustment model is too narrow when it comes to "scope," i.e., the range of aid that a researcher should be expected to provide. In particular, several have suggested that participant conditions known to the researcher prior to the study can warrant being treated no less than those discovered in the course of the study (e.g., Olson 2016).

[10] A third possible reply is to suggest that the duty to aid in the present case is not a special one, but rather, an instance of a duty to rescue.

3.9 References

Appiah, A. 1998, 'Ethical Systems, African', *Routledge Encyclopedia of Philosophy*. E. Craig (ed.), Routledge, London.

Bujo, B. 1997. *The Ethical Dimension of Community*, trans. C. N. Nganda, Paulines Publications, Nairobi.

Gyekye, K. 2004. *Beyond Cultures: Ghanaian Philosophical Studies, III*, The Council for Research in Values and Philosophy, Washington, D. C.

Gyekye, K. 2010. African Ethics. *Stanford Encyclopedia of Philosophy*, E. Zalta (ed.), https://plato.stanford.edu/entries/african-ethics/, Stanford California.

Iroegbu, P. 2005. Beginning, Purpose and End of Life. In *Kpim of Morality Ethics*, P. Iroegbu and A. Echekwube (eds.), 440–445, Heinemann Educational Books, Ibadan, Nigeria.

Kasenene, P. 1998. *Religious Ethics in Africa*, Fountain Publishers, Kampala, Uganda.

Masolo, D. A. 2010. *Self and Community in a Changing World*, Indiana University Press, Bloomington Indiana.

Metz, T. 2007, 'Toward an African Moral Theory', *Journal of Political Philosophy* 15 (3): 321–341, Revised version in 2017, *Themes, Issues and Problems in African Philosophy*, I. Ukpokolo (ed.), 97–119, Palgrave Macmillan, London.

Metz, T. 2010a, 'African and Western Moral Theories in a Bioethical Context', *Developing World Bioethics* 10 (1): 49–58.

Metz, T. 2010b, 'An African Theory of Bioethics: Reply to Macpherson and Macklin'. *Developing World Bioethics* 10 (3): 158–163.

Metz, T. 2013, 'The Western Ethic of Care or an Afro-communitarian Ethic?: Finding the Right Relational Morality', *Journal of Global Ethics* 9 (1): 77–92.

Metz, T. 2016, 'An African Theory of Social Justice: Relationship as the Ground of Rights, Resources and Recognition', in *Distributive Justice Debates in Political and Social Thought: Perspectives on Finding a Fair Share*, C. Boisen and M. Murray (eds.), 171–190, Routledge, New York.

Mokgoro, Y. 1998, '*Ubuntu* and the Law in South Africa', *Potchefstroom Electronic Law Journal* 1 (1): 15–26. http://www.nwu.ac.za/p-per/volume-1-1998-no-1-1 - Articles.

Olson, N. 2016, 'Medical Researchers' Ancillary Care Obligations: The Relationship-based Approach', *Bioethics* 30 (5): 317–324.

Richardson, H. 2012, *Moral Entanglements: The Ancillary-care Obligations of Medical Researchers*, Oxford University Press, Oxford.

Richardson, H. 2015, Correspondence with the author, December 6.

Richardson, H. and Belsky, L. 2004, 'The Ancillary-care Responsibilities of Medical Researchers', *Hastings Center Report* 34 (1): 25–33.

Singer, P. 1972, 'Famine, Affluence, and Morality', *Philosophy and Public Affairs* 1 (3): 229–243.

Slack, C. et al. 2005, 'Provision of HIV Treatment in HIV Preventive Vaccine Trials: A Developing Country Perspective', *Social Science & Medicine* 60 (6): 1197–1208.

Stobie, M. and Slack, C. 2010, 'Treatment Needs in HIV Prevention Trials: Using Beneficence to Clarify Sponsor-investigator Responsibilities', *Developing World Bioethics* 10 (3): 150–157.

Tutu, D. 1999, *No Future without Forgiveness*, Random House, New York.

Wertheimer, A. 2010, *Rethinking the Ethics of Clinical Research*, Oxford University Press, Oxford.

Chapter 4

Personhood, Autonomy and Informed Consent

Martin Ajei
University of Ghana

Nancy O. Myles
University of Ghana

Abstract

Examines the concept of informed consent from a Ghanaian Akan perspective. The authors examine assumptions of the notion of informed consent as a principle of bioethical practice and points to inherent inconsistencies within it. The chapter then proceeds to gesture toward the view that when examined, these assumptions indicate that the process of obtaining and validating informed consent should be contextually derived, and that theories of personhood and beliefs about the structure of existence are pivotal in the contextual knowledge that sustains these processes and validation.

Key Words: Personhood, autonomy, informed consent, individuality, communality, communitarian, relational.

4.1 Introduction

The idea of informed consent has become integral in contemporary medical ethics and practice. It is not only considered an ethical and legal requirement for research involving human beings for diagnostic, therapeutic, interventional or socio-behavioral studies, but more importantly, it has become a necessary aspect of the administration of health to patients; at least since the beginning of the twentieth century. Consent, when informed, is understood to entail a process of steps of information by the caregiver, and understood by the care-seeker, the end product of which is the consent to, or rejection, by the care-seeker of a prospective outcome (treatment) suggested by the caregiver. The caregiver is required to make every effort to ascertain that the care-seeker understands the purpose, benefits, and risks involved in the proposed outcome.

This chapter aims at a couple of things. It examines assumptions of the notion of informed consent as a principle of bioethical practice and points to inherent inconsistencies within it. The chapter then proceeds to gesture toward the view that when examined, these assumptions indicate that the process of obtaining and validating informed consent should be contextually derived and that theories of personhood and beliefs about the structure of existence are pivotal in the contextual knowledge that sustains these processes and validation. Accordingly, we suggest that ontological perspectives in African philosophical thought should be foundational in determining whether the consent of a patient or subject of a scientific study is informed, and that such an approach is likely to diffuse notable frictions inherent in the conjunction of 'informed' and 'consent' in biomedical narratives, and in maintaining that the subject and object of informed consent is an autonomous person.

4.2 Informed consent, autonomy and ethics

Since the ruling in 1914 of the New York Court of Appeals in the case of Schloendorff vs. Society of New York Hospital, the provision of informed consent by mentally competent patients or their chosen legal representatives is a strict and universal requirement in medical care. In his ruling, the presiding judge made the following assertion: "Every human being who is capable of reasoning, has the right to decide what is being done with his body…." (Faden and Beauchamp 1986: 123). The basis of informed consent as an ethical doctrine can be inferred from the judge's reasoning. As an ethical doctrine, informed consent can be explained in simple terms as a process of communication which enables a patient *with extant capacity to reason* to make informed and voluntary decisions whether to accept or decline medical care. Understood as such, appending one's signature to a form to declare assent in a single episode where the physician provides information and the patient or proxy indicates a choice to the physician's proposal cannot constitute informed consent. Neither would a short conversation that occurs just before treatment suffice for the required consent because such a context would not adequately make room for a change of mind upon re-consultation in the event of changes in information, treatment and diversification. The ethical doctrine entails the requirement that a patient be informed at every stage of treatment in health delivery, where possible, in a language which is easily understood by him or her, that she is made to appreciate why the treatment is being offered, made aware of the potential risks and benefits and the alternatives to the proposed therapy, and that all is done with reasonable belief in the ability of the patient to comprehend and process the information being given. In simple terms, the ethical doctrine requires the process of traditional informed consent to this pattern: disclosure, comprehension, analytical competence and voluntary consent or refusal.

Likewise, obtaining consent prior to a clinical trial entails informing the human subject about his or her rights, including the right to withdraw from the study; about key elements and the purpose of the proposed study; the procedures to be undertaken; potential benefits and risks of participating in the study and extent of confidentiality of personal identification and demographic data, among several others. Thus, the consent of a patient or participant in a clinical trial is considered to be informed if it is judiciously derived.

The requirement of informed consent implies therefore that patients have a right to refuse medical therapy on religious, cultural or other grounds because *they are competent to choose to do so*. Health care providers, it is argued, cannot subject patients to diagnosis, or prognosis or alternative treatment plans without such *understood* basis of their informed consent (see Isles 2013: 38; Fink, et al. 2010: 27- 36). The absence of such a basis would mean the patient's decision amounts to an imposition, goes the argument. The ultimate goal of understood informed consent is thus to protect and promote the dignity (Shuster 1997: 1436-1440) of the patient and it is presumed that this will be realized by observing her autonomy, freedom and rights through the affirmation of her right to information and to self-determination.

On the other hand, the ethics of medical care is not only based on the tenets of respect for autonomy and justice. They are as well based on two fundamental principles; the principle of nonmaleficence, which prescribe – avoiding an action that causes harm to the patient; and the principle of beneficence in respect of which an action ought to be taken only if it benefits the patient (Beauchamp 2013: 7). It has been argued that equal recognition of all four tenets earlier mentioned (McCormick 2017) is necessary for doctors, caregivers and families to work together towards the common goal of health care delivery for patients without conflict (Weise 2016: 88-94; Beauchamp and Childress 2001). To uphold the joint principles of beneficence and nonmaleficence require that physicians do all they can to aid or benefit the patient while preventing harm.

However, there remains a fundamental ethical dilemma entailed in the simultaneous demand for 'understood' or 'informed consent' on the one hand, and the requirement for 'beneficence and nonmaleficence' on the other. This fundamental tension is more complicated than is often admitted in actual medical practice. The underlying conflict stems from the ethical obligation on the physician to respect patient autonomy (upon which the patient's right to make decisions regarding his or her own welfare is based) and the demand placed on the physician to respect beneficence *and* nonmaleficence. To restate, in the name of respecting, protecting and promoting the patient's autonomy, dignity (Shuster 1997: 1436-1440) and right to self-determination, medical ethics demands *understood* informed consent as an antidote to any form of coercion. Yet, at the same time, the physician is also ethically obliged to uphold the joint principles of beneficence and nonmaleficence as a matter of uttermost importance.

Two levels of tension arise in these demands. At one level, there is fundamental tension inherent in the notions of 'informed' and 'consent' in informed consent. This tension arises in the fact that the patient is expected to depend on another (the learned health-giver) for knowledge on available options on which basis he or she can then make a supposed 'informed' choice of consent or refusal. It is reasonable to suppose that such 'enlightened understanding'[1], of the knowledgeable expert, in the practical situation of care, often does more than merely influence the supposed 'unenlightened' patient's choice of consent or refusal; that it is likely to dictate choice or refusal. The patient's choice is supposed to be based on her autonomy, yet it is not autonomously derived. This is because her choice is dependent on *options informed* by the authoritative other (physician) from which this patient is to choose, even if he or she bears ultimate responsibility for that choice. In other words, even if the patient is considered a free and rational adult capable of choice (i.e. medically competent), the concept of autonomy, which the demand for informed consent seeks to preserve, protect and promote, already entails the assumption that all patients are *ab initio* incompetent. So the notion of informed consent presumes *a priori* that a patient is medically 'incompetent' and so needs the tutoring of the competent physician to make a competent choice.

Another level of tension can be found in the demand in medical care ethics that *both* informed consent and the requirements of 'beneficence and nonmaleficence' should operate simultaneously. This is because the idea of autonomy is foundational to the framework that prescribes informed consent as a requirement in medical care ethics. But if, as argued, informed consent indicates paternalism that vitiates or denigrates the autonomy of the patient; then clearly, informed consent would in most cases be at odds with beneficence (which morally justifies an action only if it benefits the patient), and in some cases conflict with the principle of nonmaleficence (by virtue of which an action that causes harm to the patient ought to be avoided). The fact that patient autonomy could come into conflict with physician's beneficence becomes explicit in the several instances when the patient disagrees with the recommendation of the professional health-giver on what is in the patient's best interest medically speaking.

The implication from the foregoing is that it would be a conceptual error to define patient autonomy *solely* in terms of patient's *capacity* of choice as is assumed by the prevailing understanding of informed consent. A meaningful conception of autonomy, capable of diffusing both tensions, must necessarily entail available options presented to the patient by competent relational other(s) (the learned health-giver in this context). Dispelling this misconception is necessary for understanding and dealing with a fundamental concern about general medical practice and its preoccupation with individual autonomy mostly to the disregard of the relational (social and cultural) content of both patient and physician. The discussion on understanding personhood in the subsequent section is aimed at giving a relational account of personhood (in place of the predominant underlying individualist thought) that takes account of the *equal* values of *communality* and solidarity and allows consideration for the role of competent significant others in impacting the lives and health of those they know and care about without undermining the essential and fundamental inalienable rights of *individuality*.

The ethical dilemma deepens in the situation where a family member, health care provider or an insurance company[2] has to make decisions that supposedly remain the ethical right of the patient because she is incapable of doing so as required by the principle of informed consent. Incapacity that arises as a result of impairments to reasoning and judgment[3] renders the patient incapable of clearly appreciating and understanding all the relevant facts, implications and consequences of the decisions he or she is to make and therefore incompetent. Since such patient incompetence undermines the essence of understood informed consent, obtaining consent from a surrogate is permitted in medical practice. Surrogates such as parents or legal guardians of a child (though usually with informed assent from a minor child), and conservators for the severely mentally disordered, are generally authorized to give consent on behalf of such incompetent patients.

It is worth mentioning that in pursuing beneficence and nonmaleficence, a physician is allowed to assume a patient's informed consent through the doctrine of implied consent. This happens where an unconscious person will lose his or her life if not given immediate medical treatment, for instance. Here, the concluding part of the American judge Justice Benjamin Cardozo's statement remains relevant, "...This is true except in cases of emergency where the patient is unconscious and where it is necessary to operate before consent can be obtained...." (Faden and Beauchamp 1986). In circumstances where physicians are confronted with religious and/or cultural ethical challenges which interfere with the principles of beneficence and nonmaleficence, informed consent could be justifiably waived as urged by Benjamin Rush: "yield to patients in matters of little consequence, but maintain an inflexible authority over them in matters that are essential to life" '(Rush1786).

Instances in which patient autonomy would come into conflict with physician's beneficence have been noted earlier in this section. In such scenarios, different societies approach the conflict differently. While generally standard Western medical practice is likely to defer to the wishes of the Western conception of a mentally competent patient to make their own decisions even if the professionals believe such decisions may not be in the patient's best interest, non-Western contexts such as Africa is more likely to prioritize a social understanding of beneficence over the individualist conception of the autonomy of a person.[4]

The following section aims at offering an alternative understanding of informed consent that hinges on a pragmatic conception of a person as a being that is naturally and necessarily constituted by both the capacity or property of *individuality*, expressed in the characteristics of autonomy, freedom[5] and right-bearing on one hand; and on the other hand an equally natural and necessary property of *communality* or relationality, without restricting persons to a fixed immutable, unitary and fraternal community.

4.3 Understanding Personhood: individua*lity and* communa*lity*

The sort of relation that should exist between an individual and community has been an intractable problem for all contexts, including health delivery. The problem arises because on the one hand, in some societies the belief is prevalent that a person *naturally* has autonomy, freedom and dignity; and that these are values that are not only worth respecting and preserving by the society but are also inviolable. On the other hand, the belief predominates in other societies that an individual is also at the same time a *natural* member of the human society who also needs a society for the realization of his or her individual potential in living a life most worthwhile. Neither perspective denies that the social structure plays a role in providing the framework for the realization of the goals, hopes, and potentials of members of human society. So the question to ask is what is the moral status of a person (or the self)? Is a person an atomic, self-sufficient individual whose being is ontologically prior to the society she lives in and thus does not need to depend on her relationships with others for the realization of her ends?[6] Or is a person by nature a communal being, having natural and essential relationships with others and whose individuality is a secondary fact about him or her (Kenyatta 1965: 188, 297) such that she is a member of a collective "communion of souls rather than an aggregate of individuals?" (Senghor 1964: 93-94)

The ethical questions engendered by informed consent in health care delivery include (1) the status of the rights of the individual (patient and physician alike) – whether these rights are detached from an equal right to communality, such that they cannot be over-ridden under any circumstances; and (2) the place of such rights (for patient and physician alike) in relation to the interests and welfare of relational others.

The ethical question of the moral status of a person has attracted rival responses chiefly from religion, philosophy and the various sciences. Nonetheless, however one looks at it, it is obvious that a human being only comes to realize in some time of life that she exists as a person, with presumed others, some of whose decision(s) it is, more or less that she exists, living a life she did not ask or choose to live, in a world that she does not recall opting to live in. Yet, as it is, persons after coming to this self-realization also recognize that they are necessarily condemned to the freedom of choosing to guard this inexplicable life that seems to cease just as it came, by ensuring its continuous survival and flourishing as they best could; or choosing not to choose to guard same until it ceases by itself; or yet still, taking this life out in ways learnt to be effective for such a purpose. Since the continuous survival of persons anywhere is an empirical indication of their choosing to keep and guard this life in the best ways possible, the right to one's own life and its continuous survival and flourishing is arguably considered sacred to living persons everywhere, regardless of linguistic, territorial or cultural difference. But what this idea of personhood entails, and what the implications of the accompanying idea of a person's inalienable right to a surviving and flourishing life is, in relation to other presumably equal lives, is a normatively complicated matter whose resolution continues to engage religion, philosophy and science.

4.3.1 Individuality of Persons.[7]

Notwithstanding the variety of perspectives attending the conception of personhood and the fundamental divergences in perspectives, one theme is more or less central to the philosophical discourse on personhood and thus can be reasonably assumed as a basis to its conception: a person is a living human being with a moral status; she is a right-bearing entity. For it cannot be reasonably doubted that the need for each person to preserve and promote the sanctity of her life, argued in the foregoing section, would be fundamental to any rational conceptualization of personhood. This need would in turn require that before a person recognizes her obligations to other persons, who her self-realization naturally attaches to as living a shared-life within very significant respects, each person would behold herself and would have to be beheld by the other person(s) as a being that naturally bears the very basic right to her own life and its preservation first and foremost. But to be a bearer of this right to life implies that a person must be presumed to have certain capacities or properties for, a person would be able to bear rights only if she *can* be a rights-bearing being at all. That is to say one cannot be assumed to be a bearer of a right without a pre-requisite assumption of having the *capacity* to bear that right. Thus, the right-bearing person must be presumed to have certain capacities that ground or allow for the bearing of that right. This presupposition then leads to the fundamental question of what capacities or properties human beings must necessarily possess to make them capable of right-bearing–chiefly, right to the preservation of their lives.

The response to this question should lead philosophical discussions to the reasoned judgment that a right-bearing person would have to have as a necessary precondition a set of attributes; i.e., a capacity of self-sensing, the faculty of thought, reason, or intelligence, the ability to make choices, the capacity to hold values and make moral judgments, and some such related notions. These basic, arguably, less contentious notions, couched in highly convoluted philosophical terms of consciousness, rationality, autonomy and moral capacity respectively, are capacities that would have to be presupposed as more or less basic to the ontology of a person if she can be meaningfully identified as a distinctive right-bearing moral[8] person. And there seems to be an overlapping consensus among philosophers as to the minimally necessary account of basic capacities definitive of the human person. Consciousness would have to be presupposed as a basic requirement for the ontology of a person, seeing that one has to be aware of her being in some sense if she can bear rights at all. And, the conscious self would have to be in some sense contiguously linked to her past, present and future conscious self. She would also have to be presumed to have the rational capacity to know not only her self-consciousness and some sense of its contiguity, but must also be rational and intelligent enough to reflect on the options and arrangements that would best encourage the preservation, sustenance and flourishing of her own life. By the assumption of the capacity of autonomy, and consequent creativity, originality and innovation, she would make reasoned intelligent choices towards this same end [goal] of life preservation. And persons as moral beings presuppose that every such person would have to be presumed to be endowed with the *capacity* to make not only reasoned choices but correct, good, or right choices that would promote the preservation of her life primarily but also the lives of other persons who are necessarily and naturally a part of the life she has been condemned to choose to live.

Particularly, the distinctiveness of each person, which is crucial to the bearing of this right to life for the ultimate aim of life preservation and wellbeing earlier argued, would have to be recognized as hinging on the privacy of these capacities to each person's own 'subjective experience'. That is to say, these properties or capacities of a person, just like her life, would not have to be transferable to others, nor alienable. Neither would the subjective *experiencing* of these capacities be accessible to other human persons regardless of how harmonious or distorted their shared-life and communal bonds are. In other words, the faculties of consciousness, reason, autonomy and moral capacity, among other such 'private' and 'internal' dimensions of a person would have to be regarded and respected as *distinctive* subjectively privileged properties of each person to the extent that they are faculties directly accessible *only* to the sensing, thinking, choosing, or judging self. It is only the thinking self that can think of its own thought, for instance. Not even the expression of a feeling to another person by the person herself can guarantee its sincerity or certainty. So that even if a person's physical, objective properties suggest a certain thinking or feeling, it would still remain what it is–a suggestion–for, only a person can be aware of her thinking of that thought or her feeling of that 'mental' state such as pain.

However, it must be acknowledged that practically speaking, some of these identified defining private capacities may present themselves to the 'external' observing person as unfamiliar, handicapped or even damaged capacities or faculties in instances when a person is described as inept, mentally retarded, unconscious or even suffering from amnesia. Yet, even in such claimed objective circumstances, these instances would not take from nor undermine *subjectivity* as a fundamental faculty, aspect or dimension of the being of a person for the reason that the truth of such an assessment would always lie with the person herself. This is enough justification that a person is distinguished by her *exclusive* capacity to access her subjective experiences including but not limited to her consciousness, autonomy, thoughts and freedoms.

It is worthy of note that it is even possible for the self to be deceived of itself unwittingly to some extent. But even in such instances, it is the same self alone that is *able* to detect such self-deception of itself since, in the final instance, and often after consultation with others, only the self has such privileged access to itself. The point sought to be made with the foregoing argument is a very important one that a person is distinguished from others only by her *sole* privileged access to her fundamental capacities of consciousness, reason, autonomy and moral intuitions. This subjectively experienced faculty of a person is what refers to the *individuality* of a person. A person's *individuality* is the ultimate source of creativity, originality and innovation. It remains an extremely potent and active, yet covert, *capacity* of a person until such elusive moments of overtness mostly upon provocation–positive or negative–such as to resist an oppression of her autonomy or to register an appreciation or disapproval of a value she considers worthwhile or reprehensible respectively.

4.3.2 Persons as naturally communal: a revised moderate communitarian view

But the contents of the operations of a person's individuality always arise from her other nature of communality. That is to say, what defines the individuality of a person is simply the capacity of privileged access persons have to their own consciousness, thought, autonomy, rationality and some such notions in operation. But the content of this capacity, namely, what thought is about, or autonomy entails, or yet still morality prescribes, for instances, are necessarily relational. This defines the other aspect of the ontology of persons, which is persons' natural and necessary relationality–communality. Thus, an accurate conception of personhood must include its other aspect, namely, communality since, a person is not only constituted naturally by individuality but a person is also naturally and thus, necessarily communal.

A strong consensus exists within the corpus of Africa philosophy that the interpretation of the idea of the communality of persons takes two forms. In one model, the relationality of persons is interpreted to mean that a person is by nature inseparable from community ties in the sense that community 'defines the person as person… and personhood is something which has to be achieved, and is not given simply because one is born of human seed' (Menkiti 1984: 172). From this perspective, therefore, in defining herself as a communal being, the individual can only say: "I am because we are, and because we are therefore I am" (Mbiti 1970: 141). Gyekye rejects this view of personhood as overstating the status of community, and elaborates another model, moderate communitarianism, that affirms both the communality and individuality of persons in like measure. In this model, Gyekye is eager to show that the ontological primacy of community should not be mistaken for a negation of the moral worth of individuality. In his view, persons depend on social relations and, yet, this does not mean that they are fully defined by social context. In Gyekye's model, promotion of the common good of shared relationships cannot merit violating individual rights or otherwise degrading the dignity of an individual human being (Gyekye 1997: 270-271). The common good equals 'the social conditions that will enable each individual to function satisfactorily in a human society' (Gyekye 1997: 64). Therefore, a 'cramped and shackled self responding robotically to the ways and demands of the communal structure' cannot be fully human (Gyekye 1997: 55-56). In the context of shared relationships, a person is an individual agent and an object of moral value. As such, her inherent individuality may lead her to reject social norms that do not accord with her moral sensibilities. Thus, persons have a dual source of the self in the moderate communitarian framework that are equally morally valuable. So - the dependence of the individual human being on a network of social relations ought not to dissolve her individuality within a broader notion of the community.

We subscribe to a revised notion of Gyekye's moderate communitarian view of personhood, and wish to add to it a perspective on relationality. Upon coming to the self-realization of her *individuality* sometimes in life, a person at the same time comes to the self-realization of her naturally *relational* character; first, with herself, but with other persons as well as the external world. These others are mostly, but not necessarily, related by kinship bonds, while others constitute her 'significant others'.

To argue that to be a person also implies that one is necessarily communal, related or naturally relational, need not translate necessarily as the need for a person to be *solely* tied to, bonded by or embedded in a collective, bounded and enclosed 'communitarian community' within which the *individuality* of persons expressed as autonomy, rationality, creativity, among others, would be non-existent or inconsequential, as Gyekye argues. For, as already argued earlier, a person's *individuality* is not only inaccessible and non-transferrable to others, it is actually inalienable as well. Not even the person herself can negate or dispense with her *individuality* such understood, for one's attempt at suppression of her *individuality* would itself be the very expression of that *individuality*. Yet, the force of a person's non-optional communa*lity* or relationality that starts naturally within herself, and consequently with other persons starting from the 'communitarian community' up to the wider external world-community, cannot be downplayed either. This is so because, just like individuality, communa*lity* is itself inalienable and not transferable to others even if some aspects of the 'communitarian community', defined in terms of kinship-ties, common history, territorial and linguistic boundaries, could be said to be transferable to a certain degree. The natural *communality* of a person is, thus, distinguishable from her natural membership in a specific community defined by kinship-ties, language, culture, history, territory, among others, yet not totally detached from it. The *communality* of a person simply refers to the naturally *relational*, related and interactive character of a person. Thus communality, for us, transcends the boundaries of belonging together as members of a geographical, linguistic, biological or ancestral community defined by the various communitarian arguments including Gyekye's. This is so because people will necessarily share in the values, aims, goals and aspirations of others who may not necessarily belong to their immediate communitarian community. Besides, in a fast-globalizing world, different persons would necessarily affect and be affected by the values, aims, goals and aspirations of such 'others' who are presumed to be external to their communitarian community. The ties and boundaries of community, properly understood, then would itself not only vary but would be very elusive. Thus, it would be more defensible to think of persons as communal–inter-relational–beings than as beings defined by and restricted to linguistic, ancestral, geographical or some such communitarian community.

The necessity of *communality* stems from the cognizance of the fact that just like individuality, *communality* or relationality is itself an imposed domain of personhood whose origin cannot be conclusively explained by science, religion or philosophy without justifiable contestations. The assertion that *communality* itself, like *individuality*, is natural and therefore not a question of choice for any person is grounded in the fact that before a person could come to the self-realization that she exists at all even as a person with individualistic dimensions, she would already have been a communal, related and inter-related being; first with herself, then with immediate 'significant others' such as family, the 'communitarian community' and its essential systems, structures, language, history, culture and particular forms of life that contribute to forming her identity, but then also with the external world (physical, quasi-physical or nonphysical) and several others in different ways some of which might be distant and yet very significant. In simple terms, the character of *communality*, like *individuality*, is discovered by a person upon her self-realization to be an imposed dimension of her being which necessarily connects her in significant ways to other people and things prior to her self-realization of her *individuality*. Inasmuch as that would not be a claim of authority of a person's communal belonging over her *individuality*, it is an acknowledgement of the very significant and active role that community, basic to a person's *communality*, plays in her life.

In the first place, her very existence is the outcome of communal interactions of various forms between and among persons. She participates in this 'community' to develop herself in a cultural, linguistic and socio-historical environment that, together with her individual dimension, moulds her very identity and self understanding (Taylor 1992: 49). This suggests that even though her *individuality* may have been present from conception, it is communal relationship and its interrelations that gives content to *individuality* and guides a person's *individuality* until it emerges or evolves at the time of life when she comes to the self-consciousness that she exists as a person; as a daughter or son, a member of a clan, tribe or neighbourhood, a citizen of a nation, each with its systems and structures, norms and precepts, roles and obligations, but also privileges and entitlements. These are natural and essential aspects of a person that are already given. Thus, *communality*, together with a person's *individuality*, constitutes her given nature. But the given undergoes constant change as it interacts with itself and others.[9]

It is important to recognize that a person, being naturally communal, derives not only from the fact that one is born from communal relation, or descended into Aristotle's political society, but more so the normative sense of personhood as a right-bearing entity itself also arises from this fact of natural *communality*. Prior to a person coming to the self-realization that she exists, and acknowledging her capacity of reason, autonomy and morals, she would have been already communally-related and community bred – linguistically, historically and culturally. Her communal nature linked to community(s), thus, gives content to her rights, autonomy, rationality and morality since this capacity extends beyond the person and stands in relation to other persons. It means that, even though she bears these individual capacities, the capacities themselves presuppose or are preconditioned by a relational status or sharing others. To illustrate, I may own my thoughts, feelings and consciousness, or even talk and interact with myself, but the meanings I ascribe to those thoughts, or the language in which I express, think or reflect on those thoughts are not created by myself prior to those thoughts, they are part of my understanding of those symbols that I reflect on. But those symbols are themselves conveyed into my thoughts by interactions with others as I come to the self-realization of my existence as a part of an on-going interactive process of life. In simple terms, it is a person's given *communality* that gives content and substance to her given *individuality*, while her *individuality* in turn creates, revises, shapes, and influences her *communality* by its creativity, innovation and originality to define personhood as an on-going interplay between *individuality* and *communality*.

Thus, even though *communality*, like *individuality*, is internal and subjectively experienced, it is, unlike individuality, overt, controlled and passive. It is the observable aspects of a person that constantly seeks to fit in, receive and obey rules; it is the part that is always conspicuous and perceivable in a person during her interactions with herself and with others; it is that dimension of a person that expresses the status-quo. Therefore, a person cannot be 'an individual' as defined by individualism. A person is a complex union of *individuality* and *communality*: her *individual* aspect–a potent, self-sufficient, yet covert force– constantly mitigated by her *communal* aspect–an acquiescent, dependent, yet overt force. That means a person should be conceived of both as a self-sufficient and dependent being who is at once free and unfree all the time, not one over the other nor sometimes free, sometimes unfree, but always both free and unfree at once. And, it is such complex beings that constitute human society.

Conclusion: Implications of relational personhood for bioethics

Bioethics is a species of applied ethics. In Aristotelian terms, it is in the realm of practical wisdom (*phronesis*), which is a virtue of practical reasoning. Practical reasoning aims at making good choices, through deliberating correctly on what can be changed and have the right desires (Nicomachean Ethics, Book 6, §2) about how to live a good life (*ibid.* §5). Thus, practical wisdom involves understanding what is required in a particular situation to achieve what is good. Wim Dekkers and Bert Gordijn are therefore right in rendering Aristotle's practical wisdom as "knowing the right thing to do in a particular circumstance through understanding the circumstance rightly, knowing what matters, and effective means-end reasoning to bring about what matters"[10]

Such knowing requires significant sensitivity to context – an understanding of the facts and demands of the situation, and how to act in it to achieve the good. However, according to Aristotle, no general or universal rules exist to guide us toward such action, except the capacity of right reasoning. And as that which can be taught is that which yields to general principles, practical wisdom is not a subject of intuition since it is contextual and depends on experience (*ibid*: §8). Practical Wisdom thus supplies reasons for action that goes beyond technical ability, and involves forms of deliberation in which contextual knowledge, reflection, attitude and life experience are combined with emotional, social, and ethical capacities.

If so, then what implications do the discussions of the nature of persons in the foregoing sections have for the ethics of medical practice, as a human endeavor that needs the guidance of practical wisdom? Two implications may be drawn. First, that it would be practically wise to derive the principles underlying informed consent from knowledge and values embedded in the context of application. What persons are, metaphysically and as social beings, then, becomes pivotal in providing philosophical justification for what constitutes informed consent. We indicated in section 2 that Western medical practice is likely to defer to the wishes of a supposed mentally competent patient to make their own decisions even if the professionals believe such decisions may not be in the patient's best interest, whereas in Africa typically, a social understanding of beneficence over individualist conception of a person's autonomy would be prioritized. The reason for this is that theories of personhood emphasize the relationality and metaphysicality of persons in ways that trump individualist conceptions of autonomy,

We have argued the relational concept of person and indicated its prevalence in African philosophical thought. Likewise accepted in African thought is the idea that the universe is composed of visible and invisible aspects, both real, and that a person is likewise constituted of visible (material) and invisible (metaphysical) components. It is well accepted that Akan thought, for instance, postulates three constituents of a person, which straddle the physical versus non-physical realms of being. The ɔkra is a transcendental attribute bestowed individually to every human being at the point of birth. It is conceived as a speck of the nature of the Supreme Being or God, and functions as the principle of life and receptacle of human destiny (Gyekye 1995: .87-94). Thus, ɔkra exhibits trans-individualist dimensions. The metaphysical idea of the human possession of a speck of the nature of God is ethically significant, as it translates into the secular reasoning that the individual possesses inviolable attributes (Silk 1990: 322). The second metaphysical attribute of persons, *Sunsum*, is considered a universal power 'manifesting itself differently in the various beings and objects of the natural world' '(Gyekye 1995: 72-73). *Sunsum* functions as the basis of the psychological constitution of a person and is particularized as a person's conscious energy (Ajei 2014: 39-42). As such, *sunsum* also exhibits trans-individualist dimensions. *Mogya*, the third element is, simultaneously, the physiological basis of individual life (Gyekye 1995: 85) and an adhesive for social bonding (*ibid*: 48-49). Accordingly, it also exhibits trans-individualist dimensions. Thus, in Akan thought, the metaphysical elements of personhood play pivotal roles at the social level. In fact, they combine to fashion the theoretical basis of the relational person of moderate communitarianism, which we endorse. They work in unison to insert persons necessarily into communal reality and to make reasonable talk of the necessary and mutual dependence of persons.

Deriving principles of informed consent from these metaphysical and social theories of persons would entail practical wisdom in elevating the status of the community in the provision of informed consent, even in situations where a patient's abilities of comprehension and reason are not impaired. If the relational person is partly communally constituted, then community partakes of her individuality. Therefore, the predominance of community in the provision of informed consent becomes philosophically justifiable in the case of the person who considers himself as relationally constituted. Likewise, a person who deems herself to be metaphysically constituted will easily concede that her capacity to understand her nature by the activity of her reason is necessarily limited. She is also likely to admit that a specialist, such as a priest/priestess of African traditional religion, trained to be a specialist in having access to the metaphysical world and paranormal cognition, has the capability to understand the metaphysical aspect of her being. If so, she would not find it an affront to her autonomy by willfully conceding to the specialist the right to inform her of the right choice to make in such instances.

In such cases, the tensions that attend to informed consent described in section 3 are more easily diffused. The friction inherent in the notions of 'informed' and 'consent' in informed consent dissipate since the patient does not consider depending on another for guidance on available options to be a restriction on her autonomy. Because of the relationality of her being, the other is constitutive of her being. Also, belief in her metaphysicality allows her to think that her spiritual counsellor's guidance would conflict neither with the principle of beneficence nor with that of nonmaleficence. Thus, the risk of the patient's autonomy conflicting with a physician's or medicine man's beneficence becomes all but erased.

4.5 Notes

[1] Compare Dahl's criteria number three (3) for democratic process in Dahl, Robert A. *On Democracy* (London: Yale University Press, 2000) Chapter 4.

[2] since the patient, by directly or indirectly joining a health insurance plan, gives up certain rights and agrees to abide by the values of the insurance company

[3] such as basic intellectual or emotional immaturity, high levels of stress such as posttraumatic stress disorder (PTSD), severe mental disorder, intoxication, Alzheimer's disease or being in a coma

[4] The source of this difference in approaches lie in the standard African conception of a person as not merely an isolated being solely defined by rationality, will or memory but a community constituted being.(See Menkiti, I. 'Person and Community in African Traditional Thought', in: Wright R. A. (ed.) (1984), *African Philosophy: An Introduction* (Lanham, Md.: University Press of Americas), pp. 171, 172, 180.

[5] Including freedom to think, analyze, criticize etc

[6] See Taylor's critique of such atomistic views which he associates with social contract theories in his *Atomism*

[7] Contributors acknowledge that substantive portions of the material in this section and the next appear in some form in the PhD dissertation (work in progress) of one of the contributors.

[8] Moral here depicts mainly the capacity to make the right choices and not necessarily making the right choices per se for, actual content of morality, I argue later, would have to be based on shared and contextual meanings even if derived from generalizable categories.

[9] Compare Mead's 'I' and 'me' in Mead, G. H. (1967 [1934]) *Mind, Self, and Society from the Standpoint of a Social Behaviorist.* (University of Chicago Press, Chicago).

[10] In their Editorial Introduction, *Medicine, Health Care, and Philosophy*, Published online 2007 Jul 11. doi: 10.1007/s11019-007-9072-4. Accessed at https://www.ncbi.nlm.nih.gov/pmc/articles/PMC2778616/ on 11th May 2018

4.6 References

Ajei, M. O. 2014. *The Paranormal: An Inquiry into some features of an African Metaphysics and epistemology* (Hamburg: MissionshilfeVerlag).

Aristotle, 1925, *The Nichomachean Ethics*, transl. W.D., Ross, Oxford, Vol.IX.

Beauchamp, J. (2013). "Principles of Biomedical Ethics". *Principles of Biomedical Ethics.* **7.** "*Bioethic Tools: Principles of Bioethics*". Depts.washington.edu. Retrieved 2017-03-21

Beauchamp, Tom L., and Childress, James F., 2001. *Principles of Biomedical Ethics* New York: Oxford University Press.

Dahl, R. A., 2000. *On Democracy* London: Yale University Press.

Dekkers, W. and Gordijn, B. *Medicine, Health Care, and Philosophy*, Published online 2007 Jul 11. doi: 10.1007/s11019-007-9072-4. Accessed at https://www.ncbi.nlm.nih.gov/pmc/articles/PMC2778616/ on 11th May 2018.

Faden, Ruth; Beauchamp, Tom L., 1986. *A history and theory of informed consent* (New York: Oxford University Press), p. 123. ISBN0195036867.

Fink A.S, Prochazka A.V, Henderson W.G, et al. 2010. Enhancement of surgical informed consent by addition of repeat back: a multicenter, randomized controlled clinical trial. *Ann Surg.* July; 252 1: 27- 36. doi:10.1097/SLA.0b013e3181e3ec61.

Gyekye, K. 1997. *Tradition and Modernity: Philosophical Reflections on the African Experience.* Oxford University Press.

.... 1995. *An Essay on African Philosophical Thought: The Akan Conceptual Scheme.* Rev. ed. Philadelphia, Pa.: Temple University Press).

Isles A.F., 2013. Understood consent versus informed consent: a new paradigm for obtaining consent for pediatric research studies. *Front Pediatr.* November 21; 1: 38 doi: 10.3389/fped. 2013.00038.

Kenyatta, J., 1965. *Facing Mount Kenya.* New York: Vintage.

Mbiti, J., 1970. *African Religions and Philosophy* New York: Doubleday, Anchor Books.

Mead, G. H., 1967 [1934]. *Mind, Self, and Society from the Standpoint of a Social Behaviorist.* (University of Chicago Press, Chicago).

Menkiti, Ifeanyi A., 1984. "Person and Community in African Traditional Thought," in Wright, Richard A.: ed., *African Philosophy: An Introduction* New York: University Press of America.

Rush, B., 1786. *An Oration ... Containing an Enquiry into the Influence of Physical Causes upon the Moral Faculty.* (Philadelphia: Charles Cist)

Senghor, L. S., 1964. *On African Socialism.* Mercer Cook (trans.), New York: Praeger.

Shuster, E., 1997. Fifty years later: the significance of the Nuremberg Code. *N Engl J Med.* November 13;337 20: 1436- 1440. doi: 10.1056/NEJM199711133372006

Silk, J., 1990. "Traditional Culture and the Prospect of Human Rights in Africa", in: An-Na'im, A. A. & Deng, M. F. (eds.). *Human Rights in Africa: Cross Cultural Perspectives.* (Washington DC: The Brookings Institution).

Taylor, C., 1992. "Atomism", in *Communitarianism and Individualism* (eds.) Avineri S., and De-Shalit A. (Oxford University Press.

Weise, Mary. 2016. "Medical Ethics Made Easy" in *Professional Case Management.* 21:88-94. doi: 10. 1097/ncm.0000000000000151

Chapter 5

Cultural Translation, Human Meaning, and Genes: Why Interpretation Matters in Psychiatric Genomics

Camillia Kong
University of Oxford

Abstract

This chapter presents the challenges in the current globalized discourse on genomics and suggests the need for attenuated forms of translational thinking. She points out that problematic linguistic and cultural translation of concepts like genes and Western psychiatric diagnoses in the African context sheds critical light on the reductivism and decontextualisation around human behavior within the conceptual framing of psychiatric genomics, where mental disorder is treated as separable from the interpretative meanings of such behavior.

Key words: cultural translation, human, meaning, genes, interpretation, psychiatric genomics, reductivism, decontextualisation, mental disorder.

5.1 Introduction

Mental health research has increasingly focused on the potential biological and genetic causes of mental disorder and intellectual disability. The field of psychiatric genomics collects and analyses genomic data through population wide association studies to explore the genotype underlying neurological and behavioral phenotypes (traits) in major psychiatric and neurodevelopmental disorders. Several aspirations fuel the rapid progress of psychiatric genomics, not least the drive to find preventative or curative interventions within a precision-medicine framework. Insel and Scolnick explain:

> To repeat an oft-used metaphor from the history of polio, while we can continue to make more and better iron lungs available, we also need to go after the vaccine. All current medical treatments for mental illnesses are palliative, none are even proposed as cures. [...] [T]o stretch the polio metaphor, we have not yet gone after the vaccine (Insel and Scolnick 2006).

Other aims of psychiatric genomics include improving the diagnostic, classificatory systems of psychiatric disorders and advancing technologies to achieve a more personalised approach to mental health so that choices around prevention and treatment are better tailored to individual circumstances.

The relevance of psychiatric genomics to African contexts may not be immediately obvious given the widespread unavailability of basic mental health treatment, such as psychosocial or drug therapies, due to issues of underfunding, underinvestment, stigma of individuals and family members, poor mental health literacy, and the lack of community services and relevant training for practitioners (Saxena, et al. 2007: 878-89; Saracheno et al. 2007: 1164-1174; Patel et al. 2013: 1–6; Jacob et al. 2007: 1061-77; Gureje et al. 2005: 436-441; Collins and Saxena. 2016: 25-7). Despite these daunting challenges, Western researchers of psychiatric genomics have begun to collect genetic samples of African people with mental and neurodevelopmental disorder, recognising that current genomic samples disproportionately represent those of white European descent. If psychiatric genomics is to have a potential *global* payoff for people with mental disorder, there is a need to ensure African genomic data is represented, compared, and included to improve diagnostic tools and clinical treatments down the line.

As laudable as these aims are, pressing issues of cultural and linguistic translation present important obstacles to their achievement. These obstacles aren't just pragmatic in nature, but revolve around fundamental issues which afflict the current *enframing* of psychiatric genomics. The problematic linguistic and cultural translation of concepts like genes and Western psychiatric diagnoses in the African context sheds critical light on the reductivism and decontextualisation around human behavior within the conceptual framing of psychiatric genomics, where mental disorder is treated as separable from the *interpretative meanings* of such behavior. Yet we risk losing sight of what mental disorder and its behavior *means* for people, particularly as psychiatric and sociogenomics research adopts increasingly deterministic or reductivist language (Bliss 2018). To counter these tendencies, I argue that *attenuated forms of translational thinking* needs to be fostered and developed. This describes an intellectual orientation where African conceptual schemes and bioethical perspectives are taken seriously as substantive contributions to our global discussions around the conceptualisation and treatment of mental disorder.

Section I outlines how a genomics perspective might lend itself to a reductive, decontextualised lens of human behavior, whilst Section II critically explores how such an epistemic orientation mistakenly treats interpretive meaning as separable from our descriptions and explanations of behavior. Section III suggests that this epistemic orientation is untenable in light of the translational issues around psychiatric genomics and Western biogenetic models of mental disorder. Finally, I suggest the importance of African thought and practice in global bioethical debates around mental health, suggesting two ways in which these perspectives can challenge the reductivist and decontextualised enframing of psychiatric genomics.

5.2 Genomic Reduction and Decontextualisation

The Psychiatric Genomics Consortium describes their overarching goal as 'deliver[ing] actionable knowledge, i.e., genetic findings whose biological implications can be used to improve diagnosis, develop rational therapeutics, and craft mechanistic approaches to primary prevention' (Sullivan et al. 2017: 16). Such approaches might include focusing on genes or gene pathways that are suitable 'druggable' targets for those who have risk susceptibility towards certain mental health conditions, thus enabling its early intervention or prevention (Seretti and Fabbri 2013: 1339-41). A genomics approach to mental disorder involves a simultaneous 'zooming-in' and 'zooming-out' of their basic unit of analysis: first, the 'zooming-in' revolves around looking at our genetic architecture and molecular environment as keys to unlocking the mechanisms which cause mental health conditions. This presumes that human behavioral phenotypes might have a genetic source (how genes work within certain organs and cell-types) or epigenetic source (how our genes express themselves differently depending on the environment). Either way, explanations of human behavior are reduced to the smallest of levels – that of the molecular level. Human persons and behavior are effectively 'molecularised'. Second, there is the methodological 'zooming-out' which involves analysing individual genetic data as a statistical number within genome-wide association studies (GWAS): this method involves analysing a large number of samples of DNA to identify genomic variations which could be correlated with risk susceptibility of certain conditions. This entails the abstraction of human persons and behavior through the use of big-data sets to identify the regions of the genome which may cause disease.

In other words, complex human behavior is simultaneously *reduced* to its genomic core and *decontextualised* within large data sets to determine gene susceptibility for mental or neurodevelopmental disorders. These reductive and decontextualised tendencies can lead to worrisome implications. First, there is a singular focus on our genes to the exclusion of other factors that contribute to mental disorder. 'An orientation towards genetic susceptibility can easily begin to dominate our ways of thinking about disease prevention, until it becomes *the way* that we come to think of the problem', cautions Troy Duster (Duster 2003: 125). Our intellectual orientation becomes so narrowed that the genetic explanation is the only one that is deemed worthy of pursuit, despite the multifactorial origins of mental disorder. Without careful reflection and vigilance, numerous environmental and structural factors that contribute to mental illness – such as poverty, gender violence, racism, adverse childhood experiences, stress – risk being minimised or disregarded in research and in the treatment and policy initiatives which follow. Though specialised fields of psychiatric genomics, such as epigenetics, recognise the importance of the gene-environment interaction, nonetheless, the focus remains on how environmental factors (such as diet, exercise, parenting style, etc.) determine our *molecular* environment so that certain altered chemical pathways regulate gene expression. These pathways might be manipulated through druggable targets in future, yet whether this is a liberating and empowering direction remains a contested question. As Catherine Bliss rightly warns, 'Yes, being able to pop sociogenomically targeted drugs may liberate a person from real social conditions that affect them. In fact, popping a pill will likely lead to a pacification, and potentially depoliticization. [...] Organizing around experiences of social injustice falls out of the picture' (Bliss, 2018: 36, 37).

I am not arguing that scientific endeavours to find genetic markers for mental disorder are in and of themselves unjustified. But the reductionist and decontextualised nature of these endeavours requires careful examination because they may be symptomatic of more fundamental issues around the conceptual enframing or intellectual ethos of psychiatric genomics. The problem with this reductive and decontextualised enframing becomes more evident when cultural and linguistic translation comes into the picture, whereby misunderstanding the deeper interpretive meaning of human action and behavior results in a loss of explanatory coherence accordingly.

5.3 The Interpretive Field of Psychiatric Genomics

Genomics is often viewed as a strict *natural* science, meaning terms correlate to an objectively observable thing which enables the prediction of phenomena. Genetic variations correspond to concrete verifiable data (i.e. the fact that genetic mutations are indeed found, like the HTT gene which causes Huntingdon's Disease). But arguably, psychiatric genomics – and psychiatry more generally – blurs the line between natural and social science due to the fact that mental disorder is comprised of complex behaviors with complicated multifactorial causes, and the ability to predict the onset of mental disorder and its attendant behaviors remains elusive. More importantly, th*e social and cultural meaning* of such behavior can determine whether or not certain behavioral traits are viewed as abnormal. As one scientist describes in Bliss,

> [B]ecause the trait events are often complex, the genome-wide association correlates may be the result of some like underlying factor or a separated factor that's correlated a sort of messy proxy that we have for the trait that we are interested in. That means there is a real lack of precision from the get-go in defining the behaviors, which on top of that are cultural and constituted behavior (Bliss, 2018: 159).

The realm of the human sciences – the cultural and linguistic meaning behind human action – is entered as soon as certain behavioral traits are isolated as warranting further genetic investigation.

Despite this, the language of genetic determinism, of reducing and decontextualising complex behavioral traits and outcomes, has proven deeply seductive. Social scientists speak of a certain predictability of human outcomes through an 'objective' analysis of our genes and risk susceptibility, whereby risk scores calculated in GWAS are used to explore how genes determine mental health, social behavior, educational attainment, criminality, etc (see Davies et al. 2016: 758-767; Belsky et al. 2016: 957-972; Tielbeek et al. 2012: e45086; Tiihonen et al. 2015: 786-792; Hong Lee et al. 2013: 984-994). Trends like these strongly suggest that the interpretive meanings of complex human behaviors start to recede as we zoom in to the smallest cause of human behavior (i.e. our genes) to the largest analyses of such units of analysis (i.e. GWAS of large populations). At the heart of psychiatric and sociogenomics is a particular epistemic orientation which claims that our understanding of complex human behavioral traits can achieve scientific certainty, verification, and impartiality. Research that adheres to these standards can expect a certain epistemic status in both the natural and social sciences. Yet, as Charles

Taylor has argued, this orientation rests on a misunderstanding of the conditions of meaningful human behavior: social, cultural, and linguistic constituents of how we make sense of our behavior and actions are hived off, treated as mere subjective views entirely separable from the behavior itself (Taylor 1985: 15-57). The science of interpretation – the hermeneutical stance – is presumed to provide no objective knowledge or understanding about the phenomena of human behavior. The methods we think are appropriate to study and understand such phenomena are narrowed accordingly.

But this belies the intrinsically holistic rather than reductive ways in which we make sense of human behavior and meaning. We are self-interpreting animals, where meaning is *for a subject, of something*, and is situated in an *interrelated field of social practice and significance*. Taylor uses the term 'shame' to illustrate this point: to understand the emotion of 'shame' one also has to refer to a certain kind of situation which gives rise to such a disposition. The specific meaning of 'hiding' in this context ('hiding in shame') will mean something entirely different from 'hiding from my pursuer'. To fully understand what the emotion of shame denotes and to make sense of the act of hiding, both have to be embedded within the full context of social meaning and practices (*ibid.*).

One might argue that terms in psychiatric genomics would lack the same contextuality as the meaning of 'shame' or 'hiding'. However, consider the word *gene* and what it denotes. On one hand, the technical, scientific definition refers to the specific sequence of nucleotides which form part of a chromosome. Equally, the term *gene* is situated and evolves within an interpretive circle: it might evoke the scientific definition in certain situations, but equally, it could be related to a sense of predestination, heritability, determinism, or a blot in the very architecture of one's being. Rather tellingly, the OED defines the extended use of gene as 'reference to qualities regarded as deeply ingrained or as inherited' (Oxford English Dictionary 2018). Even if the scientific use of the term may not necessarily denote heritability or determinism, these connotations are nonetheless strongly embedded in common, informal use. The concept of *gene* has interpretive meaning *for subjects* within an *intersubjective field of practice*.

This interpretive field becomes even more evident when we talk about genes in the context of individuals making choices, such as an expectant mother undergoing prenatal testing for example. *Gene* here might be imbued with all sorts of interpretive meanings absent in the scientific lab and cause agents to act in unexpected ways: it could be connected to feelings of expectation, responsibility or pressure, leading to actions based on these feelings (like a change in one's lifestyle) or a decision to terminate a pregnancy based on an interpretation of certain genes leading to conditions that are deemed undesirable in society. But a full understanding of what *gene* means for this expectant mother and how it moves her will elude us if our intellectual orientation remains wedded to a reductive rather than holistic approach to human behavior. As Taylor writes:

> The range of human desires, feelings, emotions, and hence meanings is bound up with the level and type of culture, which in turn is inseparable from the distinctions and categories marked by the language people speak. The field of meanings in which a given situation can find its place is bound up with the semantic field of the terms characterizing these meanings and the related feelings, desires, predicaments (Taylor1985: 25).

In other words, any science that is trying to make sense of human action cannot separate the linguistic meanings and interpretations that are bound up with those behaviors. The enframing of psychiatric genomics attempts to make precisely this type of separation, but it sacrifices deep level understanding of what these behaviors and experiences *mean* for individuals as *agents and subjects*. By its very nature mental disorder is a heterogeneous experience; its meaning is subject to self-interpretation, drawing upon linguistic, intersubjective meanings and conceptual schemes. Something is inevitably lost when this type of explanation is hived off, as amply apparent in the translational issues discussed in the next section.

A couple of objections might challenge my analysis thus far: first, one could argue that psychiatric genomics as situated within a framework of personalised medicine is already (and has to be) engaged with subjects as 'self-interpreting animals'. Second, are behaviors that result from mental disorder and intellectual disability truly 'meaningful' in Taylor's sense? Are these not 'symptoms' rather than meaningful actions that reflect an intersubjective social reality?

The first objection rests on the claim that space for human interpretation and meaning is provided in the potential *clinical application* of genomic medicine. Through improvements in the explanatory and predictive potential of psychiatric genomics, individuals will be better able to make proactive choices about their mental health which suits their personal circumstances and genetic makeup, resulting in targeted drug treatments or lifestyle decisions based on their risk susceptibility towards certain disorders. Patients, in other words, are empowered to make informed, responsible choices that enhance their mental health (see Personalized Medicine Coalition 2014) . This framework of personalised medicine in and of itself implies that individuals are active, interpretive agents around their mental health care – indeed, it is the explicit purpose of genomic medicine to further empower such agency for better health outcomes.

Yet, this objection still misses the point. Even as some degree of interpretation is assumed in a model of personalised medicine, genomic information *itself* is treated as neutral data that simply requires application. Such data isn't situated and embedded within an interpretive field of purposeful action, despite the fact that its *utility* inherently depends on *predetermining* its particular meaningfulness for patients or clinicians. Indeed, the envisaged utility of neutral genomic information reveals the extent to which psychiatric genomics is itself situated within a certain conceptual and value framework which prioritises personal responsibility, empowerment, and self-actualisation. The language of empowering individual agents in their health choices makes assumptions about what it means to be 'responsible' genomic selves, to make more informed decisions about our present and future mental health as rational consumers (Novas and Rose 2000: 485-513). In turn, this picture of the responsible genomic self bears the normative and predictive weight of promises around prevention and early intervention, where assumptions of how ideal agents will act in light of their genomic information is necessary to articulate the promises of its clinical application, to ensure genomic medicine lives up to its promises. In short, this vision of genomic agency *predetermines the meaning that genomics has for agents*. Meanwhile, its prevailing epistemic orientation fails to gain any purchase on the intersubjective meaning of such information in a deep sense – namely how it is interpreted, digested, and used by agents given the values and concepts that matter *to them*, based on their social reality.

The second objection has more to do with questioning whether the behaviors and actions that result from mental disorder are truly meaningful in Taylor's sense. If they lack meaning, the envisaged problems with the enframing of psychiatric genomics would seem to disappear: we don't need to worry about what genomics means to individuals as self-interpreting beings because these biogenetically caused behaviors are not in and of themselves meaningful for subjects. In no way am I arguing that most or even any mental health clinician and researcher would put the case as strongly as it is stated here. Good clinicians often recognise that the experience of mental disorder *is* meaningful for a subject, where the desire to convey that meaning persists even as a common language or field of experience remains difficult to establish. This presumption of meaningfulness falls away nonetheless when our actions are explained in a reductive and decontextualised manner: individuals are reduced to a set of behavioral phenotypes which warrant genetic investigation because they depart from societal norms of acceptability or ideas of bodily or neurological functioning, or because they fit into certain classifications of psychiatric disorder. Understood as such, mentally disordered behaviors are symptoms rather than meaningful or intentional actions.

Yet the phenomenology of mentally disordered behaviors and actions indicates the contrary. Such behaviors and actions *are* often meaningful in a deep sense, giving shape to a person's life and expressing self-narratives and self-conceptions within an intersubjective context. Sometimes the subjective meaning behind these behaviors might be inherently harmful, like disorders that rest on self-abnegating narratives and self-hatred (like borderline personality disorder). But the behaviors that follow are still meaningful in Taylor's sense. For example, successfully treating a person who cuts herself regularly requires the presumption that there is coherent meaning behind her actions. The clinical perspective might give a behavioralist slant to her actions (e.g. 'orbitofrontal cortex dysfunction causes these patients to cut themselves'). But the patient's own explanation of her self-harm will be one that is imbued with *equally valid* significance and meaning, both real and symbolic – such as exerting control over her emotions, punishment and hatred of herself, coping with her environment and relationships (Kong, forthcoming). Or take the meaning behind anorexia nervosa, where the act of not eating and starving oneself might be a form of expressive agency in light of intersubjective cultural norms around thinness or the deprivation of opportunities and substantive agency for women (Bardo 2013). These meanings around mental disorder are not simply fabricated, made up, coming from nothing, but refract the things that matter for agents and the social reality around them.

The importance of this point cannot be understated, particularly when we consider the cultural interpretation of psychiatric genomics and biogenetic models of mental disorder. The involvement of African institutions, NGOs, and local participants is viewed as a priority to advance a global agenda around mental health. Proponents of transcultural psychiatry continue to remind institutions and researchers from the West of divergent explanatory models of causation and healing. But currently lacking is a deeper understanding and reflection as to *why* these differences are so important. And without such understanding, we foreclose questions of *how* African perspectives can contribute meaningfully to our global knowledge of mental disorder.

5.4 Attenuated Forms of Translational Thinking

Thus far I have expressed worries that the crucial interpretive domain is being lost in the current enframing of psychiatric genomics, where its epistemological orientation tends to reduce and decontextualise human meaning and behavior as it relates to mental disorder. What results is an inability to make coherent sense of human actions and the way we describe them – particularly those of which we might call 'disordered'. By contrast, the objective reality of lived experience and interpretive meaning has to be taken as a given if we are to answer questions around *why* someone does such and such, *why* we use this description and not others, or *what* worldview is mirrored in those linguistic descriptions. In other words, the way we describe the phenomena, the language that we use to ourselves, to those within our social community, and to clinicians treating us, are all embedded within conceptual schemes and meaningful intersubjective practices which reflect our social reality.

Problems associated with the linguistic translation of psychiatric genomics and its attendant biogenetic model of mental disorder illustrate this point well. Words like 'DNA' or 'gene' have little or no equivalent terminology in different African languages. Some translations will make up terms or piggy-back on other known references. For example, *gene* might be translated in Luganda as *endaga butonde*, meaning 'identifier of creation'. Yet, each of these words by themselves evoke different meanings: *endaga* draws on the common phrase *endaga muntu*, which refers to the unique number assigned to each Ugandan citizen on their national ID card (introduced in 2015), whilst *butonde* describes a 'natural state of anything that has tampered with', or 'a state that was created by God and cannot be tampered with', 'the nature of the earth'.[1] The common use of *butonde* stresses creation by and belief in a superior, divine being even as it does not necessarily denote specific religious views. Though in theory the conjunction of *endaga* + *butonde* means to convey the biogenetic idea of our unique genes determining whether or not we are likely to develop certain conditions, this Luganda phrase itself reconstructs an intersubjective social and political reality that is entirely removed from the scientific, secular trappings of Western conceptual schemes.

One might argue that these linguistic issues merely reflect the absence of appropriate vocabulary: an independent reality of a phenomenon can still be discovered, whether or not certain cultures have the language to describe it. The sun is still the sun, regardless of whether we use the same terms. But in the field of human behavior, this simply is not true: language reveals constitutive practices, intentions, and orientations towards life that have the status of reality for people. It is a window into the culture and total way of life of a people, which expresses not just how people worship and work and enjoy life, but also 'their ways of investigating nature and utilising its possibilities and in their ways of viewing themselves and interpreting their place in nature' (Wiredu 1980: 10). In short, it expresses a worldview and coherent set of practices within it. The meaning of *butonde* is a good example of this. In Luganda the term has a connotation of unchangeability – of refraining from tampering and changing what is already created. It describes a practical and moral orientation towards nature and creation. Yet, this interpretive meaning jars with an ethos focused on technological control and improvement which lies at the heart of Western biogenetic explanations and genomic medicine, where the aspiration is to target, change and manipulate the 'natural' state of our genes to avoid illness. This is not just a different inflection to the same meaning, but a different social reality and normative vision towards life.

To clarify, the non-existence of relevant vocabulary does not mean that all hope of translation should be abandoned. But good translation will attend to the non-equivalencies, non-symmetries, and the contextualised meanings of specific metaphors in the recognition that existing modes of thought are to be taken seriously (see Wiredu 1993: 91-2). The necessity of such *attenuated forms of translational thinking* is particularly evident in the ways in which Western descriptions of African explanatory models of illness typically appeal to the divide between the 'spiritual' and 'supernatural' vs. the 'material' and 'natural', with African modes of thought occupying the former. This way of characterising African thought and practice abounds in Western accounts, yet notably absent is any substantive engagement with the intellectual orientation underlying African thought and practices, resulting in explanatory incoherence at various levels.

Consider the case study of Ms MA, described by Ohene and Addom:

> 22 year-old Ms MA, a shop attendant, presented with a 2 month history of a sensation of worms crawling out of her nostrils, ears and through her vagina. She also felt them crawling all over her body and sometimes felt the worms squeezing her breasts. She had taken different worm expellants but felt no relief. Her brothers were also said to have seen her talking to herself, especially at night, sometimes with gestures. She had insomnia, anorexia and weight loss. She attributed her weight loss to the worms sucking her blood. MA did not have any feelings of hopelessness or worthlessness but felt very sad 'because of the worms'. She had no suicidal thoughts and was able to attend to her daily activities. […] She did not admit

to hearing voices but admitted she had been talking in her sleep since childhood (Ohene and Addom 2014: 54-55).

Imagine that MA attributes the sensation of worms to the wrathful powers of her ancestors. A Western biogenetic perspective looking on might immediately attribute MA's explanation to the superstitutious beliefs of her and her community. In relegating her explanation to the realm of superstitution, to the spiritual and supernatural, the presumption is that the *actual reality* is something else – either somatic reactions or neurologically caused delusions which suggests a formal diagnosis of depression, psychosis, schizophrenia etc.

Yet as soon as MA's own interpretation is dismissed or disregarded in favour of another alien conceptual scheme, the latter's incoherence with the social reality becomes pronounced. To attribute MA's descriptions to belief in the supernatural misunderstands the intellectual orientation that informs certain African cultural and social practices. In Akan thinking, for example, nonhuman beings and powers are thought to be an essential part of the world, existing and influencing the outcome of events, meaning that the Western meaning of 'supernatural' – as transcending the material world – clearly lacks any linguistic or intellectual resonance. Western biomedical thinking might appeal to the supernatural/natural dichotomy to explain MA's descriptions of her condition, but the cost would be its unintelligibility from the Akan perspective which takes as a given that, as part of a hierarchy of beings, non-human entities are spatially located in the world and actively interact with other orders of existents. Kwasi Wiredu describes,

> Accordingly, if an event in human affairs, for instance, does not appear explicable in human terms, there is no hesitation in invoking extrahuman causality emanating from the higher or even the lower rungs of the hierarchy of beings. In doing this there is no sense of crossing an ontological chasm, for the idea is that there is only one universe of many strata wherein God, the ancestors, humans, animals, plants, and all the rest of the furniture of the world have their being (Wiredu 1993: 50).

As such, MA's descriptions may fit and reflect an intersubjective reality where ancestors are thought to have real agency in the world. Yet as soon as alien intellectual orientations and conceptual frameworks are presumed, unintelligibility strikes both MA's and these foreign explanations. MA's explanation becomes unintelligible, reduced to a mere set of subjective 'beliefs' that can be set aside from the presumed 'reality of the situation'. Equally, descriptions using alien conceptual schemes become unintelligible and incoherent to the actual people they mean to describe, and shed little light as to how agents make coherent sense of themselves, their social practices, and motivation to act in certain ways.

Moreover, we fundamentally pre-empt the intellectual engagement and labour that is required to develop attenuated forms of translational thinking when the unintelligibility of these descriptions is ignored. It takes serious effort to seek to understand and engage with conceptual schemes that depart from ours. The willingness to be challenged and risk our own perspectives, an orientation of epistemic humility and openness to the truth contained in the frameworks of others – are all prerequisites to cultivating this type of translational thinking (Gadamer 2004, especially Part II, ch. 4; Warnke 1987: 167-174). Such efforts are required to avoid mis-describing the experiences and social reality of people within the concerns of alien conceptual schemes as well as to challenge the complacency and inertia in our own ways of thinking.

Ultimately, attenuated forms of translational thinking will need to form part of the enframing of psychiatric genomics and the biogenetic model if it is to be applied globally. As we see in the example of the linguistic challenges around vocabulary, or attempts to make sense of different explanatory models of causation around mental disorder, translation is not simply a matter of trying to find the right words or having one conceptual scheme eclipse another. Rather it means that we take the interpretive domain of human behavior seriously, recognising that mental disorder is a heterogeneous experience, where its varying linguistic meanings provide a vital lens of a people's social reality and the meaning of their practices.

5.5 The Need for African Bioethical Perspectives

So far I have argued that the translational issues in the African context are symptomatic of a broader problem with the current reductivist and decontextualised enframing of psychiatric genomics. In this final section, I want to briefly explore two ways in which an African bioethical perspective can help challenge and enrich this current enframing, particularly as genomic technologies are set to spread globally.

First, an African bioethical perspective should be used to critically examine and prevent the 'superimposition of alien categories onto African thought-structures' (Wiredu 1993). Of course, conceptual schemes of any culture do not remain static, and scientific language and vocabulary is often 'domesticated'. The accommodation of different meaning is an intrinsic part of the process of translation. But *prior* to the domestication, what is at stake for African thought and practice needs to be clarified, understood, and analysed, probing how vocabulary differences may reflect a fundamental conflict around peoples' interpretation of social reality and the values that different African societies deem important. The point of departure for such an examination has to be the rich traditions of African thought rather than Western bioethical categories and analyses which tend to be taken for granted. Western conceptual schemes have an overwhelming tendency to erect a boundary between nature and society, holding fast to the idea that there is a reality about behavior and action that can exist independently of the language that is used in a culture or society. That this boundary has little resonance in African thought is revealing and important. It is *revealing* because it suggests that an African bioethical perspective by default will take seriously the domain of human meaning and interpretation as a valid source of knowledge. A deepened understanding of cultural conceptual schemes goes hand in hand with any science that seeks to grasp the complexity of human behavior, functionalities, and potentialities. Moreover, it is *important* because such an intellectual orientation will provide a much-needed critical mirror to the enframing of Western psychiatric genomics and explanatory models of mental disorder more generally. Generating a *global* understanding of mental disorder demands engaging in a dynamic process of meaning-making, interpretation, and adaptation rather than hiving off and invalidating these endeavours.

Second, careful examination of these translational processes involves attending to certain normative claims about *value*. To illustrate this, Wiredu explores the dilemma of how to translate the Akan term *me nua*, typically rendered as 'my cousin'. However, the translation fails to express the strength of kinship bonds implied in Akan, and '[t]o continue to say "cousin" without a sense of uneasiness is to allow ourselves to be controlled by a foreign cultural model in our translations. If we do speak of the extended family, why may we not extend the sense of "brother"?' (Wiredu 1993: 93) Such translational issues aren't merely semantic, but matters of worth (Wiredu 1993: 94). It is this normative dimension where an African bioethical perspective will be vital: not just to *describe* these colliding visions and practices (e.g. divergent models of mental disorder causation; extended kinship bonds vs. more exclusive vision of the nuclear family), but to try and articulate answers to the question of what *normative vision* is right and appropriate. Just like human interpretation, the normative domain is often thought to be separable from the natural and social sciences. Despite efforts to insulate these investigations of human behavior, the normative is a constitutive part of our interpretations and use of language. Non-equivalences and non-symmetries in language reveal, not just the absence or presence of vocabulary, but a conflicting normative orientation in thought and practice.

For example, closer examination of the underlying ethos of a psychiatric genomics framework towards mental health is ripe for African bioethical investigation. Its emphasis on early intervention and prevention is often taken for granted, yet translational issues show that African thought and practice implies conflicting and equally powerful views about what is the appropriate and right approach to health, to nature, and the place of humans within nature (such as, not tampering with what is natural). African bioethical investigations could arbitrate between these conflicting visions, assessing the validity, coherence, and cultural and ethical value of each. What interpretive meaning and ethical vision is lost in some orthodox (or unorthodox) translations and adaptations? In what ways can these meanings and visions enrich our understanding and respectful treatment of people with mental disorder? And more generally, what resources in African thought can enhance our answers to these questions and how might they draw critical attention to the shortcomings in current frameworks around mental health care, research, and genomic medicine? 'Africa' in these normative investigations cannot be equated with 'local' or 'indigenous'. Though African bioethical responses to such questions may draw on the rich array of heretofore unknown normative perspectives, these need to be given due and serious consideration by both African and non-African bioethicists, so as to develop truly *global* knowledge and language around the understanding and care of mental health.

5.6 Conclusion

Psychiatric genomics is intrinsically engaged in an interpretive and evaluative endeavour by the very process of identifying certain behavioral traits as warranting deeper genetic investigation. I have argued in this paper that as psychiatric genomics becomes more global, there is need to critically reflect on its current reductivist and decontextualised enframing which ignores the interpretive meaning of human action and behavior. As soon as this enframing is taken as a given, we not only lose sight of what actions mean for agents, but we fail to identify where conceptual schemes and normative visions conflict in a deep sense, and indeed, foreclose the possibility of *learning* from those alternative schemes and visions. The consequences of such foreclosure are especially acute in the translational process of psychiatric genomics and the biogenetic psychiatric model. By its very nature the process of cultural and linguistic translation offers a glimpse of alternative worldviews, of divergent social realities and the interpretive meaning of our practices. But we cannot make sense of these differences if our epistemic orientation remains closed to the validity and significance of interpretive meaning around human behavior – indeed, these meanings are prone to being misunderstood, much like the Italian Catholic priests mistakenly preaching that the hostile spirit *Rubanga* was the divine creator of the Acholi people.[2]

Another underlying animus of my argument has been to assert the importance of substantive engagement with African conceptual schemes. So often the presumption is that African thought and practice have little or nothing to contribute in debates around mental health, such is the presumed dominance of Western biogenetic explanatory models. The rapid advance of psychiatric genomics seemingly attests to the growing divide between the technologies at the forefront of mental health research and the so-called 'backwardness' of African approaches to mental health. The purpose of my paper is to push back on this simplistic narrative. I am not dismissing the very real challenges of mental health care in Africa (all of which are documented all too well). But the equally real challenges around cultural and linguistic translation show how an exclusively genomic approach mental health presumes a particularly atomistic and potentially impoverished vision of human interpretive meaning and agency. Far from being objective and neutral, such presumptions can be challenged through productive encounters with African cultural and bioethical perspectives which attest to an altogether different social reality and normative vision.[3]

5.7 Notes

[1] My thanks to Janet Nakigudde for providing these translations and for much of her insight about the Luganda phrase for gene which has contributed to the content of this paragraph.

[2] Okot p'Bitek, *African Religions in Western Scholarship*, qtd. in Wiredu, *Cultural Universals and Particulars*, p. 62:'In 1911, Italian Catholic priests put before a group of Acholi elders the question "Who created you?"; and because the Luo language does not have an independent concept of create or creation, the question was rendered to mean "Who moulded you?" But this was still meaningless, because human beings are born of their mothers. The elders told the visitors that they did not know. But we are told that this reply was unsatisfactory, and the missionaries insisted that a satisfactory answer must be given. One of the elders remembered that, although a person may be born normally, when he is afflicted with tuberculosis of the spine, then he loses his normal figure, he gets "moulded." So he said, "*Rubanga* is the one who moulds people." This is the name of the hostile spirit which the Acholi believe causes the hunch or hump on the back. And instead of exorcising these hostile spirits and sending them among pigs, the representatives of Jesus Christ began to preach that *Rubanga* was the Holy Father who created the Acholi.'

[3] Funding for this research has been generously provided by the Stanley Center for Psychiatric Research at the Broad Institute.

5.8 References

Bardo, S., 2003, *Unbearable weight: Feminism, Western culture, and the body*, University of California, Berkeley.

Belsky, D.W., Moffitt, T.E., Corcoran, D.L., Domingue, B., Harrington, H., Hogan, S., Houts, R., Ramrakha, S., Sugden, K., Williams, B.S. & Poulton, R., 2016, 'The genetics of success: How single-nucleotide polymorphisms associated with educational attainment relate to life-course development', *Psychological Science*, 27(7), 957-972.

Bliss, C., 2018, *Social by nature: The promise and peril of sociogenomics*, Stanford University Press, Stanford.

Collins, P.Y. & Saxena, S., 2016, 'Action on mental health needs global cooperation', *Nature*, 534(7597), 25-27.

Davies, G., Marioni, R.E., Liewald, D.C., Hill, W.D., Hagenaars, S.P., Harris, S.E., Ritchie, S.J., Luciano, M., Fawns-Ritchie, C., Lyall, D. & Cullen, B., 2016, 'Genome-wide association study of cognitive functions and educational attainment in UK Biobank (N= 112 151)'. *Molecular Psychiatry*, 21(6), 758-767

Duster, T., 2003, *Backdoor to eugenics*, 2nd edn., Routledge, New York.

Gadamer, H., 2004, *Truth and Method*, trans. J. Weinsheimer & D. Marshall, Continuum, New York.

Gureje, O., Lasebikan, V.O., Ephraim-Oluwanuga, O., Olley, B.O. & Kola, L., 2005, 'Community study of knowledge of and attitude to mental illness in Nigeria', *The British Journal of Psychiatry*, 186(5), 436-441.

Insel, T. R. & Scolnick, E. M., 2006, 'Cure therapeutics and strategic prevention: Raising the bar for mental health research', *Molecular Psychiatry*, 11 (1), 12.

Jacob, K.S., Sharan, P., Mirza, I., Garrido-Cumbrera, M., Seedat, S., Mari, J.J., Sreenivas, V. & Saxena, S., 2007, 'Mental health systems in countries: Where are we now?' *The Lancet*, 370(9592), 1061-1077.

Kong, C., n.d., 'Nurture before responsibility: Self-in-Relation competence and self-harm', *Philosophy, Psychiatry, Psychology* (forthcoming).

Lee, S.H., Ripke, S., Neale, B.M., Faraone, S.V., Purcell, S.M., Perlis, R.H., Mowry, B.J., Thapar, A., Goddard, M.E., Witte, J.S. & Absher, D., 2013, 'Genetic relationship between five psychiatric disorders estimated from genome-wide SNPs', *Nature Genetics*, 45(9), 984-994.

Novas, C. & Rose, N., 2000, 'Genetic risk and the birth of the somatic individual', *Economy and Society*, 29(4), 485-513.

Ohene, S. & Addom, S., 2014, 'The Ghanaian non-medical conceptualization of mood disorders', in A. Ofori-Atta and S. Ohene, (eds.), *Changing trends in mental health care and research in Ghana*, pp. 54-55, Sub-Saharan Publishers, Cape Town.

Oxford English Dictionary, 2018, 'Gene, n.2', OED Online, Oxford University Press, viewed 28 March 2018, from http://www.oed.com/view/Entry/77473?rskey=iHQN99&result=2&isAdvanced=false

Patel, V., Belkin, G.S., Chockalingam, A., Cooper, J., Saxena, S. & Unützer, J., 2013, 'Grand challenges: Integrating mental health services into priority health care platforms', *PloS Medicine*, *10*(5), 1-6.

Personalized Medicine Coalition, 2014, *The case for personalized medicine*, 4th edn., Personalized Medicine Coalition, Washington, D.C., viewed 28 March 2018 from http://www.personalizedmedicinecoalition.org/Userfiles/PMC-Corporate/file/pmc_the_case_for_personalized_medicine.pdf

Saraceno, B., van Ommeren, M., Batniji, R., Cohen, A., Gureje, O., Mahoney, J., Sridhar, D. & Underhill, C., 2007, 'Barriers to improvement of mental health services in low-income and middle-income countries', *The Lancet*, *370*(9593), 1164-1174.

Saxena, S., Thornicroft, G., Knapp, M. & Whiteford, H., 2007, 'Resources for mental health: Scarcity, inequity, and inefficiency', *The Lancet*, *370*(9590), 878-889.

Seretti, A. & Fabbri, C., 2013, 'Shared genetics among major psychiatric disorders', *The Lancet*, *381*(9875), 1339-1341.

Sullivan, P.F., Agrawal, A., Bulik, C.M., Andreassen, O.A., Børglum, A.D., Breen, G., Cichon, S., Edenberg, H.J., Faraone, S.V., Gelernter, J. & Mathews, C.A., 2017, 'Psychiatric genomics: an update and an agenda', *American Journal of Psychiatry*, *175*(1), 15-27.

Taylor, C., 1985, 'Interpretation and the sciences of man', in *Philosophy and the human sciences*, pp. 15-57, Cambridge University Press, Cambridge.

Tielbeek, J.J., Medland, S.E., Benyamin, B., Byrne, E.M., Heath, A.C., Madden, P.A., Martin, N.G., Wray, N.R. & Verweij, K.J., 2012, 'Unraveling the genetic etiology of adult antisocial behavior: A genome-wide association study', *PloS one*, *7*(10), e45086.

Tiihonen, J., Rautiainen, M.R., Ollila, H.M., Repo-Tiihonen, E., Virkkunen, M., Palotie, A., Pietiläinen, O., Kristiansson, K., Joukamaa, M., Lauerma, H. & Saarela, J., 2015, 'Genetic background of extreme violent behavior', *Molecular Psychiatry*, *20*(6), 786-792.

Warnke, G.,1987, *Gadamer: Hermeneutics, Tradition, and Reason*, Stanford University Press, Stanford.

Wiredu, K., 1980, *Philosophy and an African culture*, Cambridge University Press, New York.

Wiredu, K., 1993, *Cultural universals and particulars: An African perspective*, Indiana University Press, Bloomington.

Chapter 6

The Practice of Traditional Medicine and Bioethical Challenges

Rose Mary Amenga-Etego
University of Ghana

Abstract

This chapter examines the life (*bio*) centeredness of traditional African belief systems and traditional medicine. It argues that African traditional medicine sees life as an interconnected chain that must not be broken (cyclical not linear that has an end-point). TM is also based on African conception of personhood—a person is made up of many things (spirit, blood, body, etc.). In the system of African TM, saving life means more than healing; it includes rescuing, delivering, restoring, protecting (e.g. from spiritual influences against recurring sicknesses), and weakening the powers of spiritual entities to prevent them from causing further harm. The author concludes that the widespread belief that illnesses have both physical and spiritual causes seems to warrant a combination of Western and traditional healing processes—western healing addressing physical problems and traditional healing addressing both physical and spiritual problems.

Key words: Life, African traditional medicine, indigenous beliefs, spiritual, ritual, personhood, destiny, mind, body, soul.

6.1 Introduction

Traditional medicine embodies a complex system of beliefs and practices aimed at restoring (curing), saving (rescuing/delivering), protecting (safeguarding) and fortifying life. The focus of traditional medicine is life. The Nankani/Gurune word *vam* and Akan, *nkwa* exemplify this. The Akan saying *su nkwa na nnsu ahonya* (cry for life not for material things) emphasizes this notion of life and its centrality in the scheme of things in the traditional African society. This perspective, however, does not limit the subject to the life of the individual sick person, group or community.

Rather, it seeks to (for the lack of an adequate expression) represent the view that understanding traditional medicine in the context of life takes into consideration a sophisticated cycle of systems, all of which are geared toward providing wholeness and wellbeing to a person, a people, and their environment. This is because, life, which embodies wellbeing or wholeness, has both physical and spiritual dimensions, and that embodies more than the physical individual or group.

6.2 The Indigenous Belief Systems and Traditional Medicine

It is evident that literature abounds in traditional medicine and the practices associated with health and healing. Some of these have employed indigenous concepts especially, those on the indigenous conceptions of the person to underpin their discussions. But the use of and interpretations of these concepts can be problematic due to the variety of indigenous societies and the nuanced perspectives embedded in their understanding, interpretations and applications (Atiemo 2013; Fortes 1950). In this section, therefore, the data from the primary and the secondary sources are integrated (Wolcott 2001:72).

According to Oduyoye (1998:55), the secular connotation of the English word 'medicine' cannot be equated with the Yoruba word "*oògùn* which is still both 'medicine' and 'magic' – supernatural skill, ability to manipulate the laws of nature and to affect what is ordinarily considered impossible." Oduyoye (1998:55-56) states that the "medicine-men were invariably also diviners" because "healing requires the ability to diagnose causes (physical and metaphysical), and to offer prescriptions for restoration to health." In conversation with Azubila (a herbalist in Bolgatanga in the Upper East Region of Ghana) on 13 May 2017, he made these interconnected roles of the medicine man clear when he noted that relying on the physical dimension for treatment neither ensures the right outcome nor secures lasting results in the healing, restoration and/or protection of the people. By his elaboration, Azubila was also naming the different components of traditional medicine. That is, apart from healing people suffering from ill health, they also protect people and communities from harm and danger, empower or fortify people spiritually, exorcise people possessed by evil spirits, and remove curses or spiritual punishments with the aid of rituals. In other words, traditional medicine includes the element of fortification (Mbiti 1975:153). This notwithstanding, the health practices associated with each of these intertwine with ritual performances.

Adogame (2008:309) made a similar declaration when he stated that "[i]n most African cosmologies, sickness, diseases, and other misfortunes are largely linked to supersensible origins such as the wrath of divinities and neglected ancestor spirits, malevolent spiritual entities, witches, and wizards and sorcerers." In addition to these are the refusals to accept religious roles and responsibilities of becoming diviners or healers, and the attraction of curses (parental or others). Thus, traditional medicine men/women may attribute or associate certain types of ill health, disease, or calamities to religious factors like broken taboos or neglected ancestral relations, witchcraft or evil spirits (Adogame 2008:309; Appiah-Kubi 1998:261-262; Brokensha 1966:155; Mbiti 1975:152). Inexperienced hunters and herbalists sometimes have their ill health attributed to neglected rituals (Bourdillo 2000:176-177), taboos or the infringement of the rights of some potent plants and animals (Amenga-Etego 2016).

The first part of the next section will outline and briefly discuss the Akan concept of the person to substantiate the statement on the interconnectedness of the physical and spiritual, and the request to take the religious dimension seriously in the discourse of African bioethics. This is followed by examples of Nankani practices of healing embodying ancestral beliefs, the concept of destiny and conscience to illustrate the intricate complexity involved in traditional medicine.

6.3 The Akan Concept of the Person

Generally in instances of separation, the Akan concept of the person is stated as having both physical and spiritual properties. The core component of an individual is known as the *okra/ ɔkra/ kra*. The commonest interpretation of this is the soul. It is believed to come from the Creator. Akans believe the *okra* is the source of vitality and life as well as the protector of an individual from harm and danger. The Akan sayings: *wo kra di w'akyi* (your soul is following you) and *wo kra yie* (your soul is good) illustrates this saving and protective perspective of the *okra*. These sayings are, in particular, uttered in situations where an individual is miraculously saved or protected from danger. The *okra* is also the bearer of destiny. This component makes the individual an indispensable part of the environment, hence, the saying "everyone is a child of the Creator, no one is a child of the earth (Appiah-Kubi 1998:259)." In terms of ill health and healing, an individual might require a ritual bath to reintegrate his/her *okra* after a long period of ill health. According to the Akan, the *okra* may leave a person temporarily during ill health. In such instances, even when treatment is complete, the person will not be whole and well unless he/she is given the *okra dware*. In an interview on 18 May 2017, Elizabeth Amoah explained that this ritual bath, which is meant to reintegrate the okra with the body, could be very crucial in instances where the sick person almost died. This is because the *okra* leaves the body to return to the Creator at death and near-death experiences can cause such separations. It is believed that if this ritual is not performed, the individual will die because the *okra* is the life-giving force. Accordingly, this ritual bath is performed on the individual's day of birth, with respect to the Akan calendar and day-naming system.

Another essential component of the person is the *mogya*. It is the element that links the individual to his/her matrilineage. It provides the individual with his/her religio-cultural, political and economic identity (Nzegwu 1996; Appiah 1992). Usually, the *mogya* is interpreted as blood. This literal interpretation has led to the notion that it is a physical (biological) property. By so doing, the understanding is that every human (foetus) is formed and nourished by the mother's blood as in the individual *mogya* and *honam* (body/flesh). This is true, but it is only one aspect of an intricate understanding of the *mogya*. This is because the *mogya* can also be associated with the traditional notion of genetics. By this, I am referring to instances where an individual's resemblance to a parent or grandparent is spoken of in terms of a strong or heavy *mogya* (*wɔ mami, papa or nana mogya yɛ du*). Sometimes, people will say their blood is strong or bitter when referring to their innate resistance to witchcraft. Yet another interpretation of *mogya* has to do with an intangible substance that can be explained as a spiritual entity. Although it seems to have no name or specific identity, it is this spiritual component of the *mogya* that enables the other two aspects to function. In other words, the traditional conception of the *mogya* is not simply the blood.

The other common spiritual component outlined by scholars is the *sunsum*, transmitted from the father. Normally referred to as the spirit, this element links the individual to his/her patrilineage. This linkage means that the individual has additional spiritual responsibilities to the spirituality associated with his/her father. It is important to note that it is through these (*mogya* and *sunsum*) linkages that the ancestors reincarnated. Therefore, wilful wrongdoings or disobedience to this area of one's spirituality can lead to ill health. It is also this spiritual element which gives the individual his/her distinct personality. Besides that, it provides spiritual protection to wives and children, especially, pregnant women, babies, and toddlers. This belief is illustrated in people prescribing to mothers of sick children whose fathers are absent to clothe the children with their father's clothing as a healing remedy. It is, therefore, an important element in traditional medicine. The statement *sunsum atwa mu* (a spirit has passed by) further illustrates another aspect of this spirituality. In this case, the word *sunsum* is associated with an unidentifiable spirit. Such unidentifiable spirits, in some instances, can cause ill health to those within their path. Yet again, the *sunsum* can be explained in three levels, one of which has been stated above. That is to say, the word *sunsum* represents shadow, as in the shadow of an individual and even though the shadow may be perceived as insignificant, it can be an important element in the discourse of health where sorcery and witchcraft are involved. In any or all of these instances, the medicine man/woman must diagnose the cause of ill health beyond the physical to ensure proper healing.

Apart from the above, some scholars have added the *honam* (body) and *honhom* (breath) as two elements to the physical and spiritual understanding of the indigenous health discourse. Writing on the subject, Blay incorporated these as:

> Nyame (Creator) bestows these material and spiritual elements on us at conception and birth; however, when we 'die,' the honam and mogya join Asase Yaa (Mother Earth), whereas the kra, honhom, and sunsum return to Nyame.
> Good health is contingent on balance and harmony between both the material and spiritual elements. If one is injured, the other is affected. When a person falls ill, Akans concern themselves not only with the physical manifestations of the illness, but the spiritual aspects as well (Blay 2008:26).

Although these two and their integration to this discourse are quite uncommon, it illustrates the diversity and/or specificity associated with the different groups of communities that make up the Akan. Similarly, it contributes to the growing scholarship and the nuanced perspectives that are brought into the existing literature. Besides, Blay's perception that the Creator bestows these elements "at conception and birth" supports the view that none of these components is purely physical.

Apart from the above components, there are also *nkrabea* (destiny) and *tiboa* (conscience). These are important components of the concept of the person with distinct physical and spiritual underpinnings (Amenga-Etego 2011:102; Appiah-Kubi 1998:259-260; Fortes 1959). In the first place, the relationship between destiny, ill health and healing is quite a complex one because of the nature of the indigenous family and kinship system. The conceptual understanding of destiny is that it is the pre-determined plan of an individual's life on earth (Quarcoopome 1987:100-101). This includes times of well-being, ill health and death. This pre-determined plan includes the individual's means of livelihood, nature of puberty, marriage, reproduction, etc. Consequently, if an individual's destiny is to be ill at particular periods of his/her life, it means the traditional practitioner must decipher that and deal with the situation as part of the healing process.

Again, the Creator gives the *tiboa*, the moral agent of the individual. The *tiboa* gives the individual the sense of right and wrong, hence, the belief that morality is intrinsic. The society only helps the individual to live it out in concrete ways through actions and interactions. The *tiboa* makes one responsible and accountable. To be human (*nipa*) is to be moral and responsible. The opposite is to be an animal (*aboa*). Thus, the simple statement *ɔyɛ nipa* (he/she is human) means the fellow has good moral qualities that society cherishes. On the other hand, the Akan would ask: *wo ye aboa anaa?* (are you an animal?), if an individual has no sense of morality. Therefore, if an individual's action or inaction causes ill health or an epidemic, it is incumbent on that individual to confess to facilitate the process of healing.

It is quite clear in this section that an understanding of an African concept of the person is crucial to the introductory view that the practice of traditional medicine is an intertwined complex cycle of life and systems. I have used the Akan concept in this paper because of the abundance of literature with diverse and nuanced perspectives. Besides, it is the most developed and documented conception of the person in Ghana and there seems to be no clear opposition to it. Rather, what is encountered from the other ethnic groups are elaborations or the provisions of nuanced perspectives on specific components and their influence or impact on difference discourses.

6.4 Some Nankani Practices of Traditional Medicine

This section exemplifies how some of the above concepts are interpreted and incorporated into individual, family and community-based practices of traditional medicine from the Nankani and their neighbours (Gurune, Kusasi and Tallensi).

According to the Nankani, *paa'la* (destiny) plays a crucial role in the practices of traditional medicine. For instance, if Lariba's destiny involves death during her first childbirth, the healer must be able to diagnose such a destiny and dialogue with it in the context of the family (husband and child's destinies) for the needed treatment to be effective. That is, the healer can only succeed in healing Lariba if he/she is able to change Lariba's destiny, the source of the ill health. Although individual destinies are fixed, it is believed that a plea for a change of destiny is possible because in marriage and pregnancy or childbirth, there is an intertwined destiny of husband, wife and child. For this reason, a ritual plea can be made for Lariba, whose destiny is not in-line with her husband and child, using her new status as a wife and would-be-mother (Amenga-Etego 2012:328). In other words, the physical and spiritual components do not simply overlap; they are also intertwined within the person. It is important to note that in this case, the change of destiny and subsequent healing of Lariba is understood and interpreted within the context of the patrilineal and exogamous marriage system of the Nankani and their neighbours. This system subsumes wives completely into their husband's families. It is also a patriarchal system in which family heads and husbands are responsible for the death of pregnant women. That is to say, either their ancestors are not protective of the descendants, or the husbands or men in the family are not spiritual enough to protect, defend or rescue their wives from possible harm. It is common knowledge that if a man loses two wives during pregnancy or childbirth, no family will be willing to give their daughter to such a fellow in marriage again.

On the other hand, if the above is carried out succesful (and destiny changes) or if there is no problem associated with the concept of destiny, yet, no cure is obtained despite various forms of rituals and treatments, the concept of the individual's conscience can become the focus. The sick person is asked to reflect on his/her past actions. In the case of Lariba, she might be asked to free her conscience through a confession. Usually, adultery is suspected of pregnant women and/or complicated delivery. In such instances, an appropriate confession with its accompanied rituals may also lead to healing and well-being.

Concerning illnesses attributed to aggrieved ancestor spirit s, a story was given of a young man, Akuo, who had to undergo a ritual of renaming because an ancestor spirit was aggrieved (G. Akurugo pers. comm., March 2012). The young man, who at that point in time exhibited unusual manners and symptoms of ill health, prompted a series of searches (divinations) to ascertain the cause of his problems. Eventually, it was diagnosed that the naming of the young man after his biological grandfather, when his elder brother was not yet recognised and honoured was the source of the spiritual problems (Toldson & Toldson 2001:404-405). In other words, this was a spiritual problem of a neglected ancestor spirit, and it was physically manifested in Akuo to draw attention.

To understand this alleged spiritual grievance, however, one needs some basic knowledge of the religio-political system of this society, a system that was put into writing by Fortes (1987) on the Tallensi. That is to say, first, it is a patrilineal society where sons and their naming are prioritised. Unfortunately, the elder brother had no son of his own. Second, it is a system in which, upon the death of their father or the reigning family head, the eldest son used to take over the leadership and responsibility of the family. In many such instances, children born during the leadership of particular family heads adopted his name as the family name. In his case, however, no child bears his name. Yet, he cared for his younger brother's children when the latter died while his sons were still very young. Thus, he fulfilled his role during his lifetime for his younger brother and family. Hence, he felt slighted or betrayed that his younger brother's grandson was not named after him.

Akuo's health problems were therefore attributed to this gross past patriarchal neglect or misrepresentation; hence, rituals of propitiation, restitution, and renaming were carried out to restore the young man to health and wholeness. Toldson and Toldson discussed this type of upheaval in an individual's personal life as one whose rhythm of life is disturbed. As they put it:

> Spirit, in the African cosmos, rhythmically shapes things, ideals, animals, and human beings together in a representative whole of its essence. When this rhythm is disturbed, the spirit is unsettled and manifests in the individual as anxiety, depression, or other describable mental or physical disorders. Restoring this rhythm to achieve an integrative harmony within the self is the goal of African-centered approaches to therapy (Toldson and Toldson 2001:404-405).

In other words, Akuo's health problems resulted from the disturbed relationship between the brothers in the ancestral world that needed to be resolved. With such examples, it is not surprising that Adogame (2008:309) would define healing as "a sustained ritual process of righting the disequilibrium generated by spiritual, natural, psychological, and social factors, which are often expressed in the form of physical or mental problems."

The above examples on destiny and ancestor spirits are significant because, as a people, all members of the family, household/homestead, clan and/or community, and their spiritual entities are expected to cooperate and behave in such a way that the ultimate goal of traditional medicine, which is life-centeredness, can be upheld. That is to say, that which is expected of humans, as members of the family or community, must take place to ensure that each has contributed his/her part to the search for wholeness. It is in this light that Shoko's (2008:310) definition of health as a state of wellbeing or "fulfilment whereby both the individual and society are spared from mental and physical discomfort and enjoy peace of mind" becomes significant. The individual is therefore supposed to ensure that wholeness and the continuity of life is part of his/her moral duty, so that the interconnected cycle of life is unbroken and sustained.

This interconnected cycle of life is not limited to the individual's inner composition. It includes his/her physical disposition as a relational being. That is, the physical component of life that traditional medicine engages with is comprised of other humans and the natural environment. The human dimension to this argument involves good human relations like the observances of the community's moral code: respect, kindness, compassion, sharing, hard work, etc. Some African scholars have employed the southern African concept of *ubuntu* to represent this notion of "compassion and consideration for others" (Lugira 2008:13). Mbiti (1990:141) summed it up succinctly with the maxim "I am, because we are; and since we are, therefore I am." Good human relations are very important to health and wholeness because cheating, greed, gossiping, fighting, etc. does not only lead to broken relationships, but also, to physical stress and ill-health. Consequently, the existence of the individual is tied to the existence of the group. Although nuanced differently, this notion of interconnectedness aligns with Tangwa's (2000:41) "eco-bio-communitation" perspective of the Nso worldview.

In terms of beliefs and traditional medicine, therefore, even though the Creator Spirit, ancestors and divinities may punish wrongdoing(s) with ill health, disease or death, they are still an essential component of the healing process. Unlike the above, sorcerers, witches/wizards, and other evil spirits either prey on human weakness or are used by other humans to cause disharmony and ill health. In this case, traditional medicine involves deliverance, healing and protection. Consequently, different resources are harnessed as part of the health-seeking practices of traditional medicine.

6.5 The Morality of Traditional Medicine

To understand the morality of traditional medicine, one needs to look at some aspects of the traditional philosophy of life. That is, the perspective that the African worldview is life-centered, whether one is reflecting on the physical, spiritual or its integrated form. Creatively expressed as communal living or solidarity, I have already explained that this notion of life centeredness is not linear but cyclical and that it is not limited to the life cycle (birth, puberty, marriage, old age, death and reincarnation). Rather, that it includes good health, good human relations, spiritual/duty consciousness, prosperity, good social dealings and respect for other people's property - all the things that make up life, bring peace, harmony and joy to people and their community. According to Elizabeth Amoah in an interview dated 18 May 2017, the core value of traditional medicine is to promote the things that make life worth living, especially those within the cycle of life. She observed that it is in this respect that she views traditional medicine as a comprehensive system of practices aimed at restoring life into total wholeness and wellbeing.

Speaking on these interconnected principles, Amoah stated:

> Apart from the knowledge I have acquired from my academic career, the memory from my grandmother, who was a traditional healer, is that the essence of traditional medicine is life, *nkwa*. However, *nkwa* in this context includes animals, farm produce, successes, and prosperity; in fact, all the things that promote life. For this reason, when an Akan says *nkwa* even when all is well, he/she is calling for more of the above mentioned, as a matter of fact, all that is good and desirable. So, whether it is childbearing, good health or abundant harvest, more is desired because it is believed they contribute to the promotion of good health, life, and life in the hereafter (ancestor hood)
> (E. Amoah pers. comm., 18 May 2017).

Perhaps, it is this moral principle that underpins the practice of not simply focusing on the individual and his symptoms or manifest disease, but also, the psychic and religious disposition of the individual, his/her associates, and the community or environment. It is believed that by so doing, they are seeing to all of them as part and parcel of the interconnected whole. Thus, it becomes a moral, social and religious duty for practitioners of traditional medicine to carry out their services in such a way that it promotes the life of their people and communities. This is what Magesa (1997) implies by *African Religion: The Moral Traditions of Abundant Life*.

Again, acknowledging that traditional medicine is inclusive is the basis for the ecological dimension. In the first place, believing that the natural environment has a life of its own and that it is intertwined with the rest of creation in such a way that one cannot easily disentangle it provides this linkage with traditional medicine. Moreover, there is also the belief that one could be entangled and incur the punishment of the environment (for wrongdoing or breaking a taboo) if care is not taken. For either of these reasons, traditional medicine men and women carry out pacificatory and restorative rituals with respect to their dealings with the environment. Murove (2005:28) describes these kinds of relationships as "the individual is entangled in a web of relation." In her article on "Nankani Women's Spirituality and Ecology," Amenga-Etego (2016) observed that even though the land, trees/plants, animals/birds and water bodies are part of the environment, they are also used for housing, food, medicine and drink. Yet, some of these trees/plants, animals/birds and water bodies are believed to be so potent that they are spiritualized. Consequently, some of them have been identified as hosts of spiritual entities or deified. It is for this reason that polluting or destroying the environment is abhorred while preserving and protecting it is cherished as a moral, social, cultural, and religious duty. The latter is attributed to a good *tiboa* and is rewarded with good health, while the former is punishable with ill health.

Even so, the practice of traditional medicine is bedevilled with abuses and problems. Some traditional medicine practitioners are alleged to have used their esoteric knowledge to cause harm to others. For some respondents, it is not necessarily that the practitioner(s) is/are corrupt or inherently evil in this case; rather, the system itself is very flexible and fluid. Hence, it is susceptible to easy manipulation and corruption. So unscrupulous practitioners take undue advantage of it and cause troubles (Mbiti 1975:153-154). Besides, the problems are not limited to the practitioners; their clients are also a problem.

Azubila explained that in the past people adhered to directives given by traditional medicine men and women, however, the current situation is different. Contemporary clients subvert the system for their own selfish gains. An example was given of how herbs and herbal preparations not meant for pregnant women are now used by the current society to prevent unwanted pregnancies or for abortions. This is partly because although the indigenous belief systems, moral values and taboos continue to exert influence, they no longer command complete authority and allegiance in people's moral decision-making. The power and grip over people's lives and actions by the traditional worldview has been watered down with contemporary social change, a change that has been attributed to several factors including the influence of other religions, education, urbanization, social mobility and globalization. In other words, the morality of traditional medicine that hinges on the indigenous belief systems and its forms of judgment, especially from the ancestors and divinities, no longer command the ultimate authority for some individual Africans. Therefore, because these have waned over the years, traditional medicine has also lost the fear and respect that governed its operation and usage. Consequently, the rules and regulations that guided traditional medicine are not followed strictly, and thus opening it for various forms of abuses and misuse.

One other issue that clearly came to the fore was the need sometimes to differentiate between the system and the personalities practicing it. For though Mbiti (1990:163) states that "[t]heir personal qualities vary, but medicine-men are expected to be trustworthy, morally upright, friendly, willing and ready to serve, able to discern people's needs and not be exorbitant in their charges," not all are people of integrity. There are those who practice evil under the disguise of traditional medicine. Although these are identified as [considered to be] sorcerers and witches/wizards, it is not easy to identify them. The need to therefore carefully examine and differentiate practitioners under the general rubric of traditional medicine was called upon. Attention was also drawn to the fact that a new group of people have entered the field of traditional medicine without the full or complete training or calling (spiritual gift), but because of financial gains, most especially, because of the current resurgence in the use of traditional medicine. It was noted that this group of people may only treat the symptoms but not the root cause of the illness or disease, and definitely, they cannot provide the necessary restoration, deliverance and protection, the other aspects of traditional medicine, that makes it a composite whole.

Drawing our attention to this new class of traditional medicine practitioners whose work ethic is not governed by the traditional worldview introduces a new chapter in traditional medicine that needs to be separated and addressed differently. Such an endeavor must take note of and, perhaps, include those trained by the secular academic institutions like the Kwame Nkrumah University of Science and Technology.

6.6 Bioethical Challenges

Bioethics, which is concerned with life and the boundaries of human actions, is an emerging field of study in traditional medicine. Nonetheless, while scholars are grappling with the subject, the practitioners claim this is not a new development because they have always engaged the subject. This includes the challenges brought about by contemporary social change, western scientific advancement and globalization (Andoh 2011; Murove 2005). As evidenced in the above discussion, concerns on life and the boundaries of human actions, especially by the practitioners (healers and medicine men/women) and practices (of clients) of traditional medicine have always been a serious consideration. In the traditional context, the concerns transcend the physical to the spiritual domain, where the spirits are believed to exact punishments on disobedience or culprits from time to time.

The situation is however different with the modern scientific domain, especially with the advances in biology and western medicine, where new possibilities have led to a steady rise in controversial issues on health and the practices surrounding it. Even so, a casual look at the emerging advances in western medicine seems to suggest that all is well since the overall goal is to promote life, a perspective shared by traditional medicine. However, a careful overview of the subject matter presents some differences. That is to say, although the essence of both practices is life centred, the morality behind each practice, whether simple or complex, is different. For while western medicine is generally acknowledged as being secular, traditional medicine is intricately both spiritual and secular (Toldson & Toldson 2001:404-405). Again, whereas in western medicine, the individual, as well as the individual's self-preservation, may be paramount, in traditional medicine, although the individual and his/her preservation is essential, it is not the centre of decision-making in life treating situation.

For example, some traditional bonesetters may break a fowl's leg/wing or an animal's leg as part of their treatment mechanism for humans suffering with fractures. In other cases, the fowl or animal is sacrificed to the spirits to grant the required healing or deliverance. These forms of healing practices may be condemned as superstitious with a variety of questions concerning the rights of the fowls and animals involved (Metz 2010). However, practitioners of traditional medicine argue that in these circumstances, that which is often neglected is the perspective of the indigenous worldview. For them, these fowls or animals that are injured are also treated with care because the healing of the client is incumbent on the healing of those injured fowls and animals. With regards to the sacrificial animals, it is argued that the lives of fowls and animals are not comparable to humans. Besides, the essence of animal sacrifice in times of health crisis is the act of exchange, an exchange of one life for another. In some traditional contexts, blood and eggs represent life. Therefore, the shedding of blood (killing of an animal) in the context of a health crisis is an indication that one form of life is being exchanged for the life of another. Even though some forms of lives are involved, the practices are based on the traditional moral principle of the greater good. To further illustrate the traditional principle of greater good, it was noted that, in spite of the fact that human sacrifices have been abolished, in the past, any form of health practice that involved human sacrifices was done at the family, clan or community level. It was geared towards either warding off epidemics and other forms of calamities, or it was an atonement sacrifice to end an epidemic.

Arguably, therefore, the philosophy of traditional medicine is encompassing and its intrinsic aim is to promote life, one that is within the context of the greater good. Thus, whether it is in the private or communal context, healing is a communal thing and the aim is to seek and to support that which leads to the greater good. In these instances, the traditional sense of family and communal solidarity is applied. Sometimes, a family member(s) may be delegated to accompany or support a sick person to a healer irrespective of the distance or time involved. Consequently, each person, family, clan and/or community is expected to contribute his/her/their quota to the processes of healing and health. These different levels of contributions are essential because of the intricate notion of interconnectedness imbedded in the traditional health practices and healing as stated in this contribution as the cycle of life. This interconnectedness can be summed up with the maxim: 'I am because we are; and since we are, therefore I am' (Mbiti 1990:141). Although admirable, one wonders whether these communal expectations or contributions towards the common good are practiced because they are an essential part of the indigenous moral principles or whether it is because of some fear of incurring the displeasure of the ancestors who are not just part of the cycle of life but also the custodians of the moral principles.

It is important to note that similar concerns, which arose in the areas of abortion, family planning and euthanasia, were all projected as influences of western science and medicine that have now become serious problems for traditional societies and the practices of traditional medicine. As we have noted, the ultimate aim of traditional medicine is life centred and supports that which promotes the greater good. Family planning, abortion and euthanasia are thus abhorred, punishable not only by human authorities in the family and communities but also by the ancestors with ill health, epidemics and/or deaths. In relation to the traditional notion of the cycle of life, using these herbs to prevent the ancestors from returning to life is abhorred. Similarly, euthanasia ends lives, especially of the individual. Although death is part of life, it is not up to an individual to prevent or end it; it must take its own course to facilitate the process of ancestorhood. In the past, these practices caused calamities in the lives of individuals, families, clans and communities. Therefore, some adherents of traditional religion and practitioners of traditional medicine are gravely concerned that people are resorting to the use of herbs and herbal preparations that are not meant for pregnant women for family planning and abortions. They argue that this negates the very principles of abundant life. Consequently, these areas need serious scholarly attention.

Although the above perspectives may be commendable, they are not straightforward cases without complications. The problem, therefore, arises with complicated issues. What kinds of moral decision-making processes come into play when complications arise? The Nankani saying, *kom sa ka-ie, fu wan ma a'kye, gyi yoore-la sa gnoge, la basi-ya* (if the water pours, you can re-fetch it; but if the pot is/gets broken, then all is lost/gone) is often used when a pregnant woman miscarries. Employing this saying, I asked how do the practitioners of traditional medicine act in times of complications where the lives of both mother and foetus are in danger and only one of them has a chance of survival? The main response, repeated several times, was to seek guidance from the spiritual world (divination) to ascertain the cause of such a case and follow the guidelines offered. This is because such a case is unnatural. It implies something more than physical is happening and this needs spiritual diagnoses and solution. Another response was to let nature take its course because the medicine man or woman must not play judge and executioner. The last one was to continuously treat both and perform pacification, restoration and, sometimes, votive rituals with the hope of saving both for the greater good. It is also during occasions such as these that one is called upon to examine his/her conscience and to make the necessary confession for the needed healing. When everything is done without success, then, it is attributed to the will of the Creator.

This seeming lack of urgency, decision-making, and the over dependency on the spiritual dimension of health is an area that concerns bioethicists. Can the practitioner make decisions? Must or should he make such a decision? And, is he supposed to make such a decision? What about the client's family members? Even though I was concerned about their lack of personal agency, Azubila saw it as a form of caution. He was of the view that it prevented unscrupulous practitioners from abusing the system with their personal interests. He also noted that in such a crisis, both mother and unborn child are put in a disputed terrain. We encounter, somehow, a similar argument in Tuareg medicine where the author provides a detailed discussion on how the body is a disputed terrain in matters of healing (Rasmussen 2000:263). That is, although the unborn child is dependent on the mother for survival; it is still life, hence, has its own destiny, just as the mother has hers (Amenga-Etego 2012:324&328). In that case, the health practitioners alongside the families of the patients (mother and child) will have to enter into dialogue and negotiations with the different destinies involved for an amicable solution. Here again, we encounter the concept of destiny and its influence on traditional medicine. Although this is not of immediate concern, and although literature abounds on the subject of destiny (Amenga-Etego 2011:102-103), the concept of destiny and its influence on ill health and disease, health and healing, life and death must be an area of importance to African bioethicists (Appiah-Kubi 1998:260).

The challenges associated with contemporary practices of traditional medicine are the lack of in-depth knowledge of the intricate nuances of the herbs and other medicinal properties in use as well as their religious underpinnings. There is also the fear that unscrupulous people may pose as practitioners of traditional medicine (Mbiti 1975:154). So while some indigenous practitioners argue that depending mainly on the immediate physical medicinal properties or potency of medicinal plants is inadequate and dangerous (in fact, a sacrilege), they should begin to realize that such a transformation is already in place within their communities. Similarly, there is the need for western and African bioethicists to broaden their scope on traditional medicine because both aim to save and promote life comprehensively. Their concerns have to move beyond the apparent lack of western scientific methods of preparations, testing and measurements- in terms of the herbal preparations, dosage, shelf life, as well as the duration of each traditional medicinal intake. They should also be anxious about the lack of documentation and the transformations that are taking place because the practices of traditional medicine are not static.

6.7 Conclusion

In conclusion, the essence of being human is to sustain life. In doing so, various forms of traditional medicines and practices have evolved, relatively distinct from one another yet complementary. It is quite clear from this contribution that traditional medicine, with its claim of providing holistic health and healing for its people (clients) and communities, embodies a number of non-verifiable assertions. That is, relying heavily on the indigenous spirituality, which no longer commands full authority, especially, concerning people's decision-making or moral judgement in the contemporary society, creates serious bioethical concerns. Additionally, the communal nature of African health practices is problematic because it undermines, at times, the individual's agency and right. As illustrated in this essay, these concerns are not limited to the practitioners, but also, to their clients. These factors, together with the rapid loss of knowledge, partly due to its secretive nature, fear of the unknown and death, as well as contemporary social change and globalization call for serious attention to be paid to African bioethics.

This contribution has shown why any discourse on bioethical challenges and the practices of traditional medicine must take into serious consideration the indigenous worldview. Using the traditional concept of the person and how that undergirds a number of health practices, the study calls on African bioethicists not to simply concentrate on the challenges; but also, how the advancement of western medicine and its global dissemination, as well as promotion of ideas, are transforming the use of traditional medicine. That is to say, traditional medicines that are not recommended for specific conditions like pregnancy are now used for family planning and abortion purposes.

This notwithstanding, it is quite clear that both the Western and African health systems aim at promoting life despite their differences. Thus, there is the need to recognise the uniqueness of each health system as well as its limitations. African bioethics need to engage some of these issues to contribute contextually and appropriately to the growth of the discourse. In a nutshell, this contribution, in some respect, has responded to some of Andoh's (2011) questions on "Bioethics and Challenges to its Growth in Africa." That is, there is a possibility of an authentic growth in African bioethics.

6.8 References

Adogame, A., 'Healing', 2008, in M.K Asante & A. Mazama (eds.), *Encyclopedia of African religion*, Sage, Thousand Oaks and London, pp. 309-310.

Amenga-Etego, R.M., 2016, 'Nankani women's spirituality and ecology', *Worldviews: Global Religions, Culture and Ecology*, 20(1), 15-29.

Amenga-Etego, R.M., 2012, 'The Interplay of traditional and modern concepts of health', in H. Lauer & K. Anyidoho (eds.), *Reclaiming the human sciences and humanities through African perspectives*, (Vol. 1), pp. 321-330, Sub-Saharan Publishers.

Amenga-Etego, R.M., 2011, Mending the broken pieces: Indigenous religion and sustainable rural development, African World Press, Trenton.

Andoh, C.T., 2011, 'Bioethics and the challenges to its growth in Africa', *Open Journal of Philosophy*, 1(2), 67-75. DOI: 10.4236/ojpp.2011.12012.

Appiah-Kubi, K., 1998, 'The Akan concept of human personality', in E.A. Adegbola, (ed.), *Traditional religion in West Africa*, pp. 259-270, Sefer, Ibadan, Nigeria.

Appiah, K.A., 1992, *In my father's house: Africa in the philosophy of culture*, Oxford University Press, New York.

Atiemo, A.O., 2013, Religion and the inculturation of human rights in Ghana, Bloomsbury, London.

Blay, Y.A., 2008, 'Akan', in K.A Molefe & A. Mazama (eds.), *Encyclopedia of African religion*, Sage: Thousand Oaks, London, pp. 23-26.

Bourdillon, M.F.C., 2000, 'Witchcraft and society', in K. Olupona (ed.), African *spirituality: forms, meanings, and expressions*, pp. 176-197, Crossroad Publishing Company, New York.

Brokensha, D.W., 1966, *Social change in Larteh, Ghana*, Clarendon Press, Oxford.

Fortes, M., 1950, 'Kinship and marriage among the Ashanti', in A. R. Radcliffe-Brown & D.

Forde, *African systems of kinship and marriage* African, pp. 252-284, Oxford University Press, London, New York and Toronto.

Fortes, M., 1959, *Oedipus and Job in West African religions*, Cambridge University Press, Cambridge.

Fortes, M., 1987, '*Religion, morality and the person: Essays on Tallensi religion*'. Cambridge University Press, Cambridge.

Griaule, M., 1970, *Conversation with Ogotemmeli: An introduction to Dogon religious ideas*. Oxford University Press, London, Oxford and New York.

Hours, B., 1986, 'African medicine as an alibi and as a reality', in *African Medicine in the Modern World*, Seminar proceedings No. 27, Centre of African Studies, Edinburgh, 41-52.

Lugira, A.M., 2008, 'Africism', in M.K. Asante & A. Mazama (eds.), *Encyclopedia of African religion*, pp. 11-14, Sage, Thousand Oaks and London.

Magesa, L., 1997, *African religion: The moral traditions of abundant life*, Orbis, Maryknoll, NY.

Mbiti, J.S., 1990, *African religions and philosophy*, 2nd edn., Heinemann, Oxford.

Mbiti, J.S., 1975, *Introduction to African religion*, Heinemann, London.

Metz, T., 2010, 'African and Western moral theories in a bioethical context', *Developing World Bioethics*, 10 (1), 49-58. Doi:10.1111/j.1471-8847.2009.00273.x.

Murove, M.F., 2005, 'African bioethics: An explanatory discourse', *Journal for the Study of Religion*, 18(1), 16-36, viewed 10 May 2017, from http://www.jstor.org/stable/24764253

Nzegwu, N., 1996, 'Questions of identity and inheritance: A critical review of Kwame Anthony Appiah's *in my* father's *house*', *Hypatia* 11(1), 175-201.

Oduyoye, M., 1998, 'The medicine-man, the magician and the wise man', in E.A Ade Adegbola (ed.), *Traditional religion in West Africa*, pp. 55-70, Sefer, Ibadan.

Quarcoopome, T.N.O., 1987, *West African traditional religion*, African Universities Press, Ibadan.

Rasmussen, S.J., 2000, 'Parallel and divergent landscapes: Cultural encounters in the ethnographic space of Tuareg medicine', *Medical Anthropology Quarterly*, New Series, 14(2), 242-270, viewed 5 July 2012, from http://www.jstor.org/stable/649704.

Shoko, T., 2008, 'Health', in M.K. Asante & A. Mazama (eds.), *Encyclopedia of African religion*, Sage, Thousand Oaks and London, pp. 310-312.

Tangwa, G.B., 2000, 'The traditional African perception of a person: Some implications for bioethics', *Hastings Centre Report*, 30(5), 39-43.

Toldson, I.L. & Toldson, I.A., 2001, 'Biomedical ethics: An African-centered psychological perspective', *Journal of Black Psychology*, 27(4), 401-423.

Wolcott, F.F., 2001, *Writing Up-Qualitative Research*, Sage Publication, London and New Delhi.

Chapter 7

Ethical Concerns Regarding Right of People Living with Disabilities in Ghana

Augustina Naami
University of Ghana

Abstract

This chapter reviews studies about traditional and contemporary African beliefs and attitudes toward disability and people with disability (PWD). She focusses particularly on Ghana, and argues that Ghana is yet to align and harmonize disability laws with international laws. Because of legislative vacuum in many areas, and lack of enforcement, PWD face a lot of challenges. For example, in some cultures people with disabilities are stigmatized and associated with evil spiritual influences; they are often stigmatized as "water babies" and bad luck; they are often killed by a fetish priests (through concoctions); sometimes such rituals are carried out by family members themselves. The author concludes that aligning and harmonizing disability laws in Ghana with international laws can help minimize the dehumanizing experiences that PWD go through and secure them with good protection from abuses.

Key words: right, disability, laws, stigmatization, dehumanizing, prejudice, abuse, ritual, traditional Africa, contemporary Africa,

7.1 Introduction

The number of persons with disabilities in Ghana continues to be a bone of contention. While the 2010 Census Report estimate this population at 737,743 (Ghana Statistical Service, 2012), the 2012 Human Rights Watch Report shows a remarkable difference in the number. The statistics indicate that more than 5 million people in Ghana live with disabilities, out of which 2.8 million are people with mental disabilities. And, if we go by the World Health Organisation's (WHOs) estimation that disability affects 15-20% of every country's population (World Health Organisations,

2016) then, the estimated number of persons with disabilities living in Ghana (4.8 million) is close to that of the Human Rights Watch 2012 Report.

The Persons with Disability Act (715) of 2006 defines a person with a disability as an "individual with a physical, mental or sensory impairment including visual, hearing or speech functional disability..." The Act 715 further indicates that the physical, mental or sensory impairment could result in socio-cultural and physical barriers that could substantially limit life activities of individuals with disabilities. The etiology of disability is varied. Some forms of disability occur through road accidents, amputation and diseases such as leprosy, measles, and polio.

The 1992 Constitution of the Republic of Ghana [Article 29 (sections 1-7)] clearly states the constitutional rights of persons with disabilities. Article 29 section 8 specifically states that "Parliament shall enact such laws as are necessary to ensure the enforcement of the provisions of this article," i.e., Article 29 (Republic of Ghana 1992:19). Consequently, the government of Ghana formulated the Persons with Disability Act (715) which passed parliament on the 23rd of June 2006 and was accepted into law on the 9th of August 2006. It is also noteworthy that Ghana was the 119th country to ratify the United Nations Convention on the Rights of Persons with Disabilities (CRPD) in 2007. The goal of these efforts is to protect and promote the basic rights of persons with disabilities; rights that persons with disabilities have because they are humans, as well as rights that pertain to their unique needs (See table 2). But, Ghana has yet to domesticate local laws to harmonize and align local laws] with international laws to solidify protection for the rights of persons with disabilities. Also, the implementation of the Persons with Disability Act 715 has been slow; and this negatively impacts on persons with disabilities in Ghana. This paper discusses two main ethical concerns of persons with disabilities in Ghana: Right to life and other rights of persons with disabilities.

7.2 Right to Life and the Value of Life

Right to life is the most fundamental of all human rights and this is captured in several local and international laws (See examples in table 2). Right to life implies that no one SHOULD take another person's life. It also requires government regulations to ensure that no one takes another person's life. However, in Ghana, certain cultural beliefs and practices, which infanticide children with disabilities exist. Some cultures associate disability with evil, magical powers ("juju"), sorcery and witchcraft (Agbenyega 2002, 2008; Avoke 2002; Kassah 2008). Others consider disability as a curse from the gods due to sins committed by parents, family members or ancestors (Agbenyega 2005; Avoke 2002; Ocloo 2005). Yet, other cultures consider children with disabilities as water babies "insuoba," snake babies or other "animals" (Agbenyega 2005; British Broadcasting Corporation [BBC] 2015). Children with disabilities are also considered "bad luck" and "evil spirits" who should be "returned" to the spiritual world where they came from (BBC 2015; Ocloo 2005).

The consequence is that innocent children with disabilities, who have "inherent right to life," like everyone else, are murdered. It is important to note that these children are usually killed by fetish priests. They administer concoctions noted to be poisonous to the children to "return" them to where they came from. These priests are paid for the assignment (BBC 2015). It is also important to note that while some parents willingly subject their children with disabilities to such barbaric acts, others are compelled by family members to do so. In fact, some family members themselves perform the rituals to "return" the children to where they came from (A. Timbella, pers. comm., 13 June 2015; Ocloo 2005; BBC 2015). Sometimes, the children are left in the forest or near riverbanks to die from hunger (BBC 2015; Ocloo 2005).

Assuming that some of these children are spirit children; why are the majority, children with disabilities? Why must children with disabilities be subjected to such torture, cruel, inhuman and degrading treatment when there is virtually no documented evidence of any harm the so-called "bad luck" children who escaped the rituals cause to anyone; neither to themselves nor their families. On the contrary, there is evidence that several persons with various forms of disabilities are living fulfilled lives. Some are lecturers, lawyers, managers/directors/founders of organizations, accountants and so on. Everyone can express their freedom in practicing their beliefs, but when the lives of children are involved, it is important to reconsider such actions. Let's ponder over the questions in Table 7.1 pertaining to the infanticide of children with disabilities.

Table 7. 1: Thought provoking questions to ponder on pertaining to the infanticide of children with disabilities

Can Children with Disabilities be "Animals"	Why should children with Disabilities be Murdered?
Are these children really "animals" and only a few people with powers can see that?	Is the violence against children with disabilities a matter of their quality of life?: Thoughts that the children would be better off dead due to the undue hardships and challenges that they could experience as a result of their impairments? (Asch 2003; Carlson 2013; Encyclopedia of Bioethics 2017)
If the first question is the case, why is it that the majority of these children are those with disabilities?	Could it be due to societal attitudes and environmental barriers towards persons with disabilities and the resultant consequences? (Anum 2011; Naami 2014, 2015; Naami & Hayashi 2012; Slikker 2009)
This raises the question of "Is it because of their impairment?"	Could it be due to the fear of stigma attached to disability that the family would have to embrace? (Agbenyega 2007; Anum 2011; Ocloo 2005; Slikker 2009)
	Is it due to the fear of coping with the stress and other challenges such as emotional, physical, financial, social (risk of isolation) associated with caring for a child with a disability? (Agbenyega 2005; Anthony 2009; Anum 2011; Slikker 2009). Finances: Medical intervention for some forms of disabilities could be expensive.

The infanticide of children with disabilities could be a traumatic experience for parents who experience this phenomenon. Some of these parents, especially the mothers, might have bonded well with their children before the separation. Most times the men/husbands are not in the picture. Thus, the psychological injury could be enormous for the mothers. Even those parents, who willingly opt for the practice of "returning" their children to where they came from, could also experience some psychological issues, as well as siblings of the children (Anum 2011).

Children with disabilities who survive the violence discussed previously are subjected to other forms of violence. Some of their parents and/or family members opt for religious intervention instead of medical intervention that could help improve, manage or prevent the condition from worsening. They are taken to prayer camps for healing. But, there is evidence of physical and psychological abuse of persons with disabilities at these centers (BBC 2015; Human Rights Watch 2012). There is anecdotal evidence that some of the conditions of the children worsen by the time the parents seek medical help, further impacting on the lives of those children who later become adults with disabilities.

Other parents conceal their children or adults with disabilities from public view due to the stigma attached to disability (Avoke 2002; Naami & Hayashi 2012; Ocloo 2005; Slikker 2009) thus, denying them their right to function in society. Yet, other parents maltreat their children and adults with disabilities because they consider them as hopeless, liability and so on (BBC 2015; Slikker 2009). The result is that persons with disabilities are denied their right and freedom of freely participating in mainstream society.

Other ethical concerns regarding the right to life are advanced technological interventions such as selective abortion of fetuses with defects. This intervention is practiced in Ghana already. Another advanced technological intervention is germline modification to design babies with specially selected traits "designer babies." Although this practice has not yet started in Ghana, it may catch up with us soon and, hence, the need to consider ways to address such issues when they arise. The concern is "eugenics" of the population of persons with disabilities due to the perceptions about their quality of life (Asch 2003; Carlson 2013; Encyclopedia of Bioethics 2017) and/or the fear of stigma and other challenges of caring for children with disabilities. In fact, persons with disabilities have diverse skills and expertise which they can contribute to national development (United Nations Enable 2008). In line with "eugenics" of people with disabilities via technological advances, are the end of life issues such as mercy killing or euthanasia. From a disability rights perspective, the question will be "Do people opt to die when they acquire a disability as a result of:

- the stigma that comes with disability;
- the cost and burden of care that is involved in taking care of a person with a disability or with some forms of disabilities,
- or, quality of life issues; that is, life is no longer worth living, life is no rewarding? (Asch 2003).

In summary to the right of life discussion, it is noteworthy that language is a very important aspect of every culture. Words that we use and their connotations carry a lot of meaning and impact. Stereotyping and labeling persons with disabilities result in negative attitudes and behaviors which could have a lasting effect on them (Agbenyega 2005).

Table 7. 2: Selected Rights of Persons with Disabilities from various Laws

Provision	Article/Section	Legislation
Right to life	Article 10; Article 6	UNCRPD (2006); CRC
Right to family life and social activities	Section 1	PWDA 715 (2006)
Right of access to public places	Section 6	PWDA 715 (2006)
Right of access to public services	Section 7	PWDA 715 (2006)
Right not to exploit and discriminate against persons with disabilities	Section 4	PWDA 715 (2006)
Right to participation in political and public life	Article 29	UNCRPD (2006)
Right of access to health care	Section 31-35	UNCRPD (2006)
Right of accessible transportation	Section 23	UNCRPD (2006)
Right to autonomy	Article 12	UNCRPD (2006)
Right to respect for privacy	Article 22	UNCRPD (2006)
Freedom from torture or cruel, inhuman or degrading treatment or punishment	Article 15	UNCRPD (2006)

7.3 Ethical Concerns Relating to other Rights of Persons with Disabilities

The Universal Declaration of Human Rights lays out the fundamental rights that all human beings have by virtue of the fact that they are human. Persons with disabilities have the right to fully participate in society like everyone else. They have the right to social, cultural, economic, health, civic and political participation. However, there is evidence of barriers (see table 7. 3) that impede their full effective participation and inclusion in mainstream society regardless of the laws to protect their rights. The following is a discussion of some of the barriers and how they impact persons with disabilities.

Everyone should have equal access to health care including persons with disabilities. However, several barriers prevent persons with disabilities from fully accessing health care. These barriers include inaccessible buildings, doorways, examination tables as well as medical equipment such as mammography equipment and negative attitudes of health professionals towards persons with disabilities (McColl, 2006; Neri & Kroll 2003; World Health Organisation 2016). Other issues include the unnecessary association of the impairment to physical illness without a thorough investigation of the exact presenting medical conditions (illnesses) to adequately address them. Other important issues concern how to handle persons with disabilities and their special needs. For example, let us assume that there are two people who are due for an x-ray test; one is a person with a disability who uses crutches and the other is a person without a disability. Their needs will not be the same. The person with the disability using crutches may not be able to easily use the "one size fit all" x-ray gown. It is usually very big and could affect their movement from the dressing room to the x-ray machine due to interference with their crutches. Another example is about weighing scales. Most of the weighing scales in the hospitals are not accessible (e.g., they are not fitted to accommodate wheelchairs) to certain individuals with mobility disability such as those using crutches or wheelchairs. All of these negatively impact health care for persons with disabilities.

Another concern pertains to sexual reproductive health. Persons with disabilities experience difficulty in accessing reproductive health services (inaccessible buildings and inaccessible services) due to perceptions about disability. (Groce 2004; United Nations 2006; World Health Organisation 2011). Take for instance, a person who has a hearing disability. How do health professionals communicate with them; through third parties? If this is the case, then, that also raises issues of confidentiality, autonomy and informed consent. There is evidence that women with disabilities are at a greater risk of abuse compared to their male counterparts (Groce 2004; World Health Organisation 2011), and sometimes, they may or may not know perpetrators, especially women with virtual impairment. Other times, they know who raped them but how do they defend themselves given that they cannot see? What if the violence results in pregnancy and sexually transmitted diseases? Due to the fact that they are prone to abuse, especially, the women, it is expedient to consider their unique needs.

Other concerns relate to the National Health Insurance Scheme of Ghana. Should the scheme consider expanding existing coverage to assistive devices for persons with disabilities and other unique needs related to their disabilities? Everyone should have equal access to health care but should health insurance cover disability-related expenses since some of the expenses could be costly (World Health Organisation 2016) but necessary for the effective participation and integration of persons with disability in society. Or should there be other forms of interventions to address the cost associated with disability?

Equally important is social protection benefits and whether they effectively target persons with disabilities, given that these programs usually lumped persons with disabilities together with other vulnerable populations, regardless of the fact that their issues and needs are unique. For example, compare two beneficiary households of the Livelihood for Empowerment against Poverty initiative who receive the same stipend of GHC64. Household A has a person with a disability, while household B has no person with a disability. What is the justification for the equal amount of GHC64 given to these two households given that the person with the disability has numerous additional needs associated with the disability (e.g., a special need for services such as transportation, medical services, acquisition/repairs of assistive devices and personal assistant services)? In addition, negative perceptions and attitudes towards persons with disabilities could impact on their coverage in these programs.

The Ghanaian environment is still challenging for persons with disabilities. The majority of buildings are inaccessible to persons with disabilities due to lack of elevators and access ramps. Persons with disabilities have difficulty accessing public buildings like schools, churches, government offices, theatres, restaurants, libraries, and even public toilets. Some persons with disabilities occasionally park their assistive devices (e.g., wheelchairs and tricycles) outside these buildings and crawl or are carried inside to undertake whatever business they had to do (Naami, 2014; Tijm, Cornielje & Edusei 2011). Consider how it feels like to crawl or be carried to a place that you could easily enter with dignity when access is created?

Table 7. 3: Barriers to full effective participation of Persons with Disabilities

Category of Barriers	Examples
Social/Attitudinal	Negative socio-cultural norms and practices against persons with disabilities Stigma Prejudice/negative preconceptions about disability Stereotyping/labelling Discrimination Communicating through third party instead of the person with a disability
Environmental	Inaccessible public buildings such as schools, churches, government offices, theatres, libraries, and even toilets Lack of ramps Lack of elevators Lack of sidewalks Non-thorough side walks Sidewalks overgrown with weeds Broken sidewalks Flight of steeps Steep/narrow ramps Narrow doorways
Transportation	Inaccessible trotros and buses-no ramps/lifts Lack of facilities to make domestic airlines accessible Inaccessible bus stops Inaccessible ferries (sitting areas upstairs)
Information	Lack of learning materials in alternative format Use of small print/no large print version of material Lack of sign language interpretation Videos/televisions programs that do not include captions
Health care	Inaccessible medical equipment (e.g., Mammography machines) Inaccessible examination tables Inaccessible buildings Absence of weight scale to accommodate persons with disabilities in wheelchairs Lack of negotiable area in the examination rooms Non-disability friendly waiting area chairs

Also, sidewalks are virtually non-existent. The few available sidewalks are not thorough, the starting point may be accessible but the end may not and vice versa (Naami, 2014; Tijm et al. 2011). Sometimes the sidewalks are too narrow for wheelchair users. Other sidewalks are broken, overgrown with weeds or inhibited with obstacles, such as light poles or holes, which render them inaccessible. Thus, persons with disability are compelled to use the main roads, amidst impatient drivers, motorcycle and bicycle riders as well as pedestrians (Naami 2014; Tijm et al. 2011). Why should persons with disabilities risk their lives getting around when provisions could be made to cater for their needs to fully integrate them in the society?

Furthermore, regardless of the importance of transportation in our daily lives, none of the transportation systems in Ghana is accessible to persons with disabilities (Naami 2014; Tijm et al. 2011). Think about the buses and the "trotros" (popular means of transportation in Ghana) and just imagine a person with a mobility disability (e.g., someone using crutches or wheelchair) boarding and alighting from these vehicles amidst impatient passengers and man-made barriers they create in the vehicles. And the "*trotros*" drivers are not even prepared to transport persons with disabilities who use wheelchair (BBC 2015).

Also, there is evidence that the local airlines do not transport persons with disabilities because they claim they do not have facilities to accommodate them (Attah 2017). Imagine planning an important business trip from Accra to Tamale, which you scheduled with one of the airlines. But, upon arrival at the airport, on the day of your travel, you were told that you could not travel because there was no facility to accommodate you, though you had disclosed your condition when you booked for the fight. How would you feel? Does it mean that persons with mobility disabilities (e.g. those who use a wheelchair and/or crutches) cannot travel by air domestically like everyone else and save their time and energy? Why should persons with disabilities be subjected to such inhumane treatment?

Due to their exclusion from mainstream society as a result of barriers discussed in this paper, some persons with disabilities take solace on streets by engaging in demeaning activities such as begging (Appiagyei 2007; Kassah 2008; Naami 2014). But, the question is, "What is preventing the government and other stakeholders from working to remove barriers that hinder the inclusion of persons with disabilities in mainstream society?" Is it because of our mentality and attitudes towards disability and persons with disabilities; or it is as a result of limited resources to provide for their needs, or both?" Persons with disabilities have the same human rights as everyone else and should be given the opportunity to enjoy their freedom in every aspect of life including, social, political, economic and cultural. Their continuous exclusion from mainstream society is unfair and violates their human rights as well as impacts their psychological and overall well-being.

7.4 Research with Persons with Disabilities

Research with persons with disabilities to understand their unique needs that could inform policy and practice decisions to advance their lives is imperative. However, the most important question that emerges is how researchers should balance the issue of the dignity of persons with disabilities, specifically regarding privacy and confidentiality, with the information desired from the participants? (Carlson 2013). Let us consider the use of indirect communication by researchers (e.g., proxy, surrogate respondents, and interpreters) and whether they really represent information persons with disabilities communicate. Does the use of proxies and surrogates really represent perspectives of persons with disabilities? Use of proxies and surrogates may limit the autonomy of persons with disabilities (Carlson 2013). For example, how do we know that the individual, especially those with developmental disabilities, really want to participateant in the study? Probably if they have the capacity to say no they would say so (Carlson 2013).

The major debate about research with persons with profound multiple disabilities, according to Carlson, borders on which of them can actually consent to research studies and who cannot. They may have issues of understanding and consenting to participate in the research. Another question that arises is "What efforts do researchers make to help these individuals to understand their researches? (Asch 2003; Carlson 2013). Carson notes that researchers risk including those individuals with profound multiple disabilities who otherwise cannot actually have the capacity to participate in the studies (inclusion error) and exclude those who are capable of participating in the study (exclusion error). Other issues crop up when persons with disabilities spontaneously make revelations in the presence of third parties. This could limit confidentiality. Elsewhere, guidelines for doing research with persons with disabilities exist. Probably, it is time to consider developing one for Ghana.

7.5 Policy Implications

It is evident from this discussion that ethical concerns regarding the rights of persons with disabilities are many and varied and cut across many sectors of the economy. Thus, a multidisciplinary approach is imperative to adequately and effectively address disability-related ethical issues. Given that disability issues and persons with disabilities are still marginalized in political and other discourses in Ghana, there's a need for more awareness raising, at all levels, to highlight disability issues and the capabilities of persons with disabilities in order to enhance respect for their rights and dignity as stated in the UNCRPD Article 18. The government could mandate the National Commission on Civic Education to use its outlets, throughout the country, to run educational programs about disability rights in both English and local dialects.

There should be political will (e.g. allocation of funding to enforce disability rights laws) to address the challenges persons with disabilities encounter in the society. The government should endeavour to include persons with disabilities in decision-making processes at all levels, especially those that concern them. Persons with disabilities are experts of their disabilities and can help develop interventions that could effectively address their needs. For example, the government could appoint qualified persons with disabilities in key government positions in institutions and departments. This effort could increase their visibility as well as raise awareness about their capabilities and needs.

The government could develop and/or adjust or modify existing social protection programs specifically to target persons with disabilities and their unique needs. Another policy implication regards parents/caregivers of children with developmental disabilities who end up spending their entire life caring for their children. The government should make provisions to enable, as well as motivate them to care for their children.

7.6 References

Agbenyega, J., 2005, *The power of labelling discourse in the construction of disability in Ghana*, viewed 15 December 2011, from http://www.aare.edu.au/03pap/agb03245.pdf

Agbenyega, J., 2007, 'Examining teachers' concerns and attitudes to inclusive education in Ghana', *International Journal of Whole Schooling*, 3(1), 41-56.

Anum, P., 2011, Living with a disabled child: Experiences of families with disabled children in the Dangme West District (Ghana), Ntnu.divaportall.org/smash/get/diva2:440658/FULLTEXT01.

Appiagyei, C., 2006, 'Report: Research into street begging by persons with disabilities in Accra and Kumasi', *Ghana Society of the Physically Disabled*.

Asch, A., 2003, 'Disability, bioethics and human rights', in G. L. Albrecht, K. Seelman & M. Bury (eds.), *Handbook of Disability Studies*, pp. 297-324, Sage Publications. DOI: http://dx.doi.org/10.4135/9781412976251.n12

Attah. A., 2017, *Ghanaian airline humiliates a disabled Pastor: Throws cleric out of aircraft after boarding*, viewed from http://sunnewsonline.com/ghanaian-airline-humiliates-disabled-pastor/

Avoke, M., 2002, 'Models of disability in the labelling and attitudinal discourse in Ghana', *Disability & Society*, 17(7), 769-777.

British Broadcasting Corporation, 2015, *The world's worst place to be disabled*, viewed from https://www.youtube.com/watch?v=TFAdUtKimIQ

Ghana Statistical Service, 2012, *2010 population and housing census: Summary report of final results*. Sakoa Press LTD, Accra, Ghana, viewed from http://www.statsghana.gov.gh/docfiles/2010phc/Census2010_Summary_report_of_finalresults.pdf

Groce, N., 2004, *HIV/AIDS and disability: capturing hidden voices*, Report of the World Bank/Yale University Global Survey on HIV/AIDS and Disability, viewed from http://documents.worldbank.org/curated/en/520371468140965858/HIV-AIDS-and disability-capturing-hidden-voices

Human Rights Watch, 2017, *Ghana 2012 Human Rights Report*, viewed May 2017, from https://www.state.gov/documents/organization/204336.pdf

Kassah, A. K., 2008, 'Disabled people and begging justifications in Accra-Ghana', *Disability & Society* 23(2), 163-170.

Ocloo, A., 2005, *Comprehensive study notes on special education*, GeoWillie Publications, Winneba, Ghana.

Slikker, J., 2009, *Attitudes towards persons with disability in Ghana*, viewed 19 May 2017, from www.gfdgh.org/VSO%20Attitudes%20towards%20PWDS%20in%20Ghana.pdf

McColl, M.A., Forster, D., Shoutt, S.E.D. & Hunter, D., 2008, 'Physician experiences providing   primary care to people with disabilities', *Healthcare Policy*, 4(1), 129-147.

McColl, M.A., 2006, 'Structural determinants of access to health care for people with disabilities, in M.A. McColl & L. Jongbloed, (eds.), pp. 293–313, *Disability and Social Policy in Canada*, 2nd edn, Captus Press, Toronto,

Naami, A., 2015, 'Disability, gender, and employment relationships in Africa: The case of Ghana', *African Journal of Disability Studies*, 4(1), 1-11. file:///C:/Users/tina/Downloads/95-2186-1-PB%20(1).pdf

Naami, A., 2014, 'Breaking the barrier: Ghanaians perceptions about the social model', *Disability, CBR and Inclusive Development*, 25(1), 21-39. DOI: http://dx.doi.org/10.5463/dcid.v1i1.294

Naami, A. & Hayashi, R., 2012, 'Perceptions about disability among Ghanaian university students', *Journal of Social Work in Disability & Rehabilitation*, 11, 100-111. DOI:10.1080/1536710X.2012.677616

Neri, M.T. & Kroll T., 2003, 'Understanding the consequences of access barriers to health care: experiences of adults with disabilities', *Disability and Rehabilitation*, 25, 85–96.

Tijm, M.M, Cornielje, H. Edusei A.K., 2011, '"Welcome to my life!' photovoice: Needs assessment of and by persons with physical disabilities in the Kumasi metropolis', Ghana, *Disability, CBR and Inclusive Development*, 22(1), 55-72.

United Nations, 2006, *Convention on the rights of persons with disabilities*, viewed October 2014, from http://www.un.org/disabilities/documents/convention/ convoptprot-e.pdf

United Nations Enable, 2008, *Disability and employment*, viewed 17 July 2008, from http://www.un.org/disabilities/default.asp?id=255.

World Health Organization, 2016, *Disability and health: Fact sheet*, viewed on May 2017, from http://www.who.int/mediacentre/factsheets/fs352/en/.

Chapter 8

Bioethical Challenges in Medical Practice in Ghana: Past, Present, Future

Akis Afoko
University of Development Studies; Tamale Teaching Hospital

Abstract

This chapter discusses Western principles of bioethics and the challenges of applying them (e.g. informed consent) in the practice of medicine in the African formal and informal healthcare systems. Also, the author strongly advocates ethics training in Africa, for example through the mass media and integration of ethics into the curriculum of the medical schools. Afoko presents the day-to-day ethical challenges that medical practitioners face in Africa: relationship with traditional medicine, herbal healers and other forms of medical care. He concludes with an overview of the future challenges of biomedical healthcare in Africa.

Key words: principles of bioethics, informed consent, herbal medicine, Western medicine, Hippocratic Oath, terminating medical interventions, euthanasia, physician-assisted suicide, conflict of interest.

8.1 Traditional Herbal Medicine: Past vs. Recent Practices

Over the centuries, human populations have managed to take care of their health needs through knowledge and skills acquired individually and communally.

In traditional African communities, the "medicine" man usually is a person who understands which herbs can cure which disease. He then fetches these herbs and directs the patient on their use. Treatment failure may be considered as a curse from the gods. In that context, a traditional priest, who relies on the gods and ancestors for direction, has to take care of spiritual ailments. Families are usually required to consult traditional priests who may prescribe remedies that involve pacification of the gods and ancestors as well as the use of herbs to obtain a cure.

In the traditional set up there are rules and taboos to be observed strictly by individuals and the community as a whole. Few if any ethical problems arise in this system where personal (monetary and other) gain is not usually the motive.

In contemporary African "traditional" herbal practice, many players (including well-trained university graduates in herbal medical practice and complete charlatans) are in the business for financial gain. This sharply contrasts with the "purely" traditional set up of yesteryears. In most cases, the healer is also the (sole) manufacturer of the herbal medicines. He also diagnoses the ailments, prescribes the treatment and sells the medicines. Without doubt, such an arrangement can easily lead to a conflict of interest and raise issues bordering on bioethics. Safeguarding traditional herbal practice will require a separation of these roles through the introduction of strict regulation and appropriate legislation.

8.2 Modern Western Medical Practice

In contrast to traditional medical practice, western medical practices were brought to our communities from Europe and elsewhere. Therefore, there are no direct regulations to guide such traditional practitioners. This leaves us with the western ethical considerations for modern medical practice. Statutory professional regulatory bodies regulate Western practitioners. The pattern is the same all over Africa.

8.3 Modern Ethical Challenges for African Traditional and Herbal Medical Practice

The future of African traditional and herbal medicine will involve the use of non-traditional diagnostic approaches before treatment/healing is offered. This practice will bring ethical issues into a sharp focus. For instance, herbalists have begun testing the blood of patients for malaria parasites and salmonella typhi bacteria before administering their "cure all" anti-fever medications. The use of ultrasound scanning (sometimes with dubious interpretation or none at all) is also gaining ground. Indeed, herbalist will often be seen wearing a white lab coat with a stethoscope around the neck. These practices by themselves are not unethical and should probably be encouraged if done properly and with the right motives.

Unfortunately, many herbalists have not been trained to use stethoscopes and to interpret or even understand the findings of an ultra sound scan or other radiological imaging modality. This is what may become ethically unacceptable and indeed legally questionable.

The use of the internet for acquiring information is laudable. Merely using the internet to find the actual pathophysiology of fever and repeating the same information to patients (or potential patients) does not guarantee that an herb sold in a bus will cure the diseases it is claimed to cure. Current legislation in Ghana prohibits medical doctors in the "formal" sector from advertising themselves or their services, but does not prohibit herbalist or alternative practitioners from doing so. The renowned "MediMoses" centres for treating prostate diseases are run by a trained medical doctor (physician), who is not allowed to advertise his normal services as a doctor but can advertise his traditional medical practice on giant billboards. These are ethical challenges that need resolution with the help of appropriate legislation as well as regulation by the ministry of health.

Mobile devices have become tools for posting adverts, and many app developers have incorporated adverts that may pose ethical dilemmas. It may take a couple of years to understand the nature of these challenges and their bioethical impacts.

8.4 Ethical Challenges among Practitioners of Western Medicine

This latter group of practitioners would usually receive as part of their training during lectures on western medical ethics and indeed will swear the Hippocratic Oath before they begin their medical practice. Even though modern medical practice is based on science, the scientific basis of modern medicine is recent. The cardinal disciplines of medicine such as anatomy, biochemistry and physiology form the basis of understanding the structure and function of the healthy organism whilst pathophysiology and morbid anatomy aid the understanding of disease and its natural history. Most advances in these medical sciences were made only one and half centuries ago.

The future of medical practice is linked tightly to an understanding of genetics, the immune system and the body's response to antigens and microbes. Bioethical challenges of the 21st century, however, will span areas such as advances in biomedical technology, procedures to prolong lives of the terminally ill, deferment of death, reproductive biology including attempts at cloning of organs and tissue engineering, organ transplantation and extensive use of intensive care facilities.

Abiding by the principles of the Hippocratic Oath shall remain a big challenge as confidentiality is easily compromised by recording and listening devices, abortion is seen by many as a women's right issue, euthanasia is becoming acceptable, termination of treatment to dying patients is seen as controversial in our communities. Telling the truth is what is less contentious, but issues of fake news as the norm will put the truth under dispute.

In all of this, technology per se does not necessarily lead to bioethical controversies. It must be understood that bioethical issues are intrinsic to medical practice and have remained the same since the time of Hippocrates. In clinical practice physicians will need to deal with issues of informed consent, termination of life sustaining treatments, euthanasia and physician-assisted suicide as well as conflicts of interest.

Informed Consent. Many patients in the Ghanaian /African context do not receive adequate information to help make a decision about the treatment options that best suits them. They do not also receive enough information about alternative treatment or even complication rates as pertains to that particular surgeon and or his team.

As more patients turn to the internet to seek information, and indeed as more patients see it as an obligation to challenge the health care system and its professionals, the issue of informed consent shall be a major one and hopefully shall bring about changes in the right direction. Many more hours shall be allotted to this topic during the training of doctors and other practitioners.

Ethical challenges do arise when dealing with children and persons who are not mentally fit to make appropriate decisions. It is often left to the coroners to resolve such issues, but they are seldom available. In signing (or indeed refusing to sign), consent forms many parents/guardians/family members take into consideration any personal cost they need to bear and may make a decision that is not in the interest of the patient.

In many instances, third parties who are not directly responsible for the treatment of the patient administer consent forms. Informed consent is no more a process of providing accurate unbiased information; it has become an event, whereby a patient or guardian is made to 'thumb print' to allow for the surgery or other treatment to go on without any explanation. Nurses rather than Physicians would administer consent forms just before a surgical procedure (sometimes when the patient is already on the operating table). These practices are so widespread that they have become the norm.

Terminating Medical interventions. This problem is an old one in medicine and is one of the cardinal principles of the Hippocratic Oath. In the Ghanaian context, many relatives (especially those who bear the cost of treatment) will like to know if there will be a **good** outcome after treatment. If the answer is not a firm yes, then they will prefer the physician does less for the patient.

Many health institutions fail to stock lifesaving medications, and therefore patients or their relatives need to buy such medicines even at the time of emergencies. Institutions and senior doctors often fail to hold management to account, and this a serious ethical problem.

Another challenge arises when relatives are not sure of the outcome and do not want to spend any more money. Even though no research has been carried out specifically, there have been anecdotal instances where the "Wofase" (nephew) cannot wait to inherit his "Wofa" (uncle) and will *deliberately* refuse to buy much needed medications for the resuscitation of his uncle in the Intensive Care Unit.

On the other hand, the wishes of sick patients not to receive further treatment have to be respected. In the Ghanaian context, many physicians respect this right. A few cases have been reported where physicians refer terminally ill and moribund patients to their private facilities and offer inappropriate care against the wishes of patients and relatives. This poses an ethical challenge since the motive for such treatments is questionable. Heroic treatments are still common, especially for cancer patients whose diseases are poorly diagnosed before attempting unbeneficial treatments. Visiting physicians from foreign countries (often with little experience in managing certain conditions) may sometimes engage in these kinds of treatments and leave patients worse off after they depart. Patients may also be left without appropriate referral to tertiary centers to receive adjuvant therapy. In most cases, there is no follow up review for such patients.

Euthanasia and Physician Assisted Suicide.

These are illegal in Ghana. Besides, the sociocultural environment does not support this practice. However, research has not been carried out to find out if physicians and other health professionals may have carried out euthanasia or facilitated physician-assisted suicide. Work has also not been carried out to determine what proportion of practitioners support these practices or are willing to carry them out if these practices are legalized.

Financial Conflict of Interest. The issue of how financial gain and fees affect medical decisions is nearly as old as the modern era of medical practice. The same issues appear to be the case with some herbal /alternative practitioners of modern times. This particular ethical problem is by far the most pervasive and well known. Physicians and non-physician health managers alike find themselves in a conflict of interest situations. Bad procurement practices, 'stealing' the institution's time to do private practice are a few examples.

Selling patented products, including drugs, have become a common practice. The Ghana Medical Association had openly to chastise practitioners who sell drugs in consulting rooms. Worldwide, pharmaceutical companies have adopted aggressive tactics including the financing of randomized controlled trials, sponsorship of conferences among others. In Ghana, they often need only to organize continuing medical education (CME) programs on the use of their own Drugs & Devices and provide what is termed "item 13" – post event snacks or dinner.

The pharmaceutical companies then parade consulting rooms with souvenirs but sometimes with "brown envelopes" (money in white envelopes) to encourage the prescription of their brands to patients, who may actually not need these drugs.

There is hardly a conflict of interest when it has to do with the physician's primary duties of promoting the well-being of patients, advancing research, educating younger colleagues and medical students as well as promoting public health.

Most conflict of interest arises when physicians pursue their secondary interest such as earning income, pursuing non-vocational, non-professional interests among others. Even though these secondary interests are not necessarily malevolent or non-desirable (indeed they are mostly legitimate and admirable), a conflict of interest arises when one of these secondary interests compromises the pursuit of a primary interest, especially the well-being of a patient.

Many physicians in the public sector find themselves in this kind of situation, often leading to a compromise of judgment by the physician. Again, little research has been carried out, but anecdotal evidence is rife.

Self-referral by physicians is also common. Physicians in government hospitals often refer patients to their private clinics or laboratories. This practice needs stronger regulation as well as legislation to control.

Practitioners should be compelled to disclose all possible conflict of interest situations as far as their clinical practice is concerned. A conflict of interest management protocol should be developed and legislation should spell out which activities are prohibited.

Future Dimensions of Bioethics. As genetics moves from the research to the clinical setting, practicing physicians shall encounter issues surrounding genetic testing, counseling and treatment. The new possibilities shall also bring along new challenges.

The use of genetic tests without extensive counseling so common in research studies would alter the nature of the bioethical issues. Because these tests have serious implications for the patient and others, scrupulous attention must be given to informed consent training and in the post internship years. The bioethical issues raised by genetic tests for somatic cell changes, such as tests that occur commonly in cancer diagnosis and risk stratification, are no different from the issues raised with the use of any laboratory or radiographic test.

Ethics consultation services may be of assistance in resolving bioethical dilemmas and appropriate legislation must be formulated. Current data suggest that consultation services are used mainly for problems that arise in individual cases and are not used for more institutional or policy problems

It is unclear how we shall cope with newer challenges in medicine as we embark on new adventures in the 21st Century. How prepared are we for the following?

i) Stem Cell Research and application in the clinical setting
ii) Shared parents – three parents contributing to the procreation of one child
iii) Organ transplant (face, multiple organs, brain)
iv) Human cloning
v) Tele Medicine – Robot assisted surgeries from remote locations
vi) Relocation of humans to Space to inhabit the planets.

So far, the main limiting factor for us in Ghana is cost. Our health budget cannot support these kinds of activities. Is it ethically right to spend huge sums of money on 'Da Vinci 'robots for surgery when thousands of children are malnourished and have no access to vaccines?

8.5 Bibliography

Afoko, V., & Afoko, A., 2016, *Unpublished research data on informed consent.*

Beauchamp, T.L., & Childress J.F., 2001, *Principles of Biomedical Ethics*, 5th ed., Oxford University Press, New York.

Berg, J.W., Applebaum, P.S., Lidz, C.W., Parker L.S., 2001, *Informed consent: Legal theory and clinical practice*, 2nd ed., Oxford University Press, New York.

Brennan T, Blank L, Cohen J, et al., 2002, "Medical professionalism in the new millennium: A physician charter", *Annals of Internal Medicine*, 1136, 243-246.

Crawley, L.M., Marshall, P.A., Lo, B. & Koenig, B.A., 2002, 'Strategies for culturally effective end-of-life care'. *Annals of Internal Medicine*, 136(9), 673-679.

Goldman, L. & Ausiello, D., (eds.), 2004, *Cecil textbook of medicine*, 22nd ed., W.B. Saunders Company, Philadelphia.

Chapter 9

Bioethics, Nature, the Environment and Climate Change in Africa

Godfrey B. Tangwa
University of Yaoundé 1

Abstract

Nature/God had carved out our world, planet Earth, into different continents, each characterized by its different geologic formations, geographical features, climatic systems and distinct environmental peculiarities. The inhabitants of planet Earth include plants of myriad varieties, non-human animals of various species and human beings of many different races. If plants depend (passively) on sunlight and the minerals of the earth for their survival and flourishing, non-human animals depend on plants and other animals for their survival and well-being, while human beings depend both on plants and non-human animals for their survival and well-being. This progressive system of dependence for survival and well-being or flourishing is predicated, for each ecological environment of the earth, on an appropriate climate with suitable climatic seasons rhythmically succeeding one another with appropriate regularity. This creates a balance in nature that needs maintaining in the interest of human beings, non-human animals and plants. Once this balance is grossly upset, there is danger for all the inhabitants of the Earth. This is currently happening with what has been termed "climate change".

In this paper I discuss nature, the phenomenon of climate change, and the natural environment from the point of view and perspective of bioethics in Africa.

Key words: nature, environment, climate, Africa, bioethics

9.1 Introduction

The world in which we live (Planet Earth), and the Universe as a whole in its awe-inspiring vastness, are characterized by remarkable diversity and variety of the natural, the God-given, that is only discoverable, not inventable or fabricate-able. This is the physical, natural, or material world that has fascinated human beings from the first moment of their emergence in the world and resulted in the study of science and philosophy. In studying and learning from nature and adapting to it for survival and well-being, human beings create culture, an adaptive way of living in any given environment, and cultures create technologies as a means of mastering and controlling the environment. The dichotomy between nature and culture marks an important distinction between what we find there as simply given and what we make of and do with, what is there. Human agency in nature is what creates problems in the physical environment and makes necessary the intervention of bio-ethics.

Were it possible for human beings to refrain from all interference/ interventions in nature, it is likely that there would be little or no problem with the physical environment. On its own Nature seems to 'know' how to balance its excesses and overflowing to achieve an overall equilibrium at all times. But the problem of sheer survival, let alone well-being in the world, constrained human beings, beginning with agriculture as a better option to hunting and wild plant and fruit gathering, to intervene and interfere with nature. Ideally, if such interventions, under the guidance of human rationality had remained at the level of cautious tinkering with nature, there likely would be no alarming problems.

Unfortunately, human beings are also naturally self-centered and prone to be greedy, which is what led to the historical phenomena of omnivorous exploration and discovery of the Earth/Universe, to indiscriminate colonization, subjugation and exploitation of technologically less advanced peoples around the world. Combined with various technologies that human genius is able to create, this spirit of unrestricted exploration and exploitation, at first brandished and celebrated as human progress and civilization, reveals its hidden side as the "self-endangerment and the devastation of nature" (Beck 1995:2). And, because the well-being, comparative advantage and dominant capabilities of some very powerful nations of the world have come to depend on it, the world is saddled with a situation where these threats to nature and life are systematically "produced industrially, externalized economically, individualized juridically, legitimized scientifically, and minimized politically" (ibid.). This has now become extremely dangerous and calls for a robust system of rational control in the interest of the survival and well-being of human beings and the rest of nature as a whole. Can bioethics provide such a system of rational control?

9.2 Bioethics

The coinage and popularization of the term "bio-ethics" is generally credited to Fritz Jahr (1885-1953) and Van Rensselaer Potter (1911-2001), respectively. It connotes an extension of ethics in general (right and wrong conduct) and is meant to cover not only medical ethics to which the term tends to be restricted in some quarters today, but also environmental and agricultural ethics, in short, "the application of ethics to all of life" (Potter 1996:2). The narrow conception and understanding of bioethics as restricted to modern (Allopathic) Western medicine, biomedical research and attendant technologies, especially genetic technologies is, however, very significant because of its potential to transform the world and our lives for good or for ill and for the sudden novel problems and dilemmas that it tends to raise. Such, for example, are problems related to human reproductive technologies, stem cell research, (Vayena, Rowe & Griffin 2002), telemedicine, nanotechnology, and most recently, pharming (eds. Engelhard, Hagen & Thiele 2007) and the creation of "synthetic human entities with embryo-like features".

In "pharming" "plants or animals are genetically engineered to produce pharmaceutical proteins. It is hoped that pharming may lead to new, better and cheaper drugs" (ibid.: 3), even though this perennial hope seems to serve merely as a refrain to justify all types of experimental adventures. But the effects of such procedures on environmental and pharmacological safety, on the engineered animals or plants themselves and on human beings remain to be discovered. According to a recent article in the *New York Times*[1] scientists at Harvard University are at the point of creating synthetic human entities with embryo-like features. Such a development is probably calculated to bypass the ethical debate and problems connected with the use of human embryos in research but will surely raise novel ethical problems and concerns.

In addressing these problems and dilemmas, it is necessary to keep in mind the broader conception of bioethics, englobing concerns related to the environment, climate change and human survival and well-being, in the manner of tracing a problem to its very roots for a solution. In 1927, Fritz Jahr, a German thinker from Halle, had, echoing Immanuel Kant's "Categorical Imperative", proposed a "Bioethical Imperative" stated in the following terms: "Respect every living Being as an end in itself and treat it, if possible, as such". This is an integrative conception of bioethics, covering not only the human community, culture and health but also all the physical and material aspects of our world. Industrialized world bioethics has all but completely abandoned such a conception of bioethics in favor of a fixation on individualized autonomy and unstoppable technological innovations. Among the four canonized cardinal principles of bioethics (Beauchamp & Childress 2001), only **beneficence** from the point of view of individual **autonomy** is taken seriously; **justice** and **non-maleficence** are, at best, paid only lip service.

It is arguably the abandonment of a holistic focus, more than anything else, that has most aided and abated the recklessness of technological experimentations. Within African cultures and metaphysico-religious ideas, such an ethic encompasses eco-bio-communitarianism (Tangwa 1996:192), implying interdependence and peaceful co-existence between the Earth, plants, non-human animals and human beings. The "Ubuntu" ethic of African cultures (Battle 2009, Bujo 2001, London et al. 2014, Metz 2010, Ramose 1999) is human centered and, because it is holistic, it can easily be extended to cover non-human animals, plants and nature in general.

We might discuss and argue and, perhaps disagree, about what philosophy is, what ethics is, what bioethics is, what global bioethics is all about but it is easier to recognize problems that threaten human health and well-being, the survival of plants and animals or the physical environment. And if we can recognize the problems, we should be able to recognize what would count as good and viable solutions. Ubuntu in itself is not a philosophical or moral theory although a coherent moral theory can be derived from it, as Metz and others have demonstrated. It is an attitude and way of life or better an attitude to life embedded and anchored in a culture. If it is intuitively apprehended or demonstrated and recognized that such an attitude would provide a solution or the only solution to a global problem, then it ought to be adopted as the starting point of any further critical reasoning, philosophizing, analyses or argumentation towards the solution of the given problem. This process could take various forms but, if the focus is on the results to be achieved, then it is less important as to whether we agree or disagree on the need to "embrace the universal nature of self-critical and analytical philosophical analysis and argumentation", or whether we are simply "using seemingly philosophical approaches to give [unjustified] normative emphasis on different cultural approaches to bioethics." (Hellsten 2016).

9.3 Biodiversity and Cultural Diversity

There has been increasing global awareness of the importance of biodiversity - the great number and variety of biological forms and species that we find in the world, and this has led to a further awareness that the problems which arise in connection with preservation and exploitation of the globe's resources can only be tackled from a global perspective. The

Convention on Biological Diversity (CBD 1992, 2016) founded at the Rio Summit in 1992 as a legally binding agreement on the use and conservation of biological diversity, is an instance of addressing the world's biodiversity problems from a global perspective. What has not yet been sufficiently recognized is the importance of the cultural diversity of our world and the potential of dominated or marginalized cultures to hold important viable ideas if not prescriptions to some of the global problems plaguing the world. African culture in general, for example, has an ingrained attitude of "live and let live" towards nature as a whole. In the overarching world-view this attitude between the distinction between plants, animals and inanimate things, between matter and spirit, sacred and profane, the communal and the individual, is a slim and flexible one. Such an attitude translates into humility, caution, respect and conciliation towards other human beings, non-human animals, plants, inanimate things, superhuman spirits and even the sundry intangible/invisible forces of nature. We can canvass for the global benefits of approaching and looking at our environmental problems from such point of view and perspective, but our situation in Africa remains fundamentally rife with contradictions.

Some of such contradictions are the following: It is evident that the main causes of climate change and its effects on the natural environment emanate from high technological interventions in nature and not from the subsistence farming mostly practiced in Africa. Yet, the effects of such interventions pose greater threats of famine, natural disasters and ill-health in Africa, owing precisely to the non-availability of prompt corrective technologies. It is not possible for Africa to be indifferent to these issues and problems, and yet it is evident that the problems are exacerbated if not caused by clinging on to the European model of development and European ways of seeing and doing things, imposed by colonialism. These are the reasons why African cities have expanded uncontrollably, to the detriment of villages, the prototypes of African communal life; why both African cities and villages are drowning under discarded plastics and clogged with discarded cars, whereas everywhere there is lack of the most basic/primary necessities: potable water, sanitation, primary health care, usable roads, electricity. Can bioethics show us a way out of these contradictions? I do not know.

9.4 Conclusion

Our world, Planet Earth, is a world we human beings, share with myriad other creatures and entities - non-human animals, plants, micro-organisms, invisible/ intangible forces, inanimate things. None of the entities that comprise the furniture of our world has any more reason or right to be there, to exist, than any other. Interdependence, therefore, rationally imposes itself as the imperative mood of existence in the world. And human beings, because their rationality imposes on them the whole weight of moral agency in the world, are responsible for ensuring that balance and equilibrium are maintained in nature in the interest of the survival, if not well-being, of all the creatures of the world. Bioethics is a sophisticated science which can ensure that human beings live up to their responsibilities in the world. The impediments to the fulfillment of this role lie in human ego-centrism and greed, resulting in abuse or misuse of power, knowledge, endowments and capabilities. For the survival of our world, a global ethic that shuns greed, ego-centrism and exploitation is urgently needed. Such an ethic seems available in the cultural values of African communities.

9.5 Notes

[1] https://www.nytimes.com/2017/03/21/science/embryonic-stem-cells-synthetic-embryos-sheefs.html?_r=0

9.6 References

Battle, M.J., 2009, Reconciliation: The Ubuntu theology of Desmond Tutu, Pilgrim Press, Cleveland.

Beauchamp, T.L., & Childress J. F., 2001, *Principles of Biomedical Ethics*, 5th ed., Oxford University Press, New York.

Beck, U., 1995, Ecological enlightenment: Essays on the politics of the risk society, transl. M.A. Ritter, Humanities Press, New Jersey.

Bujo, B., 2001, Foundations of African ethic: Beyond the universal claims of Western morality, The Crossroad Publishing Company, New York.

Engelhard, M., Hagen, K. & Thiele, F., (eds.), 2007, *Pharming: A New Branch of Biotechnology*, Kollen Druck + Verlag, Bonn + Berlin.

Hellsten, S.K., 2015, 'The role of philosophy in global bioethics: Introducing four trends', *Cambridge Quarterly of Healthcare Ethics*, viewed April 2015, from DOI: 10.1017/S0963180114000498.

London L., Tangwa G., Matchaba-Hove R., Mkhize N., Nwabueze R., Nyika A. & Westerholm P., 2004, 'Ethics in occupational health: Deliberations of an international workgroup addressing challenges in an African context', *BMC Medical Ethics*, 15(48), [http://www.biomedcentral.com/1472-6939/15/48].

Metz T., 2010, 'African and Western moral theories in a bioethical context', *Developing World Bioethics*, 10(1), 49-58.

Muzur, A. & Saas, H., (eds.), 2012, Fritz Jahr and the foundations of global bioethics: The future of integrative bioethics, LIT Verlag, Münster.

Potter, V.R., 1996, 'What does bioethics mean?', *The AG Bioethics Forum*, 8(1), pp. 2-3.

Potter, V.R, 1971, *Bioethics: Bridge to the future*, Prentice Hall, Englewood Cliffs.

Ramose, M.B., 1999, *Philosophy through Ubuntu*, Mond Books, Harare, Zimbabwe.

Vayena, E., Rowe, P.J. & Griffin, D.P., 2002, Current practices and controversies in assisted reproduction: Report of a WHO Meeting, *World Health Organization*, Geneva.

Index

A

abortion, 2, 3, 4, 5, 19, 22, 36, 126, 129, 135, 148
Adogame, 114, 120, 129
Africa, v, vii, viii, ix, x, xii, 1, 2, 3, 4, 5, 8, 9, 10, 14, 15, 16, 17, 18, 19, 21, 22, 23, 24, 25, 26, 27, 28, 29, 32, 34, 36, 37, 38, 41, 42, 48, 49, 50, 52, 53, 54, 55, 60, 75, 82, 86, 91, 129, 130, 143, 145, 146, 153, 157
Agbenyega, 133, 134, 136, 142
Akan, xi, 24, 28, 44, 50, 77, 91, 113, 115, 117, 118, 122, 129
Akuo, 119, 120
Amoah, 115, 121, 122
amputation, 132
ancestor, 40, 43, 46, 115, 119, 120, 122
Andoh, viii, 18, 22, 28, 32, 36, 37, 49, 54, 124, 129
animals, ix, 18, 44, 115, 120, 122, 125, 133, 134, 153, 155, 156, 157
Appiah, 34, 39, 42, 46, 47, 54, 64, 75, 115, 116, 117, 127, 129, 130
Aristotle, 25, 28, 46, 89, 90
Asch, 134, 135, 141, 142
autonomy, viii, x, 3, 7, 19, 31, 49, 51, 52, 53, 57, 58, 66, 67, 68, 69, 70, 71, 73, 74, 78, 79, 80, 81, 82, 84, 85, 86, 87, 89, 91, 92, 136, 137, 141, 155

B

Beauchamp, 3, 22, 31, 78, 151, 156, 158

Behrens, viii, 18, 22, 28, 32, 49, 54, 74
Belsky, 66, 76, 111
beneficence, viii, 31, 60, 68, 74, 79, 80, 81, 82, 91, 92, 156
bioethics, vii, viii, ix, x, xii, xv, 1, 2, 4, 8, 15, 17, 18, 19, 20, 22, 23, 24, 25, 26, 28, 29, 31, 32, 33, 34, 35, 36, 37, 38, 47, 48, 49, 52, 53, 54, 55, 61, 115, 128, 129, 130, 142, 145, 146, 153, 154, 155, 156, 157, 158
Bliss, 111
Bogaert, ix, 29, 32, 35, 54, 56

C

caregiver, x, 31, 32, 48, 50, 51, 77
Charismatic, 9, 11
Childress, 3, 22, 31, 151, 156, 158
Christian, 9, 11, 42, 43
climate change, 153, 155, 157
clinical, 6, 35, 79, 148, 150, 151, 152
cloning, 4, 147, 151
collective, 29, 49, 50, 83, 87
colonialism, x, 1, 4, 18, 19, 20, 21, 27, 29, 37, 157
communal, 33, 49, 50, 51, 52, 53, 58, 59, 61, 62, 63, 64, 65, 67, 68, 71, 72, 83, 85, 86, 87, 88, 89, 90, 92, 121, 125, 128, 157
communality, 81, 82, 83, 86, 88, 89, 90
communitarian, x, xii, 4, 6, 20, 23, 24, 31, 32, 33, 34, 48, 49, 50, 51, 52, 53, 60, 61, 75, 86, 87, 88
communitarianism, xii, 24, 87, 92, 156
communo-cultural, x, 1, 4, 13, 14
consent, viii, xi, xii, 4, 6, 7, 8, 10, 29, 31, 33, 48, 49, 51, 52, 53,

57, 63, 67, 74, 77, 78, 79, 80, 81, 82, 83, 91, 92, 137, 141, 145, 148, 151, 152
consultation, x, 31, 32, 39, 40, 46, 48, 51, 78, 86, 151
consumerism, x, 1, 4, 17
contraception, 3, 5
corruption, x, 1, 4, 16, 17, 21, 123
cosmological, 8, 41, 43, 46
cosmology, 20, 44
cultural beliefs, viii, ix, xii, 34, 132
culture, viii, ix, x, 17, 21, 24, 27, 28, 31, 33, 34, 35, 36, 38, 41, 42, 43, 44, 45, 47, 49, 52, 53, 54, 55, 60, 88, 111, 112, 129, 136, 154, 155, 156, 157

D

death, 3, 4, 5, 26, 39, 41, 42, 116, 117, 118, 119, 121, 126, 127, 128, 147
dignity, 22, 37, 65, 79, 80, 82, 87, 138, 141, 142
disability, ix, xi, 131, 132, 134, 135, 137, 138, 139, 140, 142, 143
disease, 5, 18, 23, 42, 55, 59, 69, 70, 93, 115, 121, 122, 124, 127, 145, 147
disorder, xi, 23, 93, 95
diversity., 34
diviner, x, 31, 32, 48, 51
divinities,, 43, 123
DNA, 70

E

Earth, 117, 153, 154, 156, 157
Ebola, 14, 29, 50, 55
egalitarian, 48, 49
elders, 11, 41, 48
enframing, 19
entrustment, 57, 58, 64, 66, 67, 70, 71, 72, 73, 75
environment, vii, ix, 14, 17, 24, 34, 89, 114, 115, 121, 122, 138, 149, 153, 154, 155, 156, 157

environmental, vii, ix, x, xii, 1, 4, 27, 43, 134, 153, 155, 157
ethnic, x, 2, 8, 9, 14, 20, 23, 24, 25, 31, 32, 34, 48, 51, 60, 118
euthanasia, 20, 22, 126, 135, 148, 149
existence, xi, xii, 13, 22, 41, 43, 44, 58, 72, 77, 78, 89, 90, 121, 156, 158
experimentation, 3, 39, 48

F

family, x, xii, 12, 21, 31, 32, 41, 42, 46, 48, 49, 50, 51, 52, 53, 65, 66, 81, 88, 117, 118, 119, 120, 125, 126, 127, 129, 131, 133, 134, 135, 136, 148
forces, 8, 18, 20, 43, 44, 45, 46, 157

G

Gbadegesin, viii, 18, 20, 27, 28, 32, 34, 51, 52, 54
genes, xi, 95
genetic, 14, 20, 36, 46, 112, 151, 155
genomics, xi, 2, 19, 95, 112
globalization, viii, 4, 15, 31, 36, 49, 123, 124, 128
gods, 8, 10, 14, 43, 44, 48, 51, 133, 145
Gyekye, 2, 24, 28, 42, 49, 54, 61, 74, 75, 87

H

harmony, 23, 49, 60, 61, 117, 120, 121
healer, x, 7, 9, 10, 11, 26, 31, 32, 48, 51, 118, 122, 126, 146
healing, vii, viii, xi, 5, 7, 8, 9, 11, 12, 23, 29, 35, 38, 39, 40, 42, 43, 46, 113, 114, 115, 116, 117, 118, 119, 120, 121, 125, 127, 128, 135, 146
health, vii, viii, ix, x, xii, 1, 2, 3, 5, 6, 7, 8, 11, 12, 13, 15, 16, 17, 18, 19, 23, 24, 25, 26, 27, 28,

Index

32, 34, 35, 36, 38, 41, 42, 43, 44, 46, 47, 48, 49, 50, 51, 52, 53, 54, 58, 65, 66, 70, 77, 78, 79, 80, 81, 82, 83, 93, 111, 112, 114, 115, 116, 117, 118, 119, 120, 121, 122, 123, 124, 125, 126, 127, 128, 129, 136, 137, 138, 143, 144, 145, 147, 148, 149, 150, 151, 155, 156, 158
healthcare, vii, viii, x, xii, 13, 23, 31, 32, 35, 40, 48, 51, 52, 53, 72, 137, 138, 145, 157
herbal, xii, 7, 9, 20, 40, 42, 51, 123, 126, 128, 145, 146, 150
herbalist, 114, 146, 147
Hippocratic Oath, 147, 148, 149
HIV, ix, 16, 17, 28, 35, 55, 59, 76, 143
holistic, vii, viii, xii, 8, 9, 15, 32, 42, 46, 52, 53, 128, 156
honhom, 117

I

identity, 14, 37, 38, 49, 52, 61, 62, 88, 89, 116, 130
illness, 8, 12, 20, 38, 42, 46, 51, 68, 71, 111, 117, 124, 137
impairment, 132, 134, 137
imperialism, 37
indigenous, vii, viii, ix, 1, 8, 18, 26, 28, 32, 33, 37, 38, 40, 48, 49, 53, 54, 60, 114, 117, 123, 125, 126, 128
individualism, x, 57, 59, 90
individualistic, 1, 20, 52, 53, 88
infanticide, 132, 133, 134
insuoba, 133
interpretation, xi, 20, 43, 63, 86, 115, 116, 139, 146

J

justice, 17, 18, 79, 156

K

kinship, 50, 87, 88, 117, 129
Kuhse, 35, 54

L

libation, 43, 45

M

Macklin, 33, 34, 75
Macpherson, 33, 34, 75
magical, 26, 39, 133
Masolo, 61, 75
matrilineage, 116
Mbiti, 41, 43, 53, 55, 114, 115, 121, 123, 126, 128, 130
menstruation, 14
metaphysical, 5, 13, 15, 20, 91, 92, 114
Metz, v, viii, x, 2, 18, 19, 29, 32, 33, 49, 55, 58, 61, 63, 74, 75, 125, 130, 156, 158
mogya, 116, 117
Murove, 18, 22, 122, 124, 130
Muslim, 9, 11
mystical, x, 9, 31, 32, 38, 39, 43, 44, 45

N

Nankani, 113, 115, 118, 122, 126, 129
nationalism, 37
natural, x, 1, 4, 8, 9, 17, 18, 24, 27, 39, 40, 41, 43, 44, 46, 61, 82, 86, 88, 89, 91, 120, 121, 122, 147, 153, 154, 157
naturalistic, 42, 44, 46
negritude, 37
Nkrumah, 37, 49, 55, 124
nonmaleficence, viii, 79, 80, 81, 92
Nyerere, 37, 49, 55
Nyika, ix, 29, 32, 35, 39, 54, 55, 56, 158

O

obligations, x, 50, 57, 58, 59, 60, 64, 65, 66, 67, 68, 70, 71, 72, 73, 74, 84, 89
Ocloo, 133, 134, 135, 143
Okpako, 38, 39, 42, 55

ontology, 24, 43, 45, 53, 84, 86
oracle, 39, 51
Oruka, 34

P

participants, 5, 6, 25, 57, 58, 59, 64, 65, 66, 67, 68, 69, 70, 72, 73, 141
paternalism, 3, 7, 63, 80
patriarchal, 119, 120
patrilineage, 116
pharmaceutical, 9, 15, 16, 66, 150, 155
physiological, 6, 8, 14, 92
plants, 8, 115, 122, 128, 153, 155, 156, 157
pluralism, x, 2, 23, 31, 37, 38, 47, 53
policy, x, 6, 24, 26, 141, 142, 151
polio, 132
pollution, 17, 18
pregnancy, 39, 118, 129, 137
principlism, viii, 21, 31
privacy, 14, 19, 51, 57, 58, 67, 68, 75, 85, 136, 141
psychiatric, xi, 11, 14, 19, 29, 95, 111, 112
puberty, 14, 39, 117, 121

R

Ramose, 156, 159
randomized, 13, 150
rationality, 45, 84, 86, 87, 89, 93, 154, 158
reductivism, xi, 95
relational, x, 6, 57, 58, 59, 60, 63, 66, 67, 68, 70, 71, 74, 81, 83, 86, 87, 89, 90, 91, 92, 121
relationality, 82, 86, 87, 88, 91, 92
religion, 42, 43, 46, 83, 88, 92, 126, 129, 130
religious, viii, ix, x, 3, 5, 8, 9, 11, 13, 23, 25, 26, 31, 34, 38, 39, 41, 43, 47, 53, 60, 79, 82, 115, 122, 123, 127, 130, 135, 156
reproduction, 3, 36, 55, 117, 159

research, vii, ix, 2, 3, 4, 6, 21, 59, 63, 65, 67, 73, 77, 111, 141, 149, 150, 151, 155
researcher, 57, 58, 59, 64, 65, 66, 67, 68, 69, 70, 71, 72, 73, 74, 75
resources, x, 1, 4, 5, 6, 16, 17, 18, 24, 27, 34, 50, 57, 58, 59, 66, 121, 140, 156
responsibility, 10, 28, 49, 50, 67, 69, 74, 80, 111, 119
Richardson, x, 57, 58, 59, 66, 67, 68, 69, 70, 71, 72, 73, 74, 76
rights, ix, 2, 3, 9, 13, 15, 19, 27, 49, 50, 52, 58, 67, 79, 81, 83, 84, 87, 89, 93, 115, 125, 129, 132, 136, 141, 142, 144
ritual, 9, 10, 41, 47, 114, 115, 118, 119, 120
rituals, xi, 14, 26, 38, 39, 45, 114, 115, 119, 120, 122, 127, 131, 133

S

self, xii, 6, 49, 52, 73, 79, 80, 83, 84, 85, 86, 87, 88, 89, 90, 111, 120, 154, 156
Senghor, 37
Singer, 35, 54, 65, 76
spirit, xi, 9, 12, 24, 43, 46, 113, 115, 116, 119, 120, 133, 154, 157
spiritual, vii, xi, 4, 7, 8, 9, 10, 11, 12, 13, 20, 24, 40, 42, 43, 44, 45, 46, 92, 113, 114, 115, 116, 117, 119, 120, 121, 123, 124, 125, 127, 133, 145
Sub-Saharan, x, 1, 16, 27, 28, 33, 34, 52, 58, 60, 61, 62, 63, 64, 72, 111, 129
suicide, 4, 21, 28, 148, 149
sunsum, 92, 116, 117
supernatural, 8, 20, 38, 39, 40, 41, 43, 44, 45, 47, 114
superstition, 39

T

taboos, 14, 115, 123, 146

Tangwa, v, viii, ix, xii, 18, 21, 22, 29, 32, 35, 39, 40, 49, 55, 121, 130, 156, 158
Taylor, 28, 55, 93, 112
technology, 36, 147, 148
therapeutic, 11, 39, 40, 77
Toldson, 119, 120, 125, 130
traditional, vii, viii, ix, x, xi, xii, 5, 7, 8, 9, 10, 14, 20, 22, 24, 29, 31, 32, 35, 37, 38, 39, 40, 41, 42, 43, 44, 45, 46, 47, 48, 49, 50, 51, 52, 53, 54, 55, 56, 79, 92, 113, 114, 115, 116, 118, 120, 121, 122, 123, 124, 125, 126, 127, 128, 129, 130, 145, 146, 147
traditional medicine, vii, viii, ix, x, xi, xii, 5, 8, 9, 10, 29, 31, 32, 35, 38, 39, 40, 41, 42, 47, 53, 54, 55, 56, 113, 114, 115, 116, 118, 120, 121, 122, 123, 124, 125, 126, 127, 128, 145
traditions, ix, 1, 2, 3, 20, 21, 22, 23, 24, 25, 26, 34, 64, 130
traits, 135
tribal, 13, 14, 34, 42
trokosi, 14, 48
Tuskegee, 48
Tutu, 60, 76, 158

U

ubuntu, 50, 121
universe, 12, 41, 44, 91

V

vaccines, 151
values, viii, ix, 18, 22, 24, 25, 32, 33, 34, 37, 38, 47, 48, 49, 52, 54, 60, 61, 70, 72, 74, 81, 82, 84, 88, 91, 93, 123, 158

W

wellbeing, 50, 85, 114, 117, 119, 120, 122, 150
wheelchairs, 137, 138, 139
wholeness, 114, 120, 121, 122
Wiredu, 29, 43, 45, 49, 50, 56, 112
witchcraft, 39, 115, 116, 117, 133
witches, 115, 121, 124

Y

Yoruba, x, 1, 20, 31, 32, 43, 48, 51, 52, 54, 114

www.ingramcontent.com/pod-product-compliance
Lightning Source LLC
Chambersburg PA
CBHW051101230426
43667CB00013B/2388